Practicum in

COUNSELING

Practicum in

COUNSELING

A Developmental Guide

MARIANNE WOODSIDE

University of Tennessee–Knoxville

CHAD LUKE

Tennessee Tech University

cognella® | ACADEMIC PUBLISHING

Bassim Hamadeh, CEO and Publisher
Amy Smith, Project Editor
Abbey Hastings, Associate Production Editor
Emely Villavicencio, Senior Graphic Designer
Sara Schennum, Licensing Associate
Jessica Hillstrom, Interior Designer
Natalie Piccotti, Director of Marketing
Kassie Graves, Vice President of Editorial
Jamie Giganti, Director of Academic Publishing

BRIEF CONTENTS

DETAILED CONTENTS

PREFACE

If you are reading this text, *Practicum in Counseling: A Developmental Guide,* we assume that you are either an instructor and/or supervisor for practicum student or you are a counselor in training (CIT) and are enrolled in your practicum course and beginning the practicum in counseling. This text can become a vital part of this exciting and challenging experience of practicum. You will find in this preface the goals of the text, a brief bio of the authors, an outline of the text format, and a description of the key elements that help students learn.

Goals for this Text

Since this text, *Practicum in Counseling: A Developmental Guide,* is written to accompany students in the practicum experience, there are seven goals that focus on this endeavor.

GOAL 1: *Utilize a developmental approach to empower students.* The process of becoming a counselor is developmental in nature. Learning to be a counselor requires purposeful work over a period of time to gain the knowledge, skills, and values that allow the student to assume the role of a professional counselor. This means students can reflect on and practice the critical knowledge, necessary skills, and values and ethics of the profession learned thus far through graduate study. Participating in the practicum experience represents the next step. In fact, as a counselor, students learn that professional development is a lifelong process (Ronnestad & Skovolt, 2003; Stoltenberg & McNeil, 2009). All students are encouraged to commit to professional growth and the development of their counselor identity.

GOAL 2: *Assist students to develop their professional identity as a counselor as they apply relevant concepts and skills working with clients.* By now, students understand that the primary purpose of their academic program is to move from deciding to study counseling to "learning to be a counselor" (Woodside, Cole-Zakrzewski, Oberman, & Carruth, 2007, p. 1), and then to developing an identity as a professional counselor. In fact, working with clients is a primary responsibility of practicum. Gradually assuming the role of a counselor during practicum, students learn more about who they are as a counselor and what are the professional and work-related aspects of the work.

GOAL 3: *Assist students in the development of individual and group counseling skills.* While in a counseling academic counseling program, students have been engaged in classes that provide them with opportunities to understand the helping and counseling process and develop skills to counsel others. And, students have had the opportunity to practice their newly gained skills by participating in role plays, responding to case studies and YouTube videos, conducting a counseling session(s) with a peer, and/or working in a pre-practicum experience. The next stage of their development is to counsel a client while under supervision. In practicum, students will sit face to face with an individual or group of individuals and conduct an individual or group counseling session, with the help of an instructor and site supervisor. Instructors and students will have material that will help develop counseling skills, reflect and act on ethical and multi-cultural considerations, and continuously assess strengths and areas for improvement.

GOAL 4: *Guide students toward an appreciation for and infusion of ethical, legal, and cultural considerations in the provision of counseling services.* One key aspect of becoming a counselor is learning about and practicing in an ethical, legal, and culturally sensitive manner. A three-aspect approach to developing an understanding of ethical, legal, and cultural considerations provides a useful approach to integrating these into the daily work of being a counselor: (a) becoming aware of the ethical, legal and cultural dimensions of counseling; (b) engaging in critical reflection; and (c) seeking supervision. This text helps students develop each of these aspects related to ethical, legal and culturally sensitive professional practices.

GOAL 5: *Cultivate self-advocacy through the use of models and processes of supervision.* Just as a counselor's responsibility is to empower clients to support or promote their own interests, a counselor's professional responsibility includes advocacy for self in the counseling role and advocacy for the counseling profession. Supervision as a key component of advocacy and self-advocacy. Instructors and students will find support in learning about the foundations of supervision, how to use supervision effectively, and how to ask for effective supervision.

GOAL 6: *Assist students to successfully conclude practicum and transition to the internship experience.* Counseling academic training and education includes two field-based experiences, a practicum and an internship. The requirements for each reflect the developmental nature of professional growth as a counselor. In practicum, students develop and use counseling skills to work with individual clients. How they leave practicum reflects a sense of professionalism and care for the counseling work and client work. In internship, professional growth includes an extended period of time at an internship site, supervision, counseling clients, and performing other important roles as a member of an agency or school. The conclusion of practicum is an ideal time to assess personal and professional development as a counselor and establish goals for continued professional growth and development during internship.

GOAL 7: *Provide instructors and students with a tool/mechanism for addressing the Council for Accreditation of Counseling and Related Educational Programs (CACREP) and other counseling-related standards relevant to the professional practice and entry-level specialty areas.* CACREP is an organization charged with ensuring the quality of counseling academic programs, supporting program self-review and evaluation, promoting the counseling profession, and providing support to counseling programs and their students and graduates. In each of our chapters, there is a note about how the content and activities help meet CACREP standards, thus supporting accreditation and self-review and evaluation. Included is a table that links specific chapters with ASCA national standards and multicultural competencies.

Meet the Authors

Marianne Woodside and Chad Luke are both counselor educators. Marianne is Professor Emerita at the University of Tennessee, Knoxville and Chad is Associate Professor at Tennessee Technology University, Cookeville, Tennessee. This work together reflects their interest in meeting the needs of their students engaged in field experiences and recognizing the unique needs of the practicum counseling student.

Marianne graduated from the Ohio State University with a master's in counseling and from Virginia Tech with an EdD in counselor education. She was a professor of counselor education at the University of Tennessee, Knoxville. Her specific research interests include the following: burnout; mindfulness; discourse in teaching, learning, and research; case management; and supervision. She has published numerous texts focused on human services, case management, and internship. She is married with three children and one small dog. Hiking, music, writing, and photography represent her interests.

Chad Luke has a PhD in counselor education from the University of Tennessee and is an associate professor of counseling at Tennessee Tech University in Cookeville, Tennessee and a clinical supervisor. He teaches courses in career counseling, career development, neuroscience for counselors, theory, multicultural counseling, group counseling, and practicum and internship. He has clinical experience with addictions, children and adolescents, the homeless, college students, and other adults. He is married and has a daughter, and his interests include gaming, writing, and the outdoors.

Authors' Commitments

Before we present the format and the content of the text, we would like to share three commitments we, Marianne and Chad, have to both instructors and students.

WRITING WITH ONE VOICE. Although as individuals, in speech and in writing, we can represent our own knowledge and viewpoints as scholars and teachers, in this text, we speak with one voice. This means that during the process of the text development, we (Marianne and Chad) spent time together constructing the outline of the text. We wrote each chapter of the text in a similar way. Here is the strategy we used:

1. After considerable discussion, either Marianne or Chad would write the first draft of a chapter.

2. Then, we would meet and review each section and each paragraph. We would talk through what we were trying to say and describe why it is important.

3. After writing a second draft, we exchanged drafts of each chapter multiple times to continue to integrate our values, knowledge, skills, and teaching philosophies.

The result is this text, which we offer as a guide to student counselor identity development and professional development as a counselor.

WRITING WITH STUDENTS IN MIND. We hope that students are engaged in reading and working through this text. Throughout the text, we address the student directly, using the term "you" to indicate a conversation we are having together. We present information about practicum and topics relevant to that experience such as beginning the practicum work, making introductions to a site, working with first clients, and participating in supervision. We also offer topics of interest such as ethical, legal and multicultural considerations, participating in critical incidents, working with clients, and participating in an assessment and evaluation of professional work. We present multiple ways students can engage with the text to support their day-to-day work in the world of practice.

USING EFFECTIVE TEACHING STRATEGIES. This text provides students with a way to build on their previous experience and current knowledge and integrate those with student experiences in practicum. Participating in practicum offers students time to counsel clients and use that experience to develop a personal and professional understanding of the role and responsibilities of a counselor. And, as students integrate their experiences of counseling clients, working with instructor and site supervision, participating in the practicum seminar, and studying this text, they will enhance their understanding of the counseling profession. In the text, we suggest ways and provide opportunities for students to think critically, engage in personal and professional reflection, expand their learning experiences, and collaborate with instructor and site supervisors, clients, and peers. We believe that this type of engagement during practicum will help students develop their counseling skills and expand their understanding of professional considerations and challenges.

What to Expect from this Text

Practicum in Counseling: A Developmental Guide, includes four sections and thirteen chapters. Although the four sections reflect a specific understanding of the practicum experience (e.g., introduction to practicum, beginning the practicum work, fostering counselor development, and taking leave, termination, and transition), it is also possible to read and study the chapters according to the unique requirements of the practicum course. Let's look in more detail at the format and the content of the text.

The Format

The four sections of the text include Introduction to Practicum, Beginning the Practicum Work, Fostering Counselor Development, and Taking Leave, Termination, and Transition (see Figure 0.1). As per Figure 0.1, learning represents a non-linear path. This means students will be continually referring to earlier and later chapters as they integrate the content of the text. For example, students may learn about the goals of practicum in the first week of practicum (see Chapter 2), yet need to return to study those goals more carefully as they approach mid-term of practicum and begin the assessment and evaluation of student performance (see Chapter 11).

FIGURE 0.1 Four Sections of *Practicum in Counseling: A Developmental Guide*

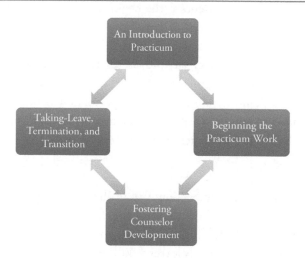

The Content of the Text

As instructors and students begin to use this text, it will be helpful to know more about its contents. This preview helps students see the breadth and depth of the projected professional growth and development the content reflects. In some ways, the table of contents, or summary of the aspects of the text, provides a road map for what students will learn during their practicum experience, both in individual and group supervision and at the practicum site. The metaphor of "the journey" describes a practicum experience whose coursework and work has a definite beginning and end. As completion of the practicum approaches, instructors will help students with the transition to the internship experience. Instructor, site supervisor, and this text serve as guides to help students prepare to assume many roles and responsibilities of a professional counselor and have a clearer professional identity. Let's look at the specific content of *Practicum in Counseling: A Developmental Guide.*

Section I

The first section of the text focuses on *an introduction to practicum.* There are two chapters in this section, each presented to help instructors and students establish a positive practicum site in which students can grow and develop.

In Chapter 1, "Now You Are in Practicum," there is a description of the goals for this text and an introduction of the authors. Students then address two difficult questions: "Is the profession of counseling right for me?" and "How will I/can I know that I am ready?" Students begin to understand their role as the bridge between the academic world and the world of practice. As a way to introduce students to their practicum experience, our cast of characters (four practicum students) explain how relevant terms reflect their own beginning in practicum and help students think about ways to enhance their own practicum experience with the practicum contract and plan ways of giving back to the practicum site.

Chapter 2, "Beginning Practicum," focuses on practicum students as they enter the site during the first few weeks of practicum. Concrete recommendations about how to share information about practicum with a site supervisor and how to establish a tone of professionalism when entering the site support students at the beginning of their work. Ideas focus on how to prepare for the first days or first week of practicum including practical aspects of setting up the work space and using electronic connections and social media. Students also learn about foundational documents they will create and use as they began to work with clients. These include professional disclosure statements, informed consent, and permission to tape. Students also learn about how to demonstrate positive and personal attributes to those in the world of practice. Finally, students identify their trajectory of work, over time, at their practicum site, from orientation to shadowing their site supervisor, to counseling clients.

Section II

As instructors and students move to Section Two of the text, "Beginning the Practicum Work," five chapters support the work of the practicum student. Students will learn how to make contact with their first client and identify and work through ethical issues relevant to practicum. They will also begin to apply previously learned skills to this client work. They will also consider multicultural issues and how they influence the work with clients. In addition, students will learn how to recognize the occurrence of critical incidents and work through them in a professional way.

In Chapter 3, "First Contact with a Real Client," students learn how to manage their expectations and anxieties of meeting their first client. They explore what they can expect from themselves (e.g., students will be both more prepared than they expect and less prepared than they expect), the default stances that students may take during their initial experiences with clients, and what silence means to students and their clients. Students also examine their expectations for their clients and the accuracy of these expectations. Learning how to view counseling from the client's perspective, students look at what the client may be expecting from their counseling and learn ways they can address the client's expectations. And, finally, students explore ways they can teach their clients how to be clients.

Chapter 4 focuses on "Making and Maintaining Contact with Clients." This chapter offers concrete suggestions about how to prepare for meeting the client for the first time, such as understanding the purpose of a session structure and how to structure the initial session and subsequent sessions. Students are then introduced the influential markers of change that support the counseling process and the aspects of the working alliance that enhance the helping relationship. The development of trust and the act of being in the moment with the client is explored and its positive outcomes confirm the development of a relationship with the client. A review of basic helping skills helps students use these skills as they transition from classroom skill development to a practical use of skills with clients.

In Chapter 5, "Ethics in Practicum," ethics in counseling beyond the classroom and into the practicum experience is explored. Discussed is the critical nature of ethical practice and described are some challenges that the practicum student may face. The presentation of an ethical model of decision making offers to practicum students some guidelines for working through ethical issues. Helpful transcripts illustrate the discussion of ethics during supervision and reinforce the importance of consulting with supervisors and others when confronted with ethical dilemmas. Considering ethical and legal issues as they relate to student work in practicum is extremely important for clients, the agency or school, the academic program, and the student's professional development.

Chapter 6, "Diversity in Practicum," focuses on considerations of diversity in practicum, onsite and in the consulting room. Practicum is a multicultural experience where students will encounter multiple contexts of multicultural work, including cultures of self, clients, supervisors, coworkers, student peers, the practicum site, and the counseling program and group supervision environment. Specifically, practicum students learn how culture relates to their work with clients. Students examine their biases, perceptions, and positions of privilege and then expand the concept of empathy as a counter to behaviors and values of oppression.

In Chapter 7, "Critical Incidents in Practicum," students learn about the importance of the critical incident as a learning opportunity that fosters professional growth and development. Although many individuals think of a critical incident in terms of crises, the term and experience has special meaning for practicum students. For instance, a critical incident can be seen in a positive or negative light. A critical incident can command attention, cause students to question beliefs or values, provide insight, or challenge students' skills or abilities. In summary, it is an incident that influences the personal and professional development of practicum students. Students are introduced to the definition of the critical incident and learn about the categories of these incidences, such as those related to the practicum student, clients, site, or supervisor. We present these incidents from both the perspective of the supervisor and the practicum student. Students learn about ways they can identify these incidents and use supervision to help them respond with reflection, consultation, management of emotions, action, and post-incident reflection.

Section III

In Section Three of this text, "Fostering Counselor Development," students explore counselor identity development and counseling knowledge and skill development. Each reflect the developmental nature of professional growth and help practicum students understand the process of learning to be a counselor. Four chapters in this section reflect concepts and activities at the heart of student success in practicum: understanding professional identity development; understanding student developmental growth as a counselor; getting what students need from supervision; and describing a positive way to participate in assessment and evaluation.

As students grow and develop as counselors, it is critical for them to understand both their professional identity development and their knowledge and skill development. In Chapter 8, "Professional Identity Development," the process view of professional counselor identity development, developed by Gibson, Dollarhide, and Moss (2010), describes the process of professional identity development. Students learn about the aspects and become more familiar with and help their own professional identity development. In essence, this chapter allows students to learn about a theoretical model and determine how it helps them make sense of the practicum experience. Students are, in essence, turning theory into practice.

In Chapter 9, "Understanding Your Development as a Counselor" the integrated developmental model of supervision (IDM) (Stoltenberg & McNeill, 2011) helps students develop insights into the qualities and abilities they are acquiring and the successive stages of professional development. Students learn about the importance of the place of supervision as it relates to the IDM and counselor professional development.

Chapter 10, "Getting What You Need from Supervision," begins with an introduction of the concept of supervision and its goals. The concept of self-advocacy, as it applies to the students' experiences in practicum, is useful to help students view a model of self-advocacy that includes self-awareness, well-being, self-care and mutual care, and personal agency. Students also learn about both the responsibilities and the rights that practicum students have. Recognizing that not all supervision represents the best that the profession has to offer, students examine ways they can recognize good supervision and then build on it. Practicum student explore how to identify poor and harmful supervision and how to ask for help if they suspect they are in a harmful situation.

Chapter 11 focuses on assessment and evaluation. This chapter begins with defining evaluation and assessment in counselor education and describing how terms related to each relate to student work. The place that supervision has in the evaluation process is examined, and students learn how they and their supervisors can establish favorable conditions in which assessment and evaluation can occur. The integrated developmental model of supervision, introduced in Chapter 9, is re-examined as a way to help students think about assessment more deeply. We turn to the measurement of professional competencies and describe the components of an empirically validated measure of student development, the counselor competences scale-revised (CCS-R) (Lambie & Swank, 2016). The CCS-R serves as an example of a valid and reliable measurement that academic programs, site supervisors, and students can use to measure counselor-related skill level and competence.

Section IV

Section Four, "Taking Leave, Termination, and Transition," focuses on the aspects of ending practicum. Concrete guidelines offer professional approaches to leaving the practicum site (supervisor, clients, tasks and responsibilities) and concluding the practicum class (faculty and peers). The final chapter supports the transition from practicum to the final field experience, the internship.

"Taking Leave from Practicum," Chapter 12, supports the conclusion of the practicum. Ending the practicum experience in a professional way contributes to both professional development and skill building in taking leave and terminating work with clients. Students' taking leave includes transitioning responsibilities with the site supervisor and staff, helping each to continue or build on their work after leaving the agency, and terminating work with clients. Students will also be concluding their work as practicum students with their faculty supervisor and student peers, completing assignments and presenting the final documentation. In both site and classroom situations, students will want to formalize their taking leave with a summary of what they have learned and a statement of gratitude for those who have supported their development.

Chapter 13, "Transition to Internship," helps students move from practicum to internship in a positive manner. This transition to internship becomes an important part of concluding the practicum experience. Within a program framework and supported by CACREP standards, counseling students move from practicum, where the focus is on counseling clients and learning how to engage in supervision, to internship, where students continue, under supervision, to counsel clients while expanding their roles and responsibilities as a professional counselor. Prior to internship, students will want to define their readiness for internship by assessing current personal and professional knowledge, skills, and values. This assessment helps the beginning internship student clarify goals for internship. Of course, these goals include personal assessment, program and CACREP goals, and faculty and site supervisor goals.

Key Elements of the Text

The elements that we use in most chapters help instructors and students use and apply the material presented. Each of these elements presents a way to deepen the learning experience and better understand personal and professional development.

Chapter Goals

Each chapter begins with chapter goals to prime the instructor and student expectations.

CACREP-Related Goals

Each chapter provides ways that the faculty (and program) can use the text and features of the text to support the 2016 CACREP standards related to practicum and specialty areas.

Cast of Characters

In each chapter, we introduce four students, Janice, Jose, Kaisha, and Sam. All four are engaged in the practicum experience. Dr. Kim supervises these four students and engages with their site supervisors. Mr. Tabor is a site supervisor. A summary of each follows:

Janice: She is a 46-year-old, White, heterosexual female returning to school for the first time in over 20 years. Her practicum placement is in a middle school.

Jose: He is a 35-year-old, biracial (Hispanic and White) queer male. His placement is a residential treatment facility for adolescents.

Kaisha: She is a 23-year-old, biracial (White and African American), heterosexual female. Her practicum placement is an outpatient community health clinic.

Sam: He is a 26-year-old, African American, heterosexual male. His placement is with a campus clinic.

Dr. Kim: She is a 40-year-old, Asian, heterosexual female. She is a counselor education faculty member currently teaching the practicum class for school and mental health counseling students.

Mr. Tabor: He is a 53-year-old, White, gay male. He is a site supervisor working with a student in Dr. Kim's practicum class.

We present additional information about these students in Chapter 1.

Reflection Questions

There are reflection questions throughout each chapter that ask students to think about the content presented or, alternatively, appear near the end of the chapter as sentence stems for guided, written reflections. The reflection questions are based on both Bloom's taxonomy and critical thinking-based guidelines to promote higher-level thinking and a deeper understanding of both the material and the practicum experience. These reflection questions encourage students to integrate their classroom learning with their field-based experience.

Transcriptions

Transcriptions facilitate student learning related to the focus of the chapter. Transcription excerpts help students read concrete examples of counselor-client and counselor-supervisor interactions. Students read these types of exchanges and think, "Hey, I can do that!"

Experiential Activities

Experiential activities provide an opportunity for students to integrate the knowledge and skills presented in previous and current coursework and the text to their practicum experience. The goal is to help students gain new understandings and ask thoughtful questions about what they are learning in practicum, their identity development, and their professional development. This can include cases, short vignettes, guided imagery, mindfulness activities, and creative art techniques applied to a wide variety of practicum experiences. The activities suggested can be applied during the group practicum meeting, with their supervisors and clients, or in other designated settings. Experiential activities include setting goals, the engaging in the experiential opportunity, and critical reflection.

Discussions Together

"Discussions Together" provides instructors, students, and site supervisors with topics relevant to practicum and the student's developmental needs. During these discussions, instructors may draw on their experiences to offer real-life content in the immediacy of the relationship. They also encourage collaboration and teamwork during practicum group classes. In addition, directly related to student-client interaction, the ways in which students respond provide insight to the instructor about how the student perceives interaction with a client.

Modeling

This is an element embedded in the text that helps instructors and students model an interaction that is authentic, probing, positive, and accepting. Specifically, in the text, when we [the authors] ask the student a question or when the student asks a question, we ask students to consider what the answer to a question will do for them. We follow the student response with an empathic response about how important it is to feel understood and not judged. This manner of modeling reinforces both instructor interaction with students and student interaction with clients. And, this interaction can make the material more tangible and, again, models supervision. The learning device used here is scaffolding, wherein the student reconsiders their question prior to receiving a response. The instructor is then empowered to provide the level of support needed at the right time.

Ethical and Legal and Cultural Considerations

We present separate chapters related to ethical and legal considerations and cultural considerations that may emerge during the practicum experience. We also infuse relevant ethical and legal prompts for students to consider in each chapter. We highlight topics and issues highlighted by the CACREP standards, the ACA Code of Ethics, the Multicultural and Social Justice Counseling Competencies, and the American School Counseling Association.

Key Terms

For each chapter, key terms are bolded and then listed at the end of the chapter.

References

References used in the text are presented at the end of the text.

Appendices

We provide various appendices located at the publisher's learning web site.

References

Gibson, D. M., Dollarhide, C. T., & Moss, J. M. (2010). Professional identity development: A grounded theory of transformational tasks of new counselors. *Counselor Education & Supervision, 50(1), 21–38. doi:10.1002/j.1556-6978.2010.tb00106.x*

Lambie, G. W., & Swank, J. M. (2016). *Counseling competencies scale–revised (CCS–R): Training manual* (Unpublished manuscript). Department of Child, Family, and Community Sciences. Orlando, FL: University of Central Florida.

McNeil, B. W., & Stoltenberg, C. D. (2015). *Supervision essentials for the Integrative Model.* Washington, D.C.: American Psychological Association.

Ronnestad, M. H., & Skovholt, T. M. (2003). The journey of the counselor and therapist: Research findings and perspectives on professional development. *Journal of Career Development, 30*(1), 5–44. doi:10.1023/A:1025173508081

Stoltenberg, C. D., & McNeil, B. W. (2009). IDM supervision: An integrative developmental model for supervising counselors and therapists (3rd ed.). New York, NY: Brunner Routledge.

Woodside, M., Cole-Zakrzewski, K., Oberman, A., & Carruth, E. (2007). The experience of learning to be a counselor: A pre practicum perspective. *Journal for Counselor Education and Supervision, 47*(1), 14–28.

CHAPTER 1

Now You Are
IN PRACTICUM

INTRODUCTION

If you are reading this text, you are enrolled in your practicum course and beginning the practicum in counseling. What an exciting time this is for you and your peers! We are excited to accompany you through your experiences in practicum and hope to become part of the team of individuals who provide you support. Enhancing your professional counselor identity and expanding and honing the skills that facilitate your work with client will provide a foundation for your professional growth and development.

You may have heard the expression, "practice makes perfect." Actually, it may be truer to say that "practice makes *permanent*." We are what we repeatedly do, and this is true for counseling as well. Therefore, it is vital that during your first experiences counseling real-life clients, your practice is shaped through closely observed processes. After all, the term practicum itself is from the Latin meaning to practice. **Practicum** is the process of applying theory to a real-world setting, and for counselors in training, that real-world consists of real-life humans, most of whom are in some sort of pain or distress. This work is intense! Because of the nature of the work, it is important that you reflect on whether this profession may be right for you.

Supervised practice—practicum—means at least two things to/for you: The first is that as a counselor in training (CIT), you cannot be now the expert you will become. This is a developmental reality that requires patience and humility, as well as trust in those commissioned to guide you. The second meaning is you will need to approach practice in a way that reflects how you want to function "for real," in part because practice is real, and because practice makes *permanent*. So, when you think about preparing for the practicum experience, it is often helpful to consider various viewpoints such as those of faculty, site supervisors, and clients. And of course, you need to consider your own view point, that of a CIT. Each of these perspectives offers a unique way of looking at this first field-based learning experience and expanding your understanding of it. A good beginning to the work of practice is to ask two **hard questions** that you may have struggled with during your preparation for practicum: "Is the profession of counseling right for me?" and "How will I/can I know that I am ready?" Before you answer these questions, consider the goals of the chapter.

GOALS OF THE CHAPTER

- Learn about the goals for this text
- Meet the authors
- Reflect on the context in which practicum occurs
- Think about questions you have about becoming a counselor
- Enhance your practicum work

Goals for This Text

Since this text, *Empowering Practicum Counseling Students: A Developmental Guide*, is written for you, its primary purpose is to support your work as a CIT enrolled in practicum. In order to do so, the text addresses several goals. Each will help you addresses important aspects of your counselor identity development and professional growth. These goals are described in more detail in the preface.

GOAL 1: *Utilize a developmental approach to empower your work in practicum.* You will learn about where you are in the developmental process and practice relevant knowledge, skills, and values that support your work in practicum.

GOAL 2: *Assist you to develop your professional identity as a counselor.* As you gradually assume the role of a counselor during practicum, you will learn more about who you are as a counselor and what are the professional and work-related aspects of the work, or "learning to be a counselor" (Woodside et al., 2007, p. 1).

GOAL 3: *Assist you in the development of individual skills.* The next stage of your development is to counsel a client while under supervision, so this text provides you with support for this important client work.

GOAL 4: *Guide you toward an appreciation for and infusion of ethical, legal, and cultural considerations.* One key aspect of becoming a counselor is learning about and practicing counseling in an ethical, legal, and culturally sensitive manner; each of these is integrated into the daily work of being a counselor.

GOAL 5: *Cultivate self-advocacy through the use of models and processes of supervision.* Supervision is as a key component of the work of self-advocacy. You will learn about the foundations of supervision, how to use supervision effectively, and how to ask for effective supervision.

GOAL 6: *Assist you to successfully conclude practicum and transition to the internship experience.* Your academic training and education includes two field-based experiences, a practicum, and an internship, so this text will help you develop and use counseling skills to work with individual clients during practicum and then to transition to internship.

Just as the goals of the text are significant to consider, your goals for practicum are also important. In Reflection Question 1.1 we ask you to match the text goals with the ones you have established for yourself.

REFLECTION QUESTION 1.1

THIS TEXT AND YOUR GOALS

How do your professional goals align with the goals of this text?

Meet the Authors

Although we, Marianne Woodside and Chad Luke, are the co-authors, we believe that the voices of and interactions with our numerous friends, family members, professors and mentors, work colleagues, and clients add to the development and writing of this text. Our own students continue to influence our teaching and writing, and, on a daily basis, they provide us insights into their experiences of learning to be counselors. We view counselor education and training as both a personal and professional endeavor and accept the potential influence of our text on your experiences in practicum. For this reason, we want to introduce ourselves and tell you something about our experiences related to counseling and teaching. We use the interview format to provide short descriptions of ourselves and our professional work (see Transcripts 1.1 and 1.2)

TRANSCRIPT 1.1 INTERVIEW WITH MARIANNE

Talk about your early life. I was raised in East Texas and lived with my mom, dad, and my younger sister. The small town in which I was reared during the 50s and 60s afforded us lots of freedoms. We knew the people in our neighborhood and were able to wander in and out of the homes on our street. We played outside with our friends until dark and rode our bicycles to school and beyond. Because I lived in the South, the population was fairly homogeneous, White; our society was segregated, and Black ("Colored" was the term used then) families lived in their own communities. Black children attended their own schools and churches. Hidden from us were the Hispanic residents who lived in our area. It was years before I learned and understood the contributions these many diverse populations made to our way of life. When I was 16, our family moved to the Middle East and I attended the International School of Kuwait. My life in Kuwait was a much more comfortable fit for me since I had teachers and friends from countries and cultures across the globe. I used to marvel at the magic of the blending of so many cultures, and I was humbled by customs and beliefs that my friends held that were so different from my own; different yet legitimate and meaningful.

Describe your journey to becoming a counselor. I remember early in my life taking care of my sister and, as I matured, taking care of my mother. In school, I made friends with my classmates, especially those who were shunned by others. I was often leading a committee to feed or clothe those in the community who needed help. In spite of this, I didn't discover the study of the profession of counseling until I was in graduate school. My advisor sent me to Dr. Herman Peter's class at Ohio State after one of my philosophy classes had been cancelled. Enrolling in that class provided the perfect introduction to what was to become my lifelong professional commitment. I felt that my background in teacher education and human services provided me with a broad foundation for my work as a counselor.

What three critical incidents occurred during your practicum in counseling?

1. I went to visit my faculty supervisor when I was setting up my practicum. I told him that I wanted the best supervisor he knew and one who would let me work with clients immediately. The problem with the placement was that I would either have to walk or take the bus since I didn't have a car. My faculty supervisor took me at my word and found me an incredible site supervisor who worked at an inner-city school about two miles away from campus. I knew that having the best supervisor would enhance my experience and I was correct!

2. Don't laugh at this, please. Or maybe you should laugh! I can remember having to audio-tape my counseling sessions during practicum. So, I bought a tape recorder and some tapes and took them to my site. I talked with my first client about permission to tape and pushed the record button. We both soon forgot about the tape recorder. I turned off the recorder and walked back to my dorm with the recorder tucked under my arm. I couldn't wait to hear my session. I rewound the tape and then pressed the play button. And then I burst into tears. I couldn't believe what I sounded like—very Southern, female, deep and husky, and so sweet—my self-image crumbled; who was this person? I couldn't hear the exchange between me and my client as I listened to the sounds made by this complete stranger (me!) that I thought I knew so well. Honestly, I was horrified!

3. During my practicum, I initiated and conducted a group of fourth-grade girls. We had an open group. I helped the girls develop their own agenda and constructed lessons that accounted for the agenda and were flexible enough to respond to the dynamics of the group. Each week, we would have group for 45 minutes after the lunch break and then I would meet with my supervisor. One thing that troubled me during group time was how mean the girls were to each other. This was difficult for me to imagine, never mind confront.

One day in supervision, I started to talk with my supervisor about what had happened during group, and I had trouble talking about it. I was having so much trouble understanding how the girls could be so hateful, calling each other names, and singling out one of the girls to bully. Two of them even threatened to beat her up on the way home. I asked my supervisor if she and I could confront the members of the group together. I talked with the group first and told them that I had asked my supervisor to join us because of the violence threatened at our last meeting, and I asked them if we could address these threats as a group. What a learning moment. Even after a long career, I am still working on my sensitivity related to meanness and bullying.

Why is teaching important to you? In our family, we have what we call the "teacher gene." And I have it! I believe that teaching opens the door for everyone engaged. I also believe that teaching and learning go hand in hand and that by working together we all learn and grow. What is wonderful about teaching is the individual nature of the activity. And, as a teacher, you can set the learning wheels in motion, but each student determines his or her own way and destination! And I feel a commitment to my students; I believe in them, and I want to offer support and challenge.

What are your hopes for students enrolled in practicum who use this text? My hope is students who read and study this text make it their own, use it to guide their own individual journey—that of learning to be a counselor. The commitment to become a professional counselor is a sacred one. May this text support students as they work with faculty and site supervisors and clients to develop their counselor professional identity and enhance their knowledge and skills working with clients. I hope that they can develop, and, at the end of practicum, I hope they can develop compassion and respect for their supervisors and clients and for themselves.

TRANSCRIPT 1.2 INTERVIEW WITH CHAD

Talk about your early life. I am an only child, raised in Charlotte, North Carolina. I always cringe a little at that descriptor "only" child, as if "insufficient" or "incomplete" is implied. It is kind of the way many feel when described as single (meaning unmarried, or un-partnered), as if part of their identity is missing. But, I've already digressed. Being an only child was a terrific experience until I experienced my parents' divorce and had no one inside the system to talk with about it. I think that may have been the first time I realized that having someone who could understand my experience and perspective stood out to me. Moving on, I lived in a small, rural neighborhood outside the city—which was quite small compared to its current size. I always felt safe, and we rarely locked doors to cars or the house. I knew the neighbor kids—mostly White, Southern, lower middle-class folks. I was always tall and skinny (try 6'8" and 150 pounds for much of high school and my early 20s). The expectation was that I would play basketball … and get college paid for … and later make money at it! It was during my first semester at college, trying to play "for real," that I realized it was not for me.

Describe your journey to becoming a counselor. That semester of college, realizing that I lacked the killer instinct need to compete at that level in basketball, was the culminating reality that I was built for relationship, not rivalry. I took a four-year hiatus from college after that disastrous first semester at college, only to return with renewed clarity that psychology, and later counseling, were for me. I had always been a sensitive person, a helper, who loved to solve problems and nurture relationship. I cried for the homeless—humans and animals—and longed for a way to help in the world. As an undergraduate psychology major, I was mentored by a faculty member who changed my life. He walked with me through some really tough stuff in my life, and through a focus on psychology and counseling theory, I learned to have psychological and relational success. I was hooked. I had to share this with others!

What three critical incidents occurred during your practicum in counseling?

1. My practicum took place at a homeless shelter in downtown Columbia, South Carolina, in a religious-based addiction treatment program for men. My first critical incident took place in the rescue mission itself. It was a combination of sensory experiences. The first wave was the smell. I am still sensitized to the smell of stale urine and unwashed bodies. It was an assault on my nose and occurred with the sight of men lying everywhere in an open room, in a variety of states of repose. I heard the sounds of men asking for money, staff setting limits, and the soup kitchen clanking lunch preparation utensils. As I climbed the stairs to the second floor, which housed the program, I wondered what in the world I was doing here. I wanted to help people, but a certain kind of people. You know the type: clean, educated, motivated, non-threatening—the type of clients that don't exist.

2. The second critical incident took place in the classroom. We were sitting in our desks, all facing forward (more on that later), talking about our experiences. I noted that the counseling process and tasks seemed overwhelming. My instructor stopped class to focus on me and most significantly the word "overwhelming." "That's a powerful word, Chad," he said. "Let's explore that further, as it can be a sign of trouble." Or something like that. Note to self in practicum: Don't use authentic words that can get you analyzed in front of the class. Between desks facing forward and reading into my emotions based on word choice, my inner counselor educator was poked. It highlighted the power of supervision, the setting of the room, and the attending style of the instructor.

3. Lastly, I had a similar experience of my voice on audiotape as Marianne, except that I did not look forward to listening to the tape! I approached it with fear and trepidation. (I may have even waited until class to listen to it the first time). When I heard my voice, I think I experienced depersonalization—I did not recognize that guy on the tape and was not pleased by his vocal quality or the words he was saying. It was a unique experience to hear myself in third person, as if someone I knew was speaking and saying things I would.

Why is teaching important to you? It was not until my doctoral program that I finally was able to understand what had happened to me in my graduate counseling program. It was also my first understanding of counselor identity development. Teaching is important to me because it constantly pushes me to challenge my assumptions. I don't want my students to wonder about what is happening to them during their graduate training. To the best of my ability, and in concert with other counseling material, I want to tell them what might happen, talk about it with them while it is happening, and look back with them after the fact and help them reflect on what has happened.

What are your hopes for students enrolled in practicum who use this text?
Practicum is something of a trial by fire. I have joked with Marianne that the only thing you need to prior to practicum is everything. It is my hope that students will use this book as a guide to be able to zoom in and out on practicum issues. There are many things to know prior to starting practicum, but many will not be important until you begin, during which time they will take on greater significance. When this happens, you may have to revisit material previously covered. Alternately, there may be material you need to read ahead to ease your nerves. I hope readers will be able to put our experience into practice for their own success.

> **CULTURAL CONSIDERATION 1.1**
>
> Now that you have read about your authors, Marianne and Chad, take a moment and reflect on the aspects of their culture that they speak of or allude to in Transcripts 1.1 and 1.2. List these. Once you have listed these, for each, describe how you think each have influenced them. How might their aspects of culture manifest in this text?

Orienting Yourself to Practicum: Asking the Hard Questions

There are several questions that you may have as you approach your work as a CIT and are learning how to be a practicum student. These questions also relate to your process of becoming a counselor. They may be questions you have confronted prior to practicum, but certainly they become more important as you enter a real-world setting and others look to you for professional work. Two questions, relevant to your experience of starting practicum, will guide your thinking.

QUESTION # 1 *Is the Profession of Counseling Right for Me?*

Most students who enter professional counseling programs do so because they want to learn about counseling and then gain employment as professional counselors. However, at the outset of their journey of learning to be a counselor, there remain doubts about their decisions and their abilities. The doubts can intensify during the first days and weeks in practicum. As you begin practicum, you may be experiencing many of these uncertainties.

These are often expressed with thoughts such as the following:

- "What if I don't like the work?"
- "Enrolling in this program seems like a poor choice."
- "My dad told me that he would rather I go to graduate school in business."
- "Helping others sometimes makes me really sad for them."

- "I have been in school for over a semester and I still am unsure if I want to be here."

- "I helped others before by giving advice; now I know not to do that. What do I do? I am still unclear that this will work."

- "I still don't know what the profession of counseling is all about."

One of the roles of your supervisors is to aid you in these reflections and, if you conclude that the profession of counseling is not for you, to help you exit the program in the most productive, successful way possible. At times, students recognize the counseling field is not a good fit for them and they, with support, discover alternative areas of study that will likely lead to greater satisfaction.

QUESTION # 2 *How Will I/Can I Know That I Am Ready?*

A question of readiness for working in an agency or school and encountering clients face to face reflects a fear common to beginning practicum students. In fact, as you begin your practicum, your fears are realistic. As with any CIT, you will be assuming a professional role before you fully understand either your professional identity or the role you are to perform. In other words, you are embarking on a journey without being adequately equipped because you do not—and cannot—know what is needed to complete the journey, not until you have made it. You will also have support and assistance from your faculty and site supervisors, other staff, and your peers, but it can still be an anxiety-provoking time. You are entering a phase of field-based learning that uses a process of observation, experience, reflection, and evaluation to promote your professional growth.

The term "**readiness**" reflects two meanings: being fully prepared and a willingness to engage. Readiness to enter a practicum experience includes elements of both of these meanings. And, it is important that you to be willing to engage with the practicum experience and, in fact, to have a certain degree of excitement and enthusiasm for the experience. Although you may not be as prepared as a seasoned professional, the faculty in your academic program will support your preparedness in two ways. First, while meeting CACREP requirements or developing a quality counselor preparation program, the faculty designed, for you and your peers, a plan of study that prepares you for this first field-based experience. Second, during your coursework, the faculty provided feedback and evaluation that helped build your knowledge base, hone your basic helping skills, and shape your professional identity.

Still, it is important to recognize your thoughts, questions, certainties, and doubts related to your readiness for the practicum experience. Reflection Question 1.2 engages you in the question "How will I/can I know that I am ready?">

Here are some of how students have expressed their responses to this question:

- "I am not ready."

- "Some days I think I can do this. Then I get the shakes and don't think I can face that first client."

- "I am so excited. I trust that the faculty know what they are doing when they send me to my school."

- "What if I can't do what my supervisor asks me to do?"
- "What if my client doesn't want a student for a counselor?"

As you respond to Reflection Question 1.2, you will learn more about your own readiness for practicum.

REFLECTION QUESTION 1.2

HOW WILL I/CAN I KNOW THAT I AM READY?

Professional counseling is a challenging profession. How can you know the profession is right for you?

If thoroughly and authentically reflected on, these questions can be intimidating. Revisiting them from time to time is a good idea and will help you assess your professional growth. As you begin practicum, there are terms that are important for you to know. Understanding the meaning of these terms will help you talk about practicum with others, aligning your language to better ensure you, your peers, and your supervisors are talking about the same things.

ETHICAL CONSIDERATION 1.1

What is the ethical dimension of the question, "How will I/can I know that I am ready?"

How Counselors in Training Talk About Practicum
Cast of Characters

Janice, Jose, Kaisha, and Sam are four practicum students who will share their experiences in practicum throughout the text. Each of these students represents composite of students we have taught through the years. All four are engaged in the practicum experience. Dr. Kim supervises these four students and engages with their site supervisors. Mr. Tabor is a site supervisor. We repeat the summary of these cast of characters as a way of reinforcing the important part they play in your understanding of the practicum experience.

Janice: She is a 46-year-old, White, heterosexual female returning to school for the first time in over 20 years. Her practicum placement is in a middle school.

Jose: He is a 35-year-old, biracial (Hispanic and White) queer male. His placement is a residential treatment facility for adolescents.

Kaisha: She is a 23-year-old, biracial (White and African American), heterosexual female. Her practicum placement is an outpatient community health clinic.

Sam: He is a 26-year-old, African American, heterosexual male. His placement is with a campus clinic.

Dr. Kim: She is a 40-year-old, Asian, heterosexual female. She is a counselor education faculty member currently teaching the practicum class for school and mental health counseling students.

Mr. Tabor: He is a 53-year-old, White, gay male. He is a site supervisor working with a student in Dr. Kim's practicum class.

Each of these students talks about several terms that are fast becoming part of your practicum experience. They describe ideas and concepts and what they mean to them. Read their words and see if you have any information that you would like to add.

Practicum experience

Janice: "Oh. All second-year students know about the term **practicum experience**. But those of us beginning practicum don't know much. We worried about enrolling in practicum and now that we are in it, we worry about what the experience will bring. It never leaves our minds. Without being too dramatic, 'We are all in.'"

Practicum student

Jose: "Oh my, here I am at 35, back in school and learning how to be a counselor as a **practicum student**. I was a science teacher for nine years in a high school. I have gone from an expert to a man with little skill. I have to be patient with myself. What I worry about most is that, because of my teaching experience, the teens I am working with in practicum think that I know more than I do. Right now, I feel this is unearned trust."

Practicum site

Kaisha: "I am not sure I am going to like my **practicum site**. I wanted to work in a rural mental health clinic and friends in our program recommended I ask for a mental health agency that services an adjoining county. The problem for me and maybe for the clients is I am biracial. Most of the clients are White. Actually, most of the staff are White too. I am not sure that I will fit it and I fear I will have trouble gaining client trust. Beginning at this site is really difficult."

Supervision

Sam: "I am still really worried about the **supervision** piece of my practicum. I think that my supervisor likes me, but what if she really doesn't it and I find out later? And I think I like her. I handle a lot of situations with humor. And, from my work in my classes, I think that I will use it in my work with clients. I am not sure that my supervisor thinks this is appropriate? From my work in theories class, I was clear that I wanted to use person-centered counseling in practicum. My supervisor wants me to use another approach. In fact, I think she insists that I use another approach. I am not very confident about how this is going to go. But I am going to try."

Faculty supervisor

Janice: "I guess I am a "Nervous Nelly," at least that is what my friends say. I keep thinking about practicum and, even though I have started, I still have lots of questions and I keep emailing my **faculty supervisor**. She helps me with some of the questions, but others, she tells me I will have to wait and that time will take care of these questions. I have heard from the second-year students that my faculty supervisor is helpful, really helpful, and that she will help me every step of the way. I hope so."

Jose: "I was so excited to meet my **site supervisor**. Because I am an older student, I knew he was younger than I am. But he has had over nine years of experience counseling teens and counseling families. I am doing what I can to let him know that age is not important. I want to learn from him. I will consider him my teacher."

Supervision

Kaisha: "I am going to need more supervision than I am getting. I talked earlier about being bi-racial. I know I am going to need help with cultural issues. And from earlier experiences in the program, I also know that I will be surprised by what some of the issues are. Right now, I am not sure that my site supervisor is going to have enough time to give me the help that I need."

Mid-term evaluation

Sam: "I know I am going to be scared of the **mid-term evaluation**. At the same time, I am good with feedback and I have the attitude of "bring it on." Of course, I am used to doing well most of the time and I have had such good feedback in my classes. I am trying to tell myself that it is good to hear where I can improve. I do believe that, it's just I don't always want to hear it. I know that it is too early to be concerned about this. But it is important."

Final evaluation

Janice: "It is difficult for me to think about the **final evaluation** when I am in my first week of practicum. I am going to take this experience one step at a time. I know that sounds like an easy response, but really, if I get too far ahead, then I think of all of the ways that things can go wrong."

Perspectives of Practicum

As you have begun to realize, practicum takes place in two very different environments, that of the college or academic world and that of the agency or school world (see Figure 1.1), or the world of practice. In fact, as a practicum student, you will function as a **bridge** that connects these two worlds. When you met your site supervisor for the first time or visited your practicum site, you were beginning to function as the bridge, and you will continue to do so during your time in practicum.

Dodds (1986) presented the perspectives of the academic world, the two worlds, the academic program, the practicum site or the world of practice, and the student, and described the major goals, ideal supervisor, and what each hopes for. See Figure 1.1 for a depiction of Dodds's model.

FIGURE 1.1. The Three Perspectives/Worlds of the Counseling Practicum Experience

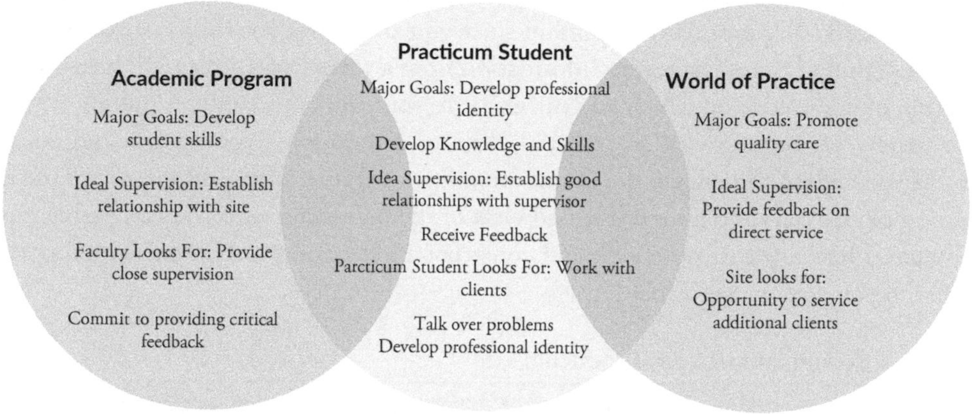

Academic Program

Major Goals: Develop
student skills

Ideal Supervision: Establish
relationship with site

Faculty Looks For: Provide
close supervision

Commit to providing critical
feedback

Practicum Student

Major Goals: Develop professional
identity

Develop Knowledge and Skills

Idea Supervision: Establish good
relationships with supervisor

Receive Feedback

Parcticum Student Looks For: Work with
clients

Talk over problems
Develop professional identity

World of Practice

Major Goals: Promote
quality care

Ideal Supervision:
Provide feedback on
direct service

Site looks for:
Opportunity to service
additional clients

Adapted from J. B. Dodds (1986) and from M. Woodside (2017)..

A key to understanding your role as a bridge that links the academic world with the practicum site is to recognize what you gain by operating within both worlds. Within the academic world you have learned and are continuing to learn the knowledge, skills, and values necessary to develop as a professional counselor. The world of practice will provide you with an opportunity to use what you have learned and enhance it as you work with clients. In Reflection Question 1.3, you will learn more about the perspectives of both worlds and your place as the bridge.

REFLECTION QUESTION 1.3

UNDERSTANDING YOUR ROLE AS A BRIDGE BETWEEN TWO WORLDS

What is your major goal for your participation in practicum?
How do you envision the ideal supervision?
What do you look for in the practicum experience (hopes and dreams)?

Early Days: Realities and Relationships

You may feel that practicum begins in a flurry, but in reality, at times, experiences in practicum begin slowly. According to practicum requirements, you will be spending 100 hours at your site over an academic term. And you may wonder, with such limited hours, if you will ever find your place at the site or establish firm and positive relationships with your site supervisor, staff, and clients. In fact, by the time you prepare to complete your practicum and leave your site, more than likely you will feel like you belong, are a part of the work team, and are making positive contributions in clients' lives. You may be reluctant to leave. For now, as a way to increase your sense of belonging and find your place, we suggest two strategies, one related to learning more about your site, the other enhancing your relationship with your supervisor.

Learning More About Your Site

You will continue to learn more about your practicum site and your site supervisor during your first few weeks. This is especially important since you are only at your site once or twice a week for a short period of time. Gathering information from a variety of sources will help you build a foundation of knowledge on which you can enhance your work. You will be looking for material from a variety of sources: written material, website descriptions, your peers, and counseling faculty. If you collect and collate the information in an organized way, by the end of the search, you have a global view and a more focused view of the practicum site. You can gather any concrete material into a file or notebook and construct an electronic document with any relevant information you gather. See Table 1.1.

TABLE 1.1. Learning about Your Practicum Site

Type of information	Information gathered	Source of information	Additional thoughts
Agency name and mission and goals			
Relevant contact information (from faculty supervisor)			
Clinical, agency, or school programs			
Support material about agency			
Populations served			
Case studies			
Funding reports			
Volunteer involvement			
Case studies (descriptions of clients who benefitted from the programs)			
Staff responsibilities			

From time to time you will want to share the information that you have gathered with your site supervisor, asking for help and clarification when needed. Review the information that you have collected about your practicum site (see Table 1.1). Look for any discrepancies in the information gathered or lack of information about the site that might be relevant to your practicum experience. Develop a list of questions you have about the site, based on the information you have gathered. With a class partner, review the information you each collected and then discuss your work. Refine your list of questions. Share these questions with your site supervisor.

Enhancing Your Relationship With Your Site Supervisor

When you conducted your initial interview with your site supervisor, you began a very important relationship. And it is one that is continuing as you begin your work in practicum. You will want to continue developing this relationship during your practicum experience. Because of the importance of this relationship, there are several conversations that you can have with your site supervisor that can support mutual dialogue and understanding. These topics are similar to those suggested when preparing for an initial interview. Addressing these topics allows you to talk about yourself, share your values and beliefs, and convey your readiness and enthusiasm for practicum and your work with clients (Center for Career Development, 2018). You will want to share more about yourself, your strengths, and your goals for practicum. Preparing to answer these questions helps you be more intentional in your dialogue with your site supervisor (see Table 1.2).

TABLE 1.2. Intentional Dialogue with Your Site Supervisor

Topic	Response
"Tell me about yourself" (Center for Career Development, 2018)	Preparing a response to this prompt helps you provide a thoughtful and reflective response and helps the site supervisor see you as a unique individual. We suggest that you share some information about your background (early life), some of your educational experiences, any volunteer and work experiences, and the reasons you are studying to become a professional counselor. You may keep your responses short, but insightful.
"What are your strengths?" (Center for Career Development, 2018)	The answer to this question you may have answered in an initial interview. We believe that focusing on strengths is an on-going conversation that you have with your supervisor. An answer to this question requires specific responses and one or two concrete examples to illustrate the points that you are making. Be sure to cite the feedback you have received from other employers or faculty. Although unasked, you also want to mention one or two areas for which you hope for growth. Practicum is about growth and development. This insight helps your site supervisor see you as competent, yet developing. You might also share strengths you have observed with your site supervisor. Provide examples that illustrate the points you are making.
"What are your goals for practicum?"	As you answer this question, you address the heart of your work with your site supervisor and clients within the site context. You can include personal goals, program goals, and practicum goals. Hearing a summary of various goals, your site supervisor can begin to plan your experiences and the supervision you will need to meet the goals. And, these goals will change during your time in practicum.

Many times, the sharing of personal information becomes a dialogue rather than question-and-answer sessions. As you begin to discuss yourself, especially as it relates to your participation in practicum, your site supervisor may self-disclose personal experiences, especially as they relate to his or her own growth and development and his or her experiences of supervision. As you engage in Reflection Question 1.4, you will begin to build your confidence in your ability to talk with your site supervisor about personal and professional topics. The responses will help you communicate more clearly and engage more effectively with your site supervisor.

Early Days: Enhancing Your Practicum

The early days and weeks of practicum represent an excellent time to not only think about beginning your work at your site, but enhancing it. This forward thinking displays motivation, initiative, and commitment, all critically important professional behaviors. Two ways to raise the level of your performance are to develop a strong practicum contract and establish a legacy project or gift.

The Practicum Contract

As you know from your experience as the bridge between the academic world and the world of practice, each world has its own expectations for your work in practicum. And, in fact, you may also have your own personal and professional goals for this first field-based experience. The **practicum contract**, an agreement among the faculty supervisor, the site supervisor, and you (as the practicum student) identifies a set of goals and objectives to be met in practicum. Outcomes that are associated with these goals are formalized in the practicum contract.

You will develop a practicum contract in the first few weeks of practicum. As we stated earlier, the document represents the integration of the three perspective we discussed at the beginning of this chapter: the academic world, the world of practice, and the practicum student. And, your negotiation of the contract that meets the needs of all three perspectives illustrates your linking or bridging responsibility. Specifically, the primary purpose of the practicum contract is to document the agreement made among the three parties related to your unique goals for practicum at your site and the roles and responsibilities you will assume. This practicum contract also helps shape the mid-term and final evaluation efforts that we will discuss later in the text. The practicum contract assumes many formats, but most include some common elements: practicum student information; specific goals; activities or tasks to meet the goals; specific ways to measure if goals are met; site supervisor, faculty supervisor, and student comments; signatures and dates.

Making a Difference: The Legacy Project

An important part of your practicum experience is what you can give to a site. In other words, what you give to your site is your legacy or legacy gift or project. To choose your **legacy gift,** you can answer the question, "What will I leave with my agency or school that would not have occurred or been developed without my work, help, or support?" In most agencies and schools, there are a list of activities or artifacts or contributions that are left undone because staff don't have time to devote to them. In spite of good intentions, often times staff use their time focusing on top priorities and attending to small and larger crises. You will want to choose at least one project that is important to the site or to clients that would not have occurred had they not been there. Janice, Jose, Kaisha, and Sam talk about choosing their legacy gifts during an online discussion board their second week of practicum.

TRANSCRIPTION 1.3. THE LEGACY GIFT

Group practicum online discussion board

Sam: What are you all going to choose as your legacy gift? I am still unsure.

Janice: I know already because my site supervisor is familiar with this assignment. She gave me four ideas and asked if any of them seemed like something that I want to do.

Sam: I am trying to decide if I should do something that builds on my strengths or stretches me. This is something that Dr. Kim says we need to consider.

Jose: My site supervisor would like for me to prepare a workshop for all staff that focuses on the opioid crisis and what the local mental health community is doing. Sort of like a cross between an education format and a community-building forum. This is a good opportunity for me to network with other community leaders and staff.

Janice: I think that I am going to start a counseling group for immigrants who are enrolled in English as a second language. The focus is going to be "developing peer friendships and finding mentors." I am also going to visit the homes of these students. This is a group that gets lost in our school.

Kaisha: Honestly, I have no idea what I am going to do. I don't think I am going to have this figured out by the time our practicum contract is due. And I don't think I have to know exactly what my legacy gift is going to be. Sam, you might have a hard time figuring something out since you are in a clinic.

Sam: I think my supervisor has some ideas but wants me to add some ideas to the list. I have an easier time thinking how others could give me a legacy gift!!!! My list of needs is great. But it is not supposed to work that way!

So, think about developing a legacy gift to your agency or school. This is a wonderful idea for your personal contribution to the site, your professional development, and a way of saying thank you to the site and supervisor who helped you during practicum.

Summary

Two questions central to your work in practicum, "Is the profession of counseling right for me?" and "How will I/can I know that I am ready?" are important to explore. Your increased understanding of the language, purpose, and approaches to practicum will assist you in addressing these questions. You can return to these core identity questions at the end of practicum and at the end of each academic semester (quarter, unit) so that you can note the differences in your responses.

Terms such as practicum, practicum student, supervision, and mid-term are important in your understanding of your practicum experience. Understanding the meaning of these terms will help you negotiate your experience with your peers and supervisors.

Because of the differences between the two worlds in which you are involved, the world of the academic program and the world of practice, you will need to act as the bridge between them, if your practicum is to be successful. Two ways that you can function effectively as a bridge are to gather materials about your site and develop an understanding of its purpose and culture and to talk with your site supervisor about your own strengths and goals.

In addition, spending time developing the practicum contract will enhance communication between your academic program and practicum site. The development of a practicum contract will serve as a roadmap for your practicum experiences. Finally, by choosing a special project or goal that helps the work of your practicum site, you can offer a legacy to those who are helping assist your development.

Key Terms

Academic world

Bridge

Dodds's three perspectives

Faculty supervisor

Final evaluation

Hard questions

Legacy gift

Mid-term evaluation

Practicum

Practicum contract

Practicum experience

Practicum site

Practicum student

Readiness

Site supervisor

Supervised practice

Supervision

World of practice

References

Center for Career Development. (2018). Gain experience. Retrieved from https://career.utk.edu/students/gain-experience/.

Dodds, J. B. (1986). Supervision of psychology trainees in field placements. *Professional Psychology Research and Practice, 17*(4), 296–300.

Woodside, M. (2017). *The human service internship experience. Helping students find their way.* Thousand Oaks, CA: SAGE.

Woodside, M., Paulus, T., & Ziegler, M. (2009). The experience of school counseling internship through the lens of communities of practice. *Counselor Education and Supervision*, *49*(1), 20–38.

CHAPTER 2

Beginning
PRACTICUM

INTRODUCTION

You may or may not have slept soundly the night before beginning your practicum experience at your site. If you are like many students, you have spent time trying to picture what you will walk into that first day. You may feel excited and nervous, since it is the next bold step in your development as a counselor. This chapter is designed to help you through those first few days and weeks, since, if your program is like many, you will begin at the site, seeing clients very soon. You will learn about some basic logistical steps, including paperwork, the philosophy behind that paperwork that will guide your growth and protect your clients, and practical considerations for the various ways you begin your practicum experience. The goals for this chapter follow.

GOALS OF THE CHAPTER

- Identify the tasks related to the first week at the practicum site
- Describe cultural norms related to the practicum site and the clients served
- Confirm your readiness for the practicum experience as you understand it at this point

Section 5. C. 2. CONTEXTUAL DIMENSIONS

a. roles and settings of clinical mental health counselors

c. mental health service delivery modalities within the continuum of care, such as inpatient, outpatient, partial treatment and aftercare, and the mental health counseling services networks" (Council for Accreditation of Counseling and Related Programs, 2016a)

Section 3: PROFESSIONAL PRACTICE—SUPERVISOR QUALIFICATIONS

N. Counselor education program faculty members serving as individual/triadic or group practicum/internship supervisors for students in entry-level programs have (1) relevant experience, (2) professional credentials, and (3) counseling supervision training and experience.

O. Students serving as individual/triadic or group practicum/internship supervisors for students in entry-level programs must (1) have completed CACREP entry-level counseling degree requirements, (2) have completed or are receiving preparation in counseling supervision, and (3) be under supervision from counselor education program faculty.

P. Site supervisors have (1) a minimum of a master's degree, preferably in counseling, or a related profession; (2) relevant certifications and/or licenses; (3) a minimum of two years of pertinent professional experience in the specialty area in which the student is enrolled; (4) knowledge of the program's expectations, requirements, and evaluation procedures for students; and (5) relevant training in counseling supervision.

Q. Orientation, consultation, and professional development opportunities are provided by counselor education program faculty to site supervisors.

R. Written supervision agreements define the roles and responsibilities of the faculty supervisor, site supervisor, and student during practicum and internship. When individual/triadic practicum supervision is conducted by a site supervisor in consultation with counselor education program faculty, the supervision agreement must detail the format and frequency of consultation to monitor student learning. (Council for Accreditation of Counseling and Relating Programs, 2016b)

Preparing Information About Practicum

As you prepare yourself to enter your practicum site for the first time, it is important that you have a clear understanding of the practicum experience, its purposes, and what it requires. This is a great time to review your academic program's handbooks, syllabus, and other paperwork related to the practicum experience. After this review, we ask that you think about the information you will want to convey to your site supervisor about practicum and your role in it. The range of preparation for practicum may vary across site supervisors. Your site supervisor may have supervised other practicum students in your program or in other programs. Or, you may be the first practicum student your supervisor has had. Regardless of your site supervisor's experience, preparing information about practicum for your site supervisor is important. Reviewing this information with your supervisor fosters a sense of collaboration and provides you both with a common understanding of the practicum experience.

In preparing information about practicum for your site supervisor, you will want to gather a set of relevant materials. Your supervisor may or may not have a copy of your counseling academic program's practicum handbook and/or the practicum syllabus. Don't worry about duplicating materials. You are gathering information for your site supervisor and preparing a folder, so information about practicum is all in one location. This information may include a summary description of practicum; the goals of practicum; the major requirements for practicum, including direct and indirect hours; expectations for supervision; and methods of evaluation.

Entering the Practicum Site

Many of you will participate in an **orientation** before you begin to assume your responsibilities as an intern. Your orientation falls on a continuum that represents a range of experiences. For example, orientation may be as extensive as a one-week orientation that is designed for all new employees, such as intensive training related to the client interventions. Or, it may be as limited as a half-day training for all volunteers and interns. Orientation may be only the time you spend with your site supervisor during the initial visit. Regardless of the nature of the orientation, it represents the time when you first enter the practicum site and begin to learn about the site, the clients it serves, and its policies and procedures. The following section describes ways you might maximize your early experiences at your placement site.

What You Do the First Few Days

The first day in practicum is both exciting and stressful. Table 2.1 provides some concrete suggestions collected from career experts that help you with **preparation for the first day** (Herman, 2018; Roos, 2014; Salpeter, 2014). Table 2.2 continues with strategies focused on practical and personal aspects of participating in practicum for the first week or two. Following these suggestions provides you a way to alleviate some of your sense of stress and helps you begin your practicum in a productive way. Many of these guidelines build on what you learned on your initial visit to the practicum site, while others relate to your status as the newest member of the agency or school team. All guidelines help you make a positive impression and assist you as you build the bridge introduced in Chapter 1 between your academic program and the practicum site (world of practice).

TABLE 2.1. Before the First Day or Week of Practicum

Before the first day or week of practicum	
Learn more about your agency or school and the population it serves	Follow up your initial visit by gaining more information about your practicum site. Begin to read about the clients with whom you will work.
Confirm travel to your agency or school	You located the site of your agency or school while making your initial visit. Think about the way you will get to your site; understand any traffic issues that may arise.
Think about alternatives if your plans go awry	Agencies, schools, and site supervisors understand that travel plans sometimes go awry. Develop backup plans.
Decide how to introduce yourself to agency staff and clients	During your first week, you will be introducing yourself to members of the agency or school, administrative staff, and clients. Prepare a way to tell these individuals who you are and your place in the agency or school.
Plan appropriate dress	During your initial visit, you had an opportunity to observe the agency or school dress and ask your site supervisor about expectations. You want to dress as an employee rather than a student.

We also provide some helpful suggestions related to **surviving the first week** of the practicum (Table 2.2). Again, career experts guide the suggestions that follow (Herman, 2018; Roos, 2014; Salpeter, 2014). These strategies help prepare you for the experience and reduce the awkwardness that you may feel as a newcomer to a setting.

TABLE 2.2. Strategies for the First Week

Strategies for the first week	
Manage your time	As you know from other jobs you have held, being on time is important. It indicates that you are serious about your commitment to the job. Work with your site supervisor to develop a calendar and a time for your practicum. Be early or on time and follow check-in procedures when you arrive. Be sure to let you site supervisor know if you encounter an unforeseen challenge. Call and provide the change in your plan for arrival or attendance. Each day before you leave, confirm your schedule for the following day or week.
Bring your own supplies	Remember the work of practicum will require supplies for notetaking, scheduling, and developing a list of tasks to be assumed and completed. Make sure you have pen, pencil, notepad, and calendar with you during the day. Or, you may use an electronic device for your notetaking. Sometimes a stressful event is lunch time. Bring your own lunch that first day or week until you understand the culture of lunch at your agency or school, and bring snacks in case you are working through the noon hour.
Think about how you will use your electronic devices	Talk with you supervisor about the use of electronic devices in the agency or school. Follow agency or school policy. Let you supervisor guide you. Even though you are accustomed to being "on call" electronically, don't use your devices for personal contacts during your work day. It is good to alert your family and friends that you will be available after work but not during work. Specifically, put your phone on vibrate or turn it off, develop a schedule for checking messages and returning them, and don't interrupt your work with your site supervisor, staff, or clients with calls or texts.
Be responsible	During the first week, you are in the learning mode. Pay attention and ask relevant questions. Learn, learn, and learn about your agency or school, its staff, and its clients. You will want to gather information and ask questions and keep a balance between the two. You might record questions that you have and ask them of your supervisor at the end of the day. And, don't forget if you do need help, be sure to ask for it. This is a great time to plan scheduled times to meet with your site supervisor.

Make some space your space	Examine where you will be working. Is the space yours alone? Do you share it? Determine what you will need. Bring in a few personal items. Keep it neat. File away any confidential information.
Respect your hours	As we stated earlier, be sure that you arrive early or on time. Also, don't leave early. Part of your professional commitment is to remain on the job during your scheduled time.

Next, let's turn our attention to how you introduce yourself and share your professional identity with the professional disclosure statement and the introduction to administration and staff. Writing these is a part of beginning practicum. It is also a step to take toward your professional identity development.

Sharing Your Professional Identity

Professional Disclosure Statement

Before you begin to see clients within the counseling context, it is important that you develop a **professional disclosure statement**. The purpose of this statement is to introduce yourself to your new clients in a formal way. Sharing a professional disclosure statement with clients provides one method of communicating with your client about your professional self and your knowledge, expertise, experience, and practicum status. You have an ethical responsibility to disclose this information to your clients. In fact, you will want them to know—in fact, it is their right to know—about your place at the clinic, agency, or school as a practicum student, to understand your engagement in supervision, and to understand the time limits of your involvement with them (e.g., 10-week or semester-long commitment). The professional statement that you compose for the practicum experience is the first among many. You will revise your professional disclosure statement as you begin practicum, and you will continue to create new statements as you gain experience, change your placement or place of employment, and increase your career expertise.

There are several sections in a professional disclosure statement and each requires different types of information about who you are as a practicum student and a developing professional counselor. These sections cover the following information: name, educational experience, previous relevant work experience, philosophy or theoretical orientation (personal or site), position as a practicum student, and the nature of supervision. In the professional disclosure statement, you can include the contact information of your faculty and site supervisors, in case of any questions or concerns.

The benefits from writing a professional disclosure statement and providing it to the client in writing are numerous. Since clients will, more than likely, not remember all the introductory information you provide them at the first session, they have a written record that they can review at their own leisure. Clients also learn about your expertise and the limits of your knowledge and experience. The professional disclosure statement marks your commitment to a profession and reminds clients that your will behave professionally and ethically. The example in Figure 2.1 also includes informed consent information and permission to tape and shows how the professional disclosure statement, informed consent, and permission to tape are combined in one form. In some instances, you might use three separate forms, or they might also be combined into one or two. Regardless of the number of documents prepared, it is crucial that all three issues be covered thoroughly with clients. Please keep in mind that the length of the form is not the most important thing. The most import thing is to use these documents to lay a foundation for the therapeutic relationship you will build and maintain over the coming weeks.

Figure 2.1 represents a sample professional disclosure statement written by a student at Northern Illinois University (n.d.).

FIGURE 2.1. Professional Disclosure Statement

Professional Disclosure and Informed Consent Statements

Community Counseling Training Center at NIU Counseling Program
Northern Illinois University
DeKalb, IL 60115 815-753-9312
Conditions of Counseling

Counseling Relationship: Unless you prefer otherwise, I will call you by your first name. During the time you and I work together, we usually will meet weekly for approximately 50-minute sessions. Although our sessions may be psychologically deep, ours is a professional relationship rather than a social one. Therefore, please do not invite me to social events, bring me gifts, ask to barter or exchange services, ask me to write references for you, or ask me to relate to you in any way other than the professional context of our counseling relationship. You will benefit the most if your interactions address your concerns exclusively.

I conduct all counseling session in English or with a translator for whom you arrange and pay. I do not discriminate on the basis of race, gender, religion, national origin, disability, or sexual orientation. If significant differences, such as in culture or belief system, exist between us, I will work to understand those differences.

Effects of Counseling: At any time, you may initiate with me a discussion of possible positive or negative effects of entering or not entering into, continuing, or discontinuing counseling. I expect you to benefit from counseling. However, I cannot guarantee any specific results. Counseling is a personal exploration that may lead to major changes in your life perspectives and decisions. These changes may affect your significant relationships, job, and/or understanding of yourself. You may feel troubled, usually only temporarily, by some of the things you learn about yourself, or some of the changes you make. In addition, counseling can result in long lasting effects. Although the exact nature of changes resulting from counseling cannot be predicted, I intend to work with you to achieve the best possible results for you.

Conditions of Ongoing Counseling: If you have been in counseling or psychotherapy during the past seven years, the CCTC may require you to sign a release so I may communicate with and/or receive copies of records from the professional(s) from whom you received mental health services, if I deem it important to do so. By signing this form, you are agreeing to disclose all previous mental health treatment and to reimburse the CCTC for any expenses charged by your previous mental health professional(s) for supplying copies of your records. While you are in counseling with me at the CCTC, you agree not to maintain or establish a professional relationship with another mental health professional unless you first discuss it with me and sign a release that enables me to communicate with the other mental health professional(s). If you decide to maintain or establish a professional relationship with another mental health professional against my advice, I may consider this your decision to change counselors and the Community Counseling Training Center at NIU reserves the right to terminate your counseling services.

Appointments and Cancellation: Our in-person contact will be limited to counseling sessions you arrange with me. My scheduled time at the Community Counseling Training Center at NIU is only 5 hours per week.

The Community Counseling Training Center at NIU (CCTC) is a training facility and maintains a strict schedule of services. If you have to miss a session, please call the CCTC at (815) 753-9312 to cancel your session as soon as possible. Please provide your name, the date and time of your session, and your counselor's name. If you miss two counseling sessions without notifying the CCTC, your services will be terminated. If you are a student seeking extra credit for participating in counseling services, you must attend a minimum of four sessions to receive your extra credit. If you are terminated you may reapply for services, pending counselor availability, however you will be required to complete four consecutive sessions.

X _____ I have read the above statements and understand the procedures regarding cancellation.

Permission to Participate and Confidentiality: I am a counselor-in-training in the counseling program at Northern Illinois University and am under the direct supervision of supervisors listed on page one (whom may be contacted at (815) 753-9312. All our counselor sessions are confidential. This means that no information will be released to persons or agencies regarding the fact that counseling has been received or the nature of the concerns without written consent. Danger to self and/or others (i.e. suicide or homicide) may necessitate the breaking of confidentiality. In addition, by law suspected child abuse and/or neglect and elder abuse and/or neglect communicated by clients must be reported to appropriate agencies by counseling staff.

X _____ I have read the above statements and understand my rights regarding my participation and confidentiality.

Recording and Observation: Counselors-in-training receive consultation and supervision. To aid in this, I must request to have your sessions recorded and/or observed. Information and recordings will be treated according to ethical standards. Confidentiality will be strictly maintained; information will not be released to any other person or agency without your written permission. In accordance with Illinois state laws, written records will be maintained for the appropriate length of time and then properly destroyed. Please read the statement below and sign if you agree. If you have questions, please talk them over with me.

X _____ I agree to the recording and/or observation of my sessions. I understand that confidentiality will be maintained, written records will be maintained, and that professional ethical standards will be observed in this process. I also understand that I may request the identities of all individuals observing my recorded counseling sessions. Recordings will be erased following supervision.

Crises: The Community Counseling Training Center at NIU is not equipped for after-hours emergencies. Any messages on the CCTC answering machine after Thursdays' hours will not be heard until Monday afternoon. If a need arises and assistance is required immediately, please contact the University Police at (815) 753-1212. If you are not a student at NIU, contact the Ben Gordon 24-Hour Community Crisis Hotline at (866) 242-0111.

X _____ I have read the above statements and understand the procedures regarding emergency situations.

In the event that I believe you are in danger, physically or emotionally, to yourself or another person, you specifically consent for me to warn the person in danger and to contact the following person(s), in addition to medical and/or law enforcement personnel:

Name Telephone Number

This professional disclosure statement comes from Northern Illinois University. Northern Illinois University. (n.d.) Professional disclosure statement. Retrieved from http://cedu.niu.edu/cctc/forms/Prof-Disclosure-Statement.pdf .

ETHICAL CONSIDERATION 2.1

As you create your professional disclosure statement, reflect on its ethical aspects. Describe how you believe the professional disclosure statement meets ethical obligations to your client, the agency you serve, the profession, and you as a student and professional counselor.

As a follow-up to review of this document, your instructor may guide you through a process of revising a version of this document to make it your own. Through this process, you will be able to own the material, expanding it in places and trimming in others.

Introduction to Administrators and Staff

One way to practice sharing your professional disclosure statement with your client is to practice it like the elevator speech. The elevator speech is a common interview preparation technique that prepares individuals to meet new people and communicate their professional identity in a brief, clear way. Luke (2018) describes using the elevator speech as an intervention for clients in a career-focused counseling environment. In Experiential Activity 2.1, we use this activity to help you prepare for meeting agency or school staff.

EXPERIENTIAL ACTIVITY 2.1
The Elevator Speech

Imagine that you enter an elevator and meet a professional who asks you to tell him or her about yourself. You have until the elevator doors open again to share this information—about 30 seconds. Determine what you will say and write out this speech. Practice this speech aloud four or five times with one of your classmates.

Engaging in activities such as Experiential Activity 2.1 have the additional benefit of assisting you as a CIT to see that you are, in fact, a professional. Gaining the skills of describing yourself as a professional may help assuage doubts about your position as a professional and reduce behaviors that made you feel like a non-professional. Sharing professional disclosure statements and other introductory documents are more effective in building rapport when they are delivered unapologetically and nondefensively; they represent the facts undergirding the clinical relationship.

Informed Consent and Permission to Tape

Informed consent is a weighty document that often intimidates students and clients alike. In response to this intimidation, CITs either tend to rush through and minimize the roles and responsibilities in the therapeutic relationship, or they spend so much time clarifying informed consent that it becomes unnecessarily daunting to the client. Therefore, active participation in the experiential activity at the end of this section, which guides you through introducing clients to the concept of informed consent, is important. You will want to review the information carefully. Both informed consent and permission to tape are documents that you will want your faculty site supervisors to approve prior to seeing and presenting these to clients.

Informed Consent

Informed consent, as described by the American Counseling Association's (ACA) Code of Ethics states,

> Clients have the freedom to choose whether to enter into or remain in a counseling relationship and need adequate information about the counseling process and the counselor. Counselors have an obligation to review in writing and verbally with clients the rights and responsibilities of both counselors and clients. Informed consent is an ongoing part of the counseling process, and counselors appropriately document discussions of informed consent throughout the counseling relationship. (ACA, 2014, p. 4)

The informed consent document includes a rationale for informed consent, information about practicum student education and training, a description of the counseling relationship, an outline of client rights and responsibilities, the nature of confidentiality and its limitations, and relevant signatures. If the practicum student is working with a minor, then informed consent is needed from the minor's parent(s) or guardian and informed assent from the minor. Essential elements of the informed consent include introduction and purpose of the informed consent, information about practicum student training, a description of what counseling entails, a description of client rights and responsibilities, limits of confidentiality, signature line, and date line.

As mentioned earlier, when the CIT is counseling a minor, the informed consent statement may be adjusted to reflect gaining parent or guardian and minor permission to counsel. Legally, minors cannot consent to their own treatment (this will vary by age and state), but assent is a way of soliciting buy-in from the client who happens to be a minor.

The following activity will help practicum students introduce the informed consent concept and form to their clients. Introducing clients to informed consent is vital to the success of work with clients. It is, oftentimes, a place where students stumble. And, when the introduction of informed consent is not conducted well, future difficulties may also arise.

One of these difficulties occurs when a practicum student must disclose client information to authorities, often to the surprise and disdain of the client. It is helpful if practicum students commit the informed consent document to memory prior to meeting with clients. Once memorized, then practice discussing informed consent with clients. Addressing the importance of the informed consent represents a developmental transition for CITs, from being able to be successful by cramming for an exam and skim the text to having direct impact on another human's well-being. Experiential Activity 2.2, Roleplaying Informed Consent, will help you prepare for introducing informed consent to your clients.

EXPERIENTIAL ACTIVITY 2.2
Roleplaying Informed Consent

Roleplaying the way in which you will introduce the informed consent will help you prepare for this experience with a real client. Once you have prepared the informed consent you will use at your practicum site, memorize the informed consent and practice explaining it to a client. Then, ask a peer to role play a client. Introduce the informed consent to the client and then respond to client questions. Client responses will range from mild disinterest, so the counselor must work to engage them, to client reluctance to sign for fear of being reported.

NOTE: In order for the signature of the client on the informed consent document to be both valid and meaningful, both components of informed consent must be clear: informed and consent. Clients must receive full and accurate information that they can understand about the parameters of the relationship. They must also consent—agree—with those conditions. Additionally, since informed consent is a living document, getting the signature at the beginning is not sufficient. The parameters must be revisited often so that clients are continually empowered throughout the counseling process.

Permission to Record

Audio or video taping work with clients requires gaining, from the client, a **permission to record**. This recording often provides a fundamental way site and faculty supervisors may review and reflect on practicum students' relationship building and skill development. In fact, the ability to record client interactions is one requirement for establishing a practicum site. Even though taping is an established part of the practicum experience, CITs are often wary of it. And, they often believe that their clients will resist being recorded and fear the recording process will impact the building of rapport and subsequent counseling (Bernard & Goodyear, 2014). As it turns out, in most cases, CITs are far more concerned about the video recorder than clients, who quickly forget about or otherwise ignore the device. It is often more the case that counselor self-consciousness about the recorder is what makes clients uncomfortable.

There are ethical considerations that must be considered to protect the client and help the client normalize the taping process. The following guidelines will help you introduce the process of taping to your clients and gain their permission to tape.

SETTING-RELATED CONSIDERATIONS. Before you begin your work with clients, work with your site supervisor to align the counseling academic program requires for taping with the agency or school's policies. It is important that both parties focus on the protection of clients, both adults and minors. Difficult situations may arise when clients are members of vulnerable populations or individual clients are reluctant to or refused to be taped.

STRUCTURING THE DISCUSSION. You can introduce the process of taping in the initial meeting with a client. Following the review of the informed consent form, the process of taping becomes an integral part of how you are learning to be a professional counselor and your need for feedback from both your site supervisor and faculty supervisor.

- Present the permission to tape form in the first counseling session.

- Assure clients that you will not tape the session without their permission.

- Explain to clients that you will stop the recording if they ask you to do so.

- Explain how important the taping is for your growth and development.

> ### CULTURAL CONSIDERATION 2.1
>
> How do you feel about taping a session with a client? Do your feelings match your client's feelings? What did you learn from gaining client permission for taping?

> ### ETHICAL CONSIDERATION 2.3
>
> Informed consent and permission to tape are documents that represent ethical and legal obligations that the academic program, you as the practicum student, and the practicum site have for the client and, in the case of a minor, the minor's parent or guardian. Why do you believe that these two documents are critical to the counseling process and the helping relationship?

- Detail how the tape is used in supervision, with the focus on your counseling rather than their role as the client.

- Clarify who listens to the tape and the nature of and limits of confidentiality.

- Describe who listens, where tapes are stored, and when they are destroyed.

One final word about reviewing and obtaining signatures for these documents is in order before we turn our attention to those first few weeks of practicum. These documents and procedures are not tasks to complete before counseling begins; they are integral to the relationship. Seek supervision and consultation from your supervisors if you have any doubts about how to practice using these documents therapeutically.

The First Weeks in Practicum

What My First Few Weeks Were Like

You first few weeks at practicum may be exciting and stressful. Because of the limited number of hours required for practicum and the press of other responsibilities such as classes, professional obligations (Chi Sigma Iota Honor Society, class projects, service learning,) as well as personal ones, it may take you some time to settle into your site and feel like you belong. Janice, Jose, Kaisha, and Sam each tell you about their first few weeks at their practicum site.

Janice: Oh my. I had forgotten what a building full of middle schoolers would be like. I spent lots of time just being in places so I could learn about middle school and the culture of the school and the kids. I watched the activity in the halls, sat in the commons during lunch, visited several classes, attended in-school suspension, and shadowed my site supervisor. I thought the whole day I was there was chaos. Absolute chaos. And noisy. I can't imagine I am ever going to adjust. Everything is so different from what I am used to. And the students are a mix of cultures. And some students speak English as a second language. And everyone is so busy, so I am not sure how I am going to meet teachers and staff in the school.

Jose: I don't know what I was expecting, but my facility was more like teaching than I thought it would be. There is a schedule and everyone, including staff, were where they were supposed to be all day. Except for my site supervisor. She does have regular counseling and groups, but she also spends a lot of time answering calls of crisis. I spent most of my time with my site supervisor in counseling sessions. I also was able to go to five groups with other members of the staff, attend two family sessions, and make one home visit. I am less worried now about working with adults. And I am reading everything I can about the therapies used here at the facility. And I am meeting a lot of staff. One concern I do have is when I get my first clients. How will I handle the fact that I am bi-racial and queer? I noticed that my site supervisor doesn't talk about ethnicity or culture at all.

Kaisha: Well, I don't look like anybody else here at the center since I look more Black than White. But that doesn't seem to matter. It is wild here. We have so many clients and so many needs. And my site supervisor just takes me with her everywhere she goes. I have only been a practicum for two days. She and I decided that it would be better if I spend one intense day a week there. And I can already see that I will always wish that I could spend more time there. When I arrived at the center, clients were already lined up to entered the door. They started asking me for help the minute that I got out of my car. And they didn't even know me. I spent time in a two-hour staffing. And then I stayed in the rec hall for two hours. I am pairing names at the rec hall with names in staffing. I thought I would be nervous, but I have been too busy to be nervous. I don't have a space yet. I hope that I can find a spot soon.

Sam: The campus clinic is very orderly. My faculty supervisor met with my site supervisor, and we mapped out my schedule. The first week, I observed several of the therapists. Three I observed in the room with them as they worked with clients. Two of them I observed behind glass in an adjoining room. I then spent an hour with my site supervisor to plan the next week. That second week, I was nervous but I saw my first client. My site supervisor observed me behind glass, and we taped my session and talked about meeting the client immediately after that. I was so intimidated at first, but the session with the client, I had to do an intake and introduce myself and review informed consent and gain permission to tape. And, my client seemed matched to my skills. We both talked about the appropriate amount (just trying to be funny here). I will see my client next week. My site supervisor and I will review my plan for the session before I see the client. And that will be the third week. So, I will also have three more clients of my own.

As you can see from hearing from Janice, Jose, Kaisha, and Sam, the first week or two in practicum can be very different at various practicum sites. One thing that they all have in common is how they are learning to work with their site supervisors, other staff, and their clients, all within the unique cultures of their practicum sites. During this time, there is time and opportunity, regardless of the agency or school and its culture and focus, to allow others to view you as a professional. You are demonstrating the way in which you work and the way you view your professional role as a counselor. And you want others to see you in a positive light! In Table 2.3, there are some guidelines about ways you can establish a reputation for hard work and commitment and demonstrating **positive personal attributes and actions** (Bajic, 2013; Herman, 2018; Roos, 2014; Salpeter, 2014).

TABLE 2.3. Positive Personal Attributes and Actions

Positive personal attributes and actions	
Lend a willing hand	Look for ways that you can support the work of your site supervisor and other staff. And, if you are asked to assume work, if you feel qualified, be willing to say yes. If you need help, ask for it.
Watch	You are new to this environment. Be observant about the culture of the site and find ways that you can help your new colleagues. Balance listening and talking.
On-going projects and new projects	You will want to find ways that you can make unique contributions to your site and to your clients. Pay attention to such phrases as "We have always wanted to do X, but never seem to have the time." You are looking for a match between what the agency or school and its clients or students need and you own knowledge and skill sets. During this time, look for ways that you might be able to contribute to the goals of the agency or school.
Pay attention to multicultural and ethical cultures and challenges	You will want to attend to the multicultural environment in which you are working. Listen and observe the culture. Find out what the particular sensitivities are in your environment. Also, pinpoint some of the ethical challenges that confront the agency or school. As a new staff member, you may have contributions to make. Watch for ways in which you can do so. Your site supervisor will be an important source for this.
Grow and develop professionally	You will want to develop professionally while you are in practicum. Consider the program goals for practicum and your own goals and ask your site supervisor for help to meet these.
Plan now	If you have goals and experiences you would like to have during your practicum, discuss this with your faculty and site supervisor. You may be so busy with the daily life of the practicum site, it would be easy only to address the goals of clients and the agency or school.

The early weeks of practicum can be hectic. They often establish a way of being at your site and a way of communicating with your site supervisor. You may establish these ways of being that promote growth and development. On the other hand, all habits may have negative outcomes. Be sure to enlist the help of your supervisors during this time.

Practicum Work Over Time

In most practicum placements, a student will assume work slowly and end practicum with responsibility for counseling clients. Practicum students will also assume several tasks that support the work of the agency or the school. The focus of practicum also changes; early in practicum, students are introducing themselves to their site supervisor and other staff, beginning to understand the nature of the practicum work, and learning about the clients and the services provided those clients. Practicum students learn about the agency or school in various ways. One activity is called **shadowing**.

Shadowing

Shadowing is a technique that is used across various professions to help new students, interns, and employees learn about the world of the work site. In the case of a practicum in counseling, a site supervisor asks the practicum students to spend several hours or days walking with them through their professional activities. Not only can the practicum student observe the work of the agency or school and the responsibilities of the site supervisor, the practicum student can also meet staff, see clients, and learn about the culture of the work environment. Shadowing might also include asking the practicum student to assume small tasks or responsibilities, not just as busy work, but as a way to contribute to the work of the agency or school. Shadowing also may include time for informal and formal supervision. The site supervisor may meet with the practicum student at the beginning of a work day to detail what the student might expect during the shadowing process. Or, the site supervisor may meet with the practicum student at the end of the day to talk about the experiences of the day. This becomes an excellent time for the practicum student to ask questions and engage the supervisor at a personal and professional level. Learning by watching means being an active learner, reflecting on the experience, and clarifying what was observed. How can you prepare for learning in this situation? Here are some questions that you can ask your site supervisor about shadowing:

- When I enter a meeting or counseling session, how will you introduce me? What would you like me to say?

- While I am with you, what should I be doing? I know that my job is to listen and observe. Would you like for me to take notes? When would that be? Other times when you would prefer I place my pen and paper in my bag?

- Are there special things that you would like for me to pay attention to during the day?

- When will we have an opportunity to talk about what I have observed?

Summary

The first days and weeks are formative times for CITs; thus, we present this chapter on making the transition from classroom learning to the experience of practicum. Included in this time is making contact with staff, presenting yourself as a professional, learning the rhythm of the site, and communicating with clients about your professional identity and the parameters of the counseling relationship. The documents described in this chapter are intended to support you in this process and to move them from being checklist items that receive limited attention to becoming an important part of your counseling work. In contrast, they have been presented in such a way that they will promote success in the counseling relationship. An important part of learning is participating in the experiential activities in this chapter and beginning to video-tape yourself. This work will help take the next steps toward growing your professional identity.

Key Terms

Informed Consent

Orientation

Permission To Record

Positive Personal Attributes And Actions

Preparation For The First Day

Professional Disclosure Statement

Shadowing

Surviving The First Week

References

American Counseling Association. (2014). ACA 2014 Code of Ethics. Retrieved from https://www.counseling.org/resources/aca-code-of-ethics.pdf

Bajic, E. (2013). Tips for stress-free first day on the job. *Forbes*. Retrieved from https://www.forbes.com/sites/elenabajic/2013/10/28/tips-for-a-stress-free-first-day-on-the-new-job/#766a8a082ac3

Bernard, J. M., & Goodyear, R. K. (2014). *Fundamental of supervision* (5th edition). Boston: Pearson.

Council for Accreditation of Counseling and Related Program. (2016a). 2016 CACREP Section 5 standards. Retrieved from https://www.cacrep.org/section-5-entry-level-specialty-areas-clinical-mental-health-counseling/

Council for Accreditation of Counseling and Related Program. (2016b). 2016 CACREP Section 3 standards. Retrieved from https://www.cacrep.org/section-3-professional-practice/

Herman, L. (2018). 8 tips for rocking your first day at a new job. *The Muse*. Retrieved from https://www.themuse.com/advice/8-tips-for-rocking-your-first-day-at-a-new-job

Luke, C. (2018). *Essentials of career-focused counseling*. San Diego, CA: Cognella.

Northern Illinois University. (n.d.) Professional disclosure statement. Retrieved from http://cedu.niu.edu/cctc/forms/Prof-Disclosure-Statement.pdf.

Roos, D. (2014). 10 tips for your first day at work. *How Stuff Works*. Retrieved from https://money.howstuffworks.com/business/starting-a-job/10-tips-for-your-first-day-of-work.htm

Salpeter, M. (2014). First day on the job: 9 ways to make a great impression. *Jobs AOL*. Retrieved from https://www.aol.com/2013/06/12/first-day-on-job-make-good-impression/

CHAPTER 3

Managing
EXPECTATIONS

INTRODUCTION

One of the most exciting and anxiety-producing events in your counseling development is making first contact with a client in your role as a counselor. The term **first contact** represents not only the first time that you have interaction with a client, this even may, in many ways, be similar to an alien encounter. It may seem alien because the term "client" conveys many meanings that represent personal and professional responsibility. You also might categorize this encounter as alien because a client might seem like another lifeform in a counseling context. You may view this event as harrowing or daunting.

What will you say? What will they say? What will you wear? How will it go? Will you perform as expected? What happens if they don't talk? What happens if they do talk? What if they are suicidal? The questions during this time are often innumerable, and all the words of encouragement from your faculty and site supervisor and classmates may fail to calm the storm of excitement and anticipation you may feel. The goals for this chapter follow.

- Identify and challenge your expectations of yourself, your client, and the counseling process
- Recognize and challenge your responses as a counselor in training when feeling stuck in a session
- Understand the roles of your client and yourself in the counseling endeavor and communicate those with your client

ASSOCIATED CACREP GOALS (CACREP, 2018)

Section 5: Entry-level specialty areas C. Clinical mental health counseling

- 2. Contextual dimensions
- 3. Practice

Managing Expectations and Assumptions

For most of us, our behaviors, thoughts, and emotions represent a temporal or time-related quality. In other words, to differing degrees we actively consider the past, the present, and the future. Before you meet with your first client, you have expectations and assumptions that guide your thoughts and feelings about this future event. These include beliefs held about yourself and the client. In other words, you may have some preconceived ideas about the encounter, and you have assumptions based on the past and your present experiences. Looking at and then addressing these expectations and assumptions help you prepare for the future and establish realistic expectations about yourself and your client.

What You Expect From Yourself

It has been said that experience is something you get just after you need it. This is certainly true of your first contact with a client. As soon as the session is over, you will know infinitely more than you did 50 minutes prior. And, practicum student responses to this first session vary. You may even find yourself wishing you could go back and do it again. Or, you may want to forget this first counseling session ever happened. It might be that you will bask in the success of this first session and how well it went—only to review the video later, and to your horror or dismay, what you remember is inaccurate or incorrect, something that never happened! Or you might just be glad that the first experience is over!

Whatever your **expectations of yourself** are as you make first contact, for the majority of you reading this book, those expectations will be wildly off the mark. How could this be? You've spent time, money, and effort preparing for the opportunity to begin your work as a counselor. You've roleplayed, rehearsed, read, studied, and put on your game face. Yet, it seems like you left Earth (as in the case of an alien experience) or, at least the classroom, and entered this foreign world of practice, that of counselor-client dynamics. You may even find yourself frustrated with your professors for not adequately preparing you for working with a client.

All these thoughts, feelings, and behaviors you have after making first contact are related to the expectations and assumptions that you held leading into first contact. Expectations are to be expected! Unfortunately, expectations about an experience that is unknown can never really be accurate. The first thing, therefore, that we want to convey to you about expectations is that you will have them and they will very likely be inaccurate. So, your first expectation should be that your expectations will not be what you anticipate.

Here is a list of some of the things you *can* accurately expect:

YOU WILL LIKELY BE MORE PREPARED THAN YOU FEEL. Throughout the process of a counselor education program, courses are sequenced and content is planned in ways that build counselor mind-sets and skills—a professional counselor identity, in other words. This process of professional counselor identity development is occurring on a day-to-day basis as you engage in your academic program, its responsibilities, and tasks; and, this process occurs often outside your awareness. There will be, of course, times in which you are very aware of moments of growth, but, in general, your growth will be so gradual that you may not even realize what you have learned and how you have grown until you sit with a client. Even then, you might not believe it until your classmates and instructor offer honest feedback about your sessions.

YOU WILL LIKELY BE LESS PREPARED THAN YOU FEEL. Since you began your academic program, you may have learned that counseling is not what you first imagined it to be. In fact, courses such as Introduction to Professional Counseling or Skills for Counselors helped you see counseling as a complex, professional activity. Your first encounter with a client further changes how you view what counseling is. How you view your preparation for this first encounter changes as well. For example, you will find yourself prepared in ways you did not expect. You may find ways in which you are less prepared than you thought. The following two examples will help you think about your own preparation. Related to your ease in social situations, in your everyday life, you may find you have an easy grace when talking with others, whether at the drive-through or the doctor's office. You really aren't concerned about beginning a conversation with a client or engaging in ice breakers. However, once you enter the counseling room and sit with your first client, you may be surprised when your mouth goes dry and you feel somewhat unsure how to interact. The second example is related to engaging a client beyond the welcoming and icebreaker stage. You may struggle to move past this casual, coffee shop talk and deepen the session toward exploring client goals. The inability to move past casual conversation is an example of the counselor default stance, which we describe later in this section.

YOU WILL HAVE YOUR OWN ISSUES (BAGGAGE) REFLECTED AT YOU. One of the foundations of counseling is developing rapport and establishing a counseling relationship. This requires honest engagement with the client and maintaining an openness and honesty with the client. In these early client encounters, you will experience some highs and lows. Resonating with a client feels good; so does experiencing a client who is happy to participate in the counseling process and is willing to discuss personal issues and vulnerabilities or express them through art or narratives; these reinforce our decision to become professional counselors. In the moment, you may even feel that clients are glorious. At the same time, clients may also reflect painful mirrors of your own humanness. Expect that, at times, clients will push your buttons—intentionally and accidentally—and they will reveal those things about you that you may not want to face. Know that experienced counselors undergo similar reflection and mirroring. As clients show us behaviors that look a lot like ours, it is often awkward. During the first client encounters, this may be extremely uncomfortable.

For example, one of our practicum students, Kaisha, was reeling from the recent divorce of her parents. In her first counseling session with a 14-year-old teen male, she admonished him for being so hard on his parents. He complained about their fighting and yelled as he told her he felt he was always in the middle of the fight. He said, "I just wish they would get a divorce." She responded, "Can't you just appreciate they are together!" He fought back as he told Kaisha, "You don't know what it is like to have parents always on the brink of divorce." At that point in the session, Kaisha told the client, "I know you are upset. I am going to get my supervisor to talk with you."

With this example, Kaisha was captured in the moment by her own feelings of her parents' divorce. Even her comment, "I know you are upset" could easily have reflected her own feelings, "I know I am upset." Kaisha may be able to follow through with this client in a later session and use self-disclosure to increase her rapport with this young teen. But, in this session, she was so overwhelmed by her own emotions, she needed her supervisor's assistance.

Each client encounter may not end in an impasse or compromising situation for you as a practicum student. Counseling encounters, however, have the power to evoke strong behaviors, thoughts, and emotions. And oftentimes those come when least expected.

> **ETHICAL CONSIDERATION 3.1**
>
> ACA Code of Ethics A.4. Avoiding Harm and Imposing Values prohibits counselors from imposing their values on their clients. This often is viewed as the "big issues" in belief (e.g., faith, abortion, infidelity, etc.), but we would like you to consider how life circumstances can evoke a powerful response from CITs in ways you might not expect. Think about the many roles you have currently and discuss the ways those roles could result in values conflicts with your clients. But do this with an open mind, without judging yourself about it.

YOU WILL REVEAL YOUR DEFAULT COUNSELOR STANCE. When buildings, bridges, or trucks are under a heavy load, they respond with cracked walls, swaying movements, or deflated tires, respectively. In fact, when pressured, physical materials in the world behave in predictable ways, often despite the best intentions of engineers. Likewise, counselors in training (CITs) experience similar **default counselor stances,** or positions or ways of responding when under the stress of the counseling session. Let's consider these default counselor stances more carefully.

Default Stance Responses

In our experience, several classic default modes, such as **asking questions, giving advice, problem solving, offering small talk, being silent,** and **blaming the client** are predictable (see Figure 3.1).

FIGURE 3.1. Default Stance Responses

We discuss the most common default stances as well as offer ideas about how to counter them.

Asking Questions

One of the more common—and insidious—default modes of responding to clients involves asking questions. When stressed, CITs may resort to asking questions, a familiar aspect of social conversation. The questions asked may take several forms. Some questions come in rapid succession, one right after the other, potentially overwhelming the client: "Why did you come in today?" "What made you choose this clinic?" "Have you ever been here before?" Clients have little or no time to respond, nor do they know which question to answer and when.

A second type of question is the one asked out of curiosity. These are not the respectfully curious questions wherein the counselor seeks to know the client and understand his or her worldview; instead, they are counselor centered and often are asked out of a need to fill the silence or to keep the conversation going or fill out an intake form. Asking questions keeps the counselor in control of the session, but to the detriment of client autonomy and self-direction. Two examples illustrate this use of questions. "Here are three services we provide. Which one do you think you need?" "I am going to lay out a plan for you. Let me know what you think."

A third and final type of question requires the classic yes-or-no response, restricting the client's answer. This type of question also splits the client's thinking into a yes/no, right/wrong, black/white mind-set, a mind-set that may have contributed to the issue(s) the client faces. Examples include, "Have you ever been to counseling before?" "Do you know anyone who has had counseling?" "Are you glad that you are here?"

Our CITs, Janice, Jose, Kaisha, and Sam, each remember struggling in their skills class to avoid asking closed questions and offering clients room in the conversation by asking open questions. Jose speaks of the impact the lesson on questions have on their skills class when he recounts the following:

> You should have seen all of us when we focused on only asking open questions. By the end of the week, we would be talking with each other and

kidding around. We developed the acronym, JETBO, which stands for "just easy to be open." While waiting for class to begin, we would hear a closed question being asked. We would yell JETBO out across the room. And we would also call it out on ourselves. And then we would laugh. We had a good time with this.

ANTIDOTE TO ASKING QUESTIONS. Shhhh … is the answer. Quiet yourself and listen, as John and Rita Sommers-Flanagan (2018) implore new counselors. Many times counselors need to be able to offer direction and, at times, redirection to clients, but they do not need to be in control of the session at all times. Counseling is about the *process*; as a counselor, you don't necessarily have to cover a certain amount of content. Often, the adage "less is more" is true for counseling.

WHEN YOU QUIET YOURSELF, IN FACT, YOU ARE TRUSTING IN THE PROCESS OF COUNSELING. As you develop your skill in process work, counseling looks a little bit like this:

a. You trust that developing a relationship is a process.

b. You believe that through the process of developing a relationship with a client, he or she will provide the information needed at the time it is needed.

c. One exception to this is, of course, in the case of a crisis or an initial intake, both of which require specific types of information at specific times.

d. With experience, when counselors lean into or use the process, clients will "land" where they need to in a session.

While this may sound a little mystical, there is nothing magical about it. Establishing the counseling relationship and using the counseling process is extremely difficult—this is why counselors are needed and friends and family are not always enough. One final note about asking questions: As a guide to using questions, ask yourself four questions.

a. What is the purpose of the question?

b. Is the question client centered or counselor centered?

c. Will the answer move the client toward wellness and success?

d. Can the question harm the client?

Giving Advice

This default stance response is also common among practicum students and, unfortunately, creates two types of challenges to client growth and wellness. First, giving advice presupposes that the counselor has the best view of both the client's concern and the "right" solution. Yet, this is not how counselors are to approach clients. Giving advice further creates dependence on the counselor by the client, fostering a need to obtain counselor approval prior to making decisions or taking action. Advice giving is a perfectly understandable default, but it is quite dangerous to the relationship and the whole counseling enterprise. Statements that begin with, "Well what about doing …"; "Listen, I've got a great idea …"; or, "You should respond by telling her …" are signals that you are giving advice rather than helping the client explore issues and responses.

Second, practicum students often feel pressure to offer their client something tangible or concrete regarding their presenting issue. Early on in our training, we are especially vulnerable to the need to feel competent, and we search for ways to confirm that we can help. And, clients often want this as well, at times asking explicitly, "What should I do?" "How should I feel? and appearing to watch and wait for the advice. Our responses often feel clumsy and inadequate, with forced feedback such as, "Counseling is not about my opinion, but yours; what are some alternatives you have considered?" Early on we aren't confident that this type of response will let to productive problem solving. It feels more natural just to provide a solution and move on.

ANTIDOTE TO GIVING ADVICE. Those first few counseling sessions with clients can be some of the most disempowering of one's life: The feelings of inadequacy in the moment can be overwhelming. Giving advice is a sure sign that the counselor in training is feeling overwhelmed and uncertain that the theory and skills learned are insufficient to help the client and carry the session. However, seeing that clients have lived with themselves their whole lives and you have known them for 10 minutes, it may be presumptuous to think anyone could offer advice that they have not heard before.

Further, giving advice is a sign of a natural insecurity one experiences in a new role, but is also one that must be addressed in supervision right away. Many times, in sessions, novice counselors, in their panic to recall what they have learned, offer the kind of support they have received or the kind of support they wish to receive. Advice giving is a clear example of this: We receive advice from others in our lives all the time! And this is why it is imperative that you not give advice in your sessions. So, the next time you feel the urge to offer a client advice, pause and ask yourself these three questions:

a. What would be the purpose of advice giving?

b. Is advice giving what is needed now?

c. What do I gain by giving advice to this client?

Problem Solving

Problem solving is a nuanced version of advice giving and can be more difficult to detect because of its relative sophistication. You will know you have defaulted into problem solving when you find yourself asking the client, "Have you tried …" or "What if you … ?" The first concern is that it these approaches represent closed questions, wherein the only responses evoked are a yes or no. As you have already learned, these questions are counselor centered and keep the counselor in control of the conversation. Problem solving also undermines the client's own capacities for finding solutions. Remember, clients have made it through their lives without our help thus far, and the capacity for change is within them.

ANTIDOTE TO PROBLEM SOLVING. Problem solving typically means that the client has "hooked" the CIT in, by playing on his or her newness in the field or through basic counter-transference. In other words, the practicum student as a counselor—for whatever reason—has allowed him or herself to feel responsible for the client's problem, or at least for fixing the problem. These clients present as helpless and often portray themselves as hapless victims in need of rescue. The CIT or novice counselor genuinely wants to help but gets drawn in to rescuing. The antidote for problem solving is "remembering your skin." What does this phrase mean for you and your role as a counselor?

Your skin is a physical barrier between your innermost self and the rest of the world. It defines you. Likewise, professional ethics and standards are our profession's skin, and they show that the client's problems are their own, as are the solutions to those problems. In other words, there is a boundary between us and the clients we serve. It is virtually always in the client's best interest to promote his or her own problem-solving skills.

Offering Small Talk

Small talk involves engaging in surface conversation past the point of rapport building and to the detriment of movement toward client goals. Small talk occurs when the practicum student is unsure, unable, or unwilling to deepen the session and move the client and the conversation past coffee shop talk. Small talk has its place in the counseling relationship, albeit a small, brief place. It is problematic when it encroaches on time and space for clients to engage in the counseling process in meaningful ways.

ANTIDOTE TO SMALL TALK. The antidote to small talk is the recognition that after an initial greeting and basic rapport building, small talk, except when used strategically with specific clients at specific times, is non-therapeutic. The client—or someone—is paying you for your time, and there are expectations that accompany that payment. Small talk does happen, and it is definitely going to occur during practicum, but it diverts us from engaging the client in a meaningful way. The client may initiate the small talk in an effort to keep the conversation superficial. Counselors in training may use small talk for the same reason.

Small talk default stance response is an example of a social role/rules trap: CITs do not have to follow these rules. In fact, they may need to actively challenge these assumptions by biting their tongue. For example, Janice was raised in the South and her interactions outside the counseling arena are steeped in the rules of polite conversation. Being female, she was taught that it is not polite to interrupt. And, she has a long tradition of letting the other lead the conversation. She related the following to her faculty supervisor.

> One of the difficulties that I had in our skill class was leading any conversation. I remember one role play in particular. My "client" (another member

of our class), talked a mile a minute and controlled the entire conversation, filling the time up with small talk. I was supposed to be practicing a brief counseling intervention. All I was able to say for our 10-minute counseling interview was, "Hello, my name is Janice, and I am a counselor in training. Can you tell me a little bit about why you have come to talk with me today?" That is all that I said for the entire 10 minutes.

After the role play, Kaisha, her "client," her classmates, and the instructor talked about the role of small talk and how clients can use the session time to divert the conversation from serious issues. As the discussion deepened, Kaisha began to see how her culture has influenced the way she approaches counseling. And she began to realize how assuming the counseling role requires her to learn new skills of interaction so she can move her talk with a client from polite to professional.

Being Silent

Silence is, in essence, the absence of sound or noise. Within a counseling session, silence occurs when neither the client nor the counselor speaks. And this silence or quiet is often an uncomfortable moment for the client or counselor or both. For a practicum student, the thought of silence or the occurrence of silence in the counseling session may produce anxiety and concern. There are positive ways that counselors may use silence therapeutically. For example, counselors may sit quietly to allow clients time in the moment to experience and process their thoughts and feelings.

When silence occurs because the counselor has nothing to say, the outcome for both counselor and client may be different. Silence of this sort is related to the to fight-or-flight response associated with anxiety or fear about a threat; in this case, the response is a freeze response. This occurs when the CIT feels overwhelmed in the moment and locks up. It becomes a problem in sessions when clients feel responsible for this reaction or doubt the counselor's competence and comfort in working with them. Jose tells us about his long-standing fear of silence.

> In my family if you were silent, then you never got any help or support. There were four kids and everyone but me was outspoken. And I finally learned to be if I was going to be heard. As a result, I was loud and rowdy at home and at school. I could push my way to the front of the line. I thought that speaking up for others who couldn't speak for themselves was my job. So, I never gave anyone a chance to speak. I thought that I was helping. I see that I did that with my own teaching, too. I was always asking them a question and then answering it for them.

ANTIDOTE TO SILENCE. Silence feels like one of the scariest occurrences in counseling. After all, many CITs believe it is the counselor's job to know what to say at all times. This means that speaking demonstrates competence! However, as we stated earlier, silence can be used effectively in counseling. Therefore, the antidote to silence is to move into the silence, rather than running from it. In counseling, running from silence means resorting to small talk or other default stance responses to escape the discomfort of silence. Moving or leaning into the silence means talking about it: "Wow, it looks like we both ran out of things to say at the same time!" or,

"Silence gives us time to pause and explore where we are in the process," or even, "Gosh, I'm at a loss for words, not because of anything you said or did." It is vital that counselors feel permission to suspend certain social roles and rules, such as keeping the conversation going. Silence in these instances provides opportunities to process these differences.

Blaming the Client

Often, students reflect the following sentiment when they explain their video-tape of a counseling session: "My video was bad because I had a really tough client; the client refused to talk." Blaming the client for a difficult session or for less than desirable outcomes is fairly common, but this response is often detrimental to the growth of both the client and the counselor. First, clients have come for help, so naturally they will have behaviors that are challenging. Second, as difficult as it is to feel confident in these first days, weeks, and months of practicum, blaming the client is not the appropriate response. You, as the counselor, are a professional, and you have power in your role in the relationship—it is important not to abuse this power by blaming the other for issues and challenges that arise.

ANTIDOTE TO BLAMING THE CLIENT. Blaming others is about perceived power. And individuals are more likely to assign responsibility for fault or wrongdoing to others when they feel powerless, inadequate, or incompetent. Many times, blame is accompanied by a lessening of respect for the other and viewing the other as undeserving. Hence, when we feel powerless in a counseling session, we are vulnerable to blaming.

Fortunately, there exists a paradox about the concept of power to assist us: Power is inherent in the role of the counselor, so any power in the session is ours to reach out and take. However, we believe that most of the power we think we have as a counselor is illusory or bad. Each of us has learned this lesson when clients "act off-script" and do things we do not expect. So, where is the power in counseling? The good news is that the authentic power that exists during the counseling session is the relationship. We can use the value of the relationship to address our own fears and subsequent blaming of the client. From this perspective, we recognize that even in our own discomfort, the client is the vulnerable one, the one who is hurting. At these moments, we can turn blame into concern.

AN ADDITIONAL THOUGHT ON BLAME. Students may have to videotape all their counseling sessions or maybe they have to just videotape one. Regardless of the number, many practicum students feel pressure to complete the videotape(s) of the session(s) required of them—to complete these and not think about them anymore. After all, the video(s) for this one course exists in a context of chaos in which exists multiple classes and assignments and multiple roles and responsibilities outside of school. However, videotaping is essential for our own personal and professional growth and development. Reflection and analysis can demonstrate how blaming the client harms the relational component of our counseling. This harm violates the ethical standard of "do no harm." Reviewing our own work with clients means revisiting our responses to clients and then seeking an alternative to blaming the client. In some sense, in a subsequent session there exists an opportunity to redo the video, own our behaviors, and demonstrate behaviors other than blaming the client.

Although you will use several of these five default stances when you encounter clients for the first time, preparing for alternative ways of interacting will help you avoid them. In Reflection Question 3.1, you will work with your peers and supervisors to develop alternative ways of initiating client interaction and responding to verbal and nonverbal client communication.

EXPERIENTIAL ACTIVITY 3.1
Alternatives to Your Default Stances

In this experiential activity, you will work with your peers to develop alternatives to your default stances.

Create a scenario you may have experienced working with clients at your practicum site. For each of the default stances, note your goal for using each. Record your feelings at the time you communicate from a default stance.

What You Expect for Your Client

Believe it or not, you will likely find that, in addition to having expectations for yourself, you will also discover that you have **expectations for the client**. These expectations may take many forms.

CLIENTS WILL KNOW HOW TO BE CLIENTS. Perhaps the most common expectation CITs have about their clients is that clients know how to be clients. In fact, you may find that this is an unquestioned assumption that you hold: "Of course, clients know how to be clients; they are clients! And they come for help."

The reality is that many, if not most, clients with whom we work—either directly or via supervision—do not, in fact, know how to be clients. Even for those who have been in counseling before, they may know how to be a client in a previous setting with another counselor, but they do not know how to be *your* client.

How is this possible? Think back to a time where you had to go to a medical specialist or a general practitioner at a new medical facility. What was that like for you? You have been to doctors' offices before, but someone at this new office felt different: You may not have known what to say to the specialist. Were you supposed to just start talking? Should you have waited for the doctor to ask you questions first? Why did you have to put on the paper gown prior to meeting with doctor? You felt vulnerable and exposed.

Similarly, clients enter the counseling center or the school counseling office feeling exposed and vulnerable, unsure what to expect, what to say, and when to say it, and how much of their story to share. Informed consent is invaluable for addressing this expectation. Returning to gaining informed consent, it is important to reiterate that informed consent is not just something to get through to get to the real counseling process. Instead, informed consent becomes an integral part of building rapport and encouraging authentic responses from your client. Even a behavior as simple as pausing after asking them if they have any questions about their intake paperwork can support the act of building trust and teaching them to be clients.

CLIENTS WILL BE MOTIVATED. One of the biggest challenges for new counselors is the contrast between their motivation to be a great counselor and some clients' limited enthusiasm for coming to counseling and being in the session. This strikingly different approach to the counseling session is understandable. By the time that CITs come to their first session, they have invested quite a lot of preparation time and energy getting ready for this professional encounter. In relation to the client perspective, what we find is that many people are ambivalent—at best— about most change. And clients feel ambivalent about seeking help long before they meet you during this first session; this ambivalence is not about you! For clients, change is difficult and represents a form of loss. In fact, your clients have likely been thinking about counseling—if they have given it any thought—at times with a sense of dread. Again, this fear or apprehension is not about you. Your client may be court mandated or even relationally mandated (by a loved one, for example) to enter counseling.

CLIENTS WILL SEE YOU AS INCOMPETENT. Whether you have seen your first client by the time you are reading this, it will come as no surprise that your confidence may not be at an all-time high. The fact is, the role for which you are training and the tasks associated with making first contact with a client are daunting, and early counseling efforts can shake your confidence. Many times, we project this lack of confidence or sense of self-efficacy onto our clients. We may find ourselves apologizing, over-compensating, or trying to control the session. This is a normal reaction to working with clients for the first time, but ultimately these are unproductive feelings that lead to less-than-effective approaches.

It is important to realize that the clients have their own issues to deal with, so they will not likely be interested in yours. Occasionally, as a result of anxiety or suspicion, a client will attempt to undermine the counselor by challenging his or her training, credentials, age, and other characteristics. Again, in these moments, it is most effective to recognize that these client behaviors are not about you, but more of a reflection of processes occurring within the client. For instance, while working at the campus clinic, one of Sam's first clients challenged him in the middle of the intake process. His client was a 22-year-old African American. In the middle of the session, this client asked, "Man you are just like me, my age, African American, male. What makes you think you can help me? You probably don't know much more than I do."

How do you respond to a client's resistant behaviors? If you respond as if the resistance is about you, you will actually make it about you by becoming defensive. In contrast, when you see this as a client dynamic, you can more easily slide back into your basic skills and reflect the client's comments back to them. For instance, you might be able to move from a defensive statement, "Well, counseling is not about me, it is about you and your goals and behaviors," to something more reflective, such as, "On top of whatever brought you here today, you're also concerned that you won't be able to work effectively with me. That must be difficult. Could we talk about this for a moment?" In fact, Sam responded to his client in a similar way. He said, "I appreciate your honesty. I'd like to hear more about your concerns." At the end of intake, both Sam and his client agreed to meet once more and then reevaluate how and if they should continue to work together.

What Your Client Expects From You and Counseling

During your first practicum experience, you will encounter **client expectations** that are low and high and that often vacillate between these two points. Both low and high client expectations have their own challenges and opportunities. Let look at a few of the more common client expectations.

THE CLIENT HAS LOW EXPECTATIONS. As you read this, you may think like Chad did during his first practicum: "Oh good, my client has low expectations, so we can only go up from here." The challenge with low client expectations, however, is that the counselor often has to work in creative and persistent ways to connect with the client. The client is neutral about counseling, at best, and is cautious making a personal investment in the counseling process. For example, clients may anticipate that engaging in counseling with you may resemble past counseling experiences—these may be ones in which they did not connect with the counselor, felt judged, or were otherwise dissatisfied with counseling. In these cases, you're not starting the relationship off on a level footing, as the client may expect that you will be like "other counselors." For this reason, it is important to explore early on with clients their previous counseling experiences and how those may influence what they expect.

Another type of low expectation a client may have for counseling is related to his or her own self-perception. Practicum students may view clients as resistant to change early in the counseling process, only to discover clients reveal later that they feel hopeless regarding change. They may believe that they are broken beyond repair or in an impossible position and that going through the motions of counseling is a waste of time. In these instances, it is important that you not internalize the client's lack of motivation and mirror a sense of hopelessness. Remember, you didn't cause this sense of despair or low motivation. In fact, you are not that powerful. On the other hand, a counseling relationship and participating in the counseling process can facilitate change and increase a client's motivation and hopefulness.

A third type of low client expectation relates to many clients' own levels of effort. Their expectations of themselves is low; they may believe that counseling involves change without challenges. During her practicum experience, Marianne discovered that not all clients wanted to work as hard as she did. She was sure that if she committed to clients and was determined to make their lives better, then they would meet her and join her in the relationship and work. Marianne was surprised when several of her clients seemed to expect that if they would "go through the motions" of the counseling process, then the issues or challenges will resolve themselves. We caution against imposing counselor expectations onto client expectations, even if those expectations for the client are positive.

In the cases where clients do not take the process as seriously as their counselors do, these clients may recoil from having discrepancies or ambiguities pointed out to them. Discrepancies, as you are learning in your academic training program, are the moments of incongruity between two statements a client makes, or between a statement and a behavior. For example, a client may state that he or she wants to take more ownership regarding creating and maintaining healthy interpersonal relationships on the one hand, then continue blaming all those around him or her for not being easier to get along with. It is not enough for clients to say, "I want change." In fact, in many cases, the only way to change is to change. And, for clients to expect to change without challenge, indicating that change requires effort is not a very welcome message. To see this more from the client's perspective, think of a recent change you tried to make; it likely did not command 100% of your commitment!

CLIENTS HAVE HIGH EXPECTATIONS. The first type of high client expectation you are likely to encounter in practicum is the client's desire for answers. "Why is this happening to me?" "What should I do about this?" "How can I stop this?" It is perfectly natural to want answers and solutions to longstanding problems. However, by virtue of their longitudinal nature, these concerns or problems take time to unfold. It is also natural for a client to have avoided or anticipated attending counseling for so long that when he or she does arrive, he or she is ready for things to change. However, he or she may still not be ready to make the changes; instead, he or she may look expectantly to you to make change happen.

Clients, like most humans, would prefer to experience change with the least effort and discomfort possible. They may expect a magic pill or a silver bullet to take away their pain or to change their circumstances. While this expectation is understandable, it is unrealistic in the context of the counseling relationship. As noted earlier in this chapter, reflecting these observations back to the client, rather than reacting defensively, can make the transition from ambivalence to greater commitment to change.

Essentially, many clients simply want to feel better, or, at the very least, to feel different. When CITs assume the client's anxiety, pressure, and/or unrealistic expectations, they short-circuit the therapeutic relationship and process, frustrating both client and CIT. Another option is for CITs to create space for clients to sit with their unrealistic expectations. Ironically, this has the effect of restoring client autonomy rather than making them dependent on the counselor for answers and solutions.

Sam is working in a campus clinic, and the first week he has been observing his supervisor work with clients. He talks about his first impressions about the first client that he saw. Once he talked with his supervisor, he was able to see alternative impressions about this client.

> Seeing my site supervisor work with clients served by this campus clinic has taught me so much. I feel I am so fortunate to be able to observe my site supervisor in counseling sessions before I have clients of my own. I have seen seven sessions. I have time to take notes after each session, and I record my questions. At the end of each day, my site supervisor and I talk about what I have observed. She also asks me to respond to three questions: What are your impressions of the client? How would you describe the session? How would you have approached this client? The first time I saw my site supervisor work with a client, I was mystified. The client was polite and involved and finally asked my supervisor, "Well what do you think that I should do? I know that this situation is complicated." The client asked this question in such a reasonable way. I was sure that my supervisor would outline some concrete choices. Instead, my supervisor said, "You see complications. What feelings do you associate with complications?"

In Experiential Activity 3.2, you have the opportunity to learn how to manage the expectations of both you and your client.

EXPERIENTIAL ACTIVITY 3.2
Managing Expectations of You and Your Client

One of the most straightforward ways to manage expectations in a session, regardless of their origin, is to expose clients to the light of reflection. If you have not met with your first client yet, prepare for that meeting by describing your expectations of yourself, your expectations of your client, and what you believe your client expects of him- or herself. If you have met with your first client, reflect on your expectations and what you knew of your client expectations prior to your meeting.

Teaching Clients How to Be Clients

Earlier we stated that one of the unproductive assumptions, described briefly previously, is that clients who enter counseling know how to be clients, and, more specifically, know how to be your client. Although this may be a bit jarring to read, this is a faulty assumption. In fact, clients are learning their own role at the same time you are learning your role as a counselor, a professional helper. You may be feeling fear, anxiety and uncertainty, but so is your client. And, the focus of the counseling session must remain on the client's well-being. To take this one step further, CITs sacrifice their right to natural self-focus when encountering clients. No matter how vulnerable you may feel in the session, it is the client who is most vulnerable, because your role carries the weight of power and professional responsibility. Therefore, it is important that you teach your client how to be a client and how to be your client. You can do this in two ways: normalizing client fears and anxieties and helping clients take the counseling process seriously.

Normalizing Fears and Anxiety

The first step in teaching a client how to be your client is an extension of informed consent, in which the counselor **normalizes fear and anxiety** or apprehension of the counseling process. Clients may not show overt signs or even state it explicitly, but it is usually safe to assume that these fears and anxieties will be part of their experience of counseling. Therefore, we look beyond our own feelings of uncertainty to extend support to our clients. This may take a variety of forms, but it begins with a cordial greeting and an awareness of body language. Are they stiff, rigid, leaning away from you, arms crossed, or making poor eye contact? During this period of acclimation to this first counseling session, it may be appropriate to point out the awkwardness that typically accompanies this first meeting. How do you help clients normalize their feelings? Perhaps the following transcription excerpt will help clarify how you can help clients normalize their fears and anxieties (see Transcription 3.1).

TRANSCRIPTION 3.1. NORMALIZING CLIENT FEAR AND ANXIETIES

Mr. Tabor: Good morning. Thank you for coming in.

Bret: Hey (fair eye contact but appears tense, reserved, perhaps guarded).

Mr. Tabor: It means a lot that you kept your appointment—not everyone makes it this far!

Bret: (smiles uncertainly)

Mr. Tabor: What I mean is that while this will come to feel like a safe place, it can also feel like a taking a risk, or feeling a bit unsure of the process. It's quite difficult to get this far, so that means a lot.

Bret: I never thought of it that way. It really has been hard to get here.

Mr. Tabor: Congratulations on taking a major step. Perhaps we could begin by chatting a bit about what you can expect now that you're here and then you can tell me more about how hard it was to get here. Would that be okay?

Bret: Sure.

This is a very simple example, one that you and your instructor will likely modify to fit your client and your counseling style. The point here is that counseling is risky, regardless of the care we take to soothe clients. You may find yourself tempted to take responsibility for the client's anxiety and try to manage it for them. There are several reasons why you would want to do this: either a lack of skill or a need to own the client's issues. Work with your faculty or site supervisor, review your audio or videos of your client work, and determine whether you lack the skill to normalize client fears or anxieties or want to assume too much ownership for the client's emotion. Learning the skill of normalizing client fear and anxiety and regulating your own emotions is developmentally appropriate for you as a CIT.

You may be asking yourself, "But what if clients are not scared, anxious, or apprehensive?" This is a reasonable question because clients may come in to the first counseling session somewhat carelessly or intrepidly, something often seen in certain types of practicum settings, such as community mental health agencies, residential settings, acute care settings, and school counseling settings. Many clients have been in counseling previously. They believe they know the process and what to expect. This, too, can be somewhat unnerving to beginning practicum students because the client may appear to know more of what to expect than the CIT. This provides an excellent opportunity to work with the client and gauge his or her expectations relative to your own. Determining expectations together promotes a positive relationship with this type of client, the **carefree client**. It may be useful to spend just a few moments learning more about any previous counseling experiences or carefree attitudes. Read through Transcription 3.2 to view an example of Kaisha's first session with a carefree client.

TRANSCRIPTION 3.2. THE CAREFREE CLIENT

Kaisha: Good morning. Thank you for coming in.

Carlo: It was such a nightmare getting here! My last therapist's office was on a more convenient bus route, but this place is hard to find.

Kaisha: Oh my, it has been challenging just to get to the … (client cuts in)

Carlo: It doesn't matter. I'm here now. My family member is driving me crazy and my doctor, who is not helping at all, said I need to get back into therapy. I just need … (client follows stream of consciousness related to his perception of the problem being in the system).

Kaisha: (slightly lifting index finger, as if half-heartedly hailing a taxi) I'm so sorry but I need to jump in for a second. (client appears momentarily stunned). I hate to cut you off because it seems like you have a lot going on… .

Carlo: That's what I was saying, my family member… .

Kaisha: (breaking back in again) Sorry to cut in again. I would like to hear more about those things, but before we jump right into them, there is a little ground we need to cover first. Could you hold onto your story for a moment longer as we cover a few preliminary things?

Carlo: I guess, but I thought you're supposed to listen.

Kaisha: Yes, very true, that is part of our work together, and I appreciate you sharing that expectation. However, in our work together, there is a little more too it, and I want to make certain that you are sure of what you say to me before you say it. Does that sound fair?

Carlo: (sighs) Sure.

Transcription 3.2 demonstrates yet another reason we as counselors educate clients about how to be our clients. From the tone of the transcription, it is easy to see that this client had his own expectations about what counseling was. This is not an uncommon occurrence. And Kaisha was able to begin to clarify with Carlo the nature of counseling. This clarification was something Kaisha had to learn how to do so. In fact, Kaisha recalls sitting in an earlier counseling session waiting as a client talked through the whole session. Kaisha made a few nonverbal acknowledgements, but really had little input in the session. Her session note reflected rapport building and empathic responding, but Kaisha concludes now that she failed to educate her client. She also believes the client made very little progress in the session through his or her verbal stream of thought. It is difficult to redirect a client early on in counseling, but nowhere near as difficult as it is later in the relationship, after ineffective habits have been formed.

Teaching clients to be clients is an ongoing process, and although there are some common aspects of the experience, such as normalizing fears and anxieties that clients experience, it is also important to respond to each client according to his or her unique needs, culture, and context.

Summary

This chapter focused on meeting your client for the first time. Enhancing your readiness means taking the time, in advance, to examine and to learn to manage the expectations you have for yourself and your client, as well as your client's expectations for you and the counseling process. For example, you learned that you will likely be more prepared than you feel, and you will be more prepared than you expect; conversely, you will be less prepared than you expect; you will have your own issues (baggage) reflected at you; and you will reveal your default counselor stance. A default counselor stance represents a common way of responding when under the stress of the practicum encounter. Many times, this is counter to what you have been taught in your skills for counseling classes. Classic default modes, such as asking questions, giving advice, problem solving, small talk, silence, and blaming the client are predictable.

As you anticipate and begin to work with clients, you will learn that you also have expectations for your clients. For instance, you may believe that clients will know how to be clients, clients will be motivated, and clients will see you as incompetent. Challenging each of these assumptions will help you as you approach a client for the first time. It is also important to note what clients expect from you and from counseling. These insights allow you to meet the client within his or her reality, rather than in concert with your own assumptions. You may assume either the client has low expectations or the client has high expectations. Either assumption will frame how you approach and work with the client; either may not accurately reflect the way the client comes to the counseling session.

We ended this chapter with discussion of how to teach your clients to be clients. We recognize that being a client is a new role for the client. You can help clients normalize their fears and anxieties or address the needs of clients who appear to know more than you. Either of these can be disconcerting to the novice counselor.

Key Terms

Asking questions

Being silent

Blaming the client

Carefree client

Client expectations

Default counselor stance

Expectations for the client

Expectations of yourself

First contact

Giving advice

Normalizing fear and anxiety

Offering small talk

Problem solving

References

CACREP Standards. (2018). *Section 5: Entry-level Specialty Areas—Clinical Mental Health*. Retrieved from https://www.cacrep.org/section-5-entry-level-specialty-areas-clinical-mental-health-counseling/

Sommers-Flanagan, J., & Sommers-Flanagan, R. (2018). *Clinical interviewing (6th ed.).* Hoboken, NJ: John Wiley & Sons.

CHAPTER 4

Making and Maintaining
CONTACT WITH CLIENTS

INTRODUCTION

Counselors in training (CITs) frequently ask during the first weeks of practicum, "What do I do when I get in the session, for real?" followed the next week by, "So, I've made contact and built rapport during the first session; now what?" The tone of these questions is often delivered in a slightly panicked voice or thought. Counselors in training also reflect uncertainty, as if they are surprised and upended by the fact that the client came back for a second session. A supervisor's response to these questions and feelings is often some variation of "It depends. What does the client want/need?" In fact, this response becomes a common theme in practicum supervision. Unfortunately, if you have asked this question of your supervisor, this response is often unsatisfying. You are looking for specific information and help about how to work with a specific client.

The challenge here is that even though you may have had a year or more of courses by the time you enter practicum, you only "know" how counseling works academically or theoretically. Until you've done the work experientially, it can be hard to *know* what to *do* next. Therefore, during practicum, the first session will resemble the subsequent sessions, in terms of refining your ability to listen fully. Right now, you may be questioning the power and validity of listening. But, by learning to listen fully, you will begin to understand its impact on establishing and maintaining a therapeutic relationship with a client. In this chapter, the process of **making contact** and **maintaining contact** with clients through the relationship, and via listening, is addressed as a way of helping you prepare for your first meeting with a client. The goals for this chapter follow.

In this chapter, you will do the following:

- Recognize the structure and purpose of the counseling session
- Enact the skills of being a counselor in the moment with real-life clients
- Understand the ways counselors can enhance their work with clients

ASSOCIATED CACREP GOALS (CACREP, 2018)

Section 5: Entry-level specialty areas C. Clinical mental health counseling.

- 2. Contextual dimensions
- 3. Practice

Preparing for That First Meeting/Being with Clients

As counselors, prior to a meeting with a client, we develop plans. Planning serves a variety of purposes that include establishing a professional stance to the session, refreshing our knowledge of the client, thinking about how to be open and present to the client and issues presented, gathering appropriate materials and/or forms needed for the work, and establishing an outline or format that supports paperwork and other documents after the session. One way to prepare for meeting with a client is to write and then envision the **structure of the session**. Seeing what a general overview of a counseling session might look like and reviewing that first session will help you conceptualize and maintain continuity of counseling with a client.

Structuring the Session

Students want to know, "How do I begin a session?" This is an important question for students to consider and articulate. The question itself represents the bridging that occurs between the academic world and the world of the agency or school and of the client. And, the ultimate function of the bridge is the practicum student sitting face to face with the client.

Unfortunately, there remains a sense amongst students that this question, "How do I begin a session?" will be perceived as silly or even ignorant. They believe if they have to ask this question, they are revealing their lack of competency and fear others will conclude that they should not be in practicum. However, the reverse is true. This is a vital early question that needs to be made explicit in supervision, by the faculty supervisor and the site supervisor, prior to making first contact. What may not be obvious to you as a practicum student is that experienced counselors continue to prepare for and structure client sessions during their professional practice.

In practicum and counseling in general, we accept the role of a professional counselor and suspend other roles, such as friend, to make contact with the client in a clinically efficacious way. It is natural to wonder how to even begin a session when we accept this new role as a professional counselor.

What does this first session with a client look like? You may have difficulty envisioning it. Over the years, we have addressed an approach to session planning by implementing a rubric for helping students think through and plan the first session and subsequent practicum sessions. The following is a rough guide to an initial 50-minute counseling session, the **initial session outline** (see Table 4.1).

TABLE 4.1. Initial Session Outline

Time	Topic	Description
Minutes 1–5	Warm-up	3-minute greeting, introductions, connection 2-minute goals for session
Minutes 5–10	Informed consent and assorted paperwork	Introduction to counseling and relationship Limits of confidentiality
Minutes 10–40	Presenting problem/client concerns	Client perspective Gathering information Offering reflection in the form of basic skills
Minutes 40–50	Wrap-up	Most important things Summary from counselor: "As we come to the end of our time today, there are a few things that stand out to me." "What will you take from this session?"

The initial session outline presented in Table 4.1 is a thumbnail sketch and should not be followed rigidly. To make this point clearer, we offer Transcription 4.1, recording the warm-up to highlight how these interactions might proceed. Mr. Tabor, a site supervisor, recorded one of his session as an illustration of an initial session warm-up.

TRANSCRIPTION 4.1. EXCERPT FROM INITIAL SESSION OUTLINE

WARM-UP

Mr. Tabor: Good morning. Thank you for coming in. I'm Jim and I am a counselor here. I'm looking forward to hearing from you, but first, there are a few preliminary items to cover. Okay?

**Please note, it is rarely helpful to ask socially normed questions such as, "How are you?" First, clients may begin to tell you prior to you setting the stage for the relationship through goal setting, informed consent, and expectations. The result is having to stop them or otherwise cut them off. Second, and more common, the client will respond with a similarly social response such as "fine" or "good," and while this is comfortable from a social exchange perspective, it intimates that counseling will proceed according to social rules, which it should not.

Mr. Tabor: As we begin, I'd like to cover a couple of important items. In this session, we will go over what counseling here looks like, ways we will work together, and perhaps most importantly, the lengths I will go to protect your dignity as a person. Along the way, I hope you will begin to feel free to share elements of your story. Does that sound fair?

Client, Sue: (sighs) Yes. I was not sure what to expect. This helps.

Mr. Tabor: I'm glad to hear it. Let's talk a little about how this relationship will be different than other relationships in your life.... .

After a first session with a client, the counselor prepares for a follow-up session. You would expect the second and subsequent sessions to differ from the initial session. You will also note similarities (see Table 4.2). Remember that this **follow-up session outline** is a guide and should not be rigidly adhered to.

TABLE 4.2. Follow-up Session Outline

Time	Topic	Description
Minutes 1–8	Warm-up	2-minute connection 1-minute emergent issues check 3-minute linking to previous session 2-minute goals for session
Minutes 8–40	"Working"	Gathering information Offering feedback in the form of basic skills
Minutes 40–50	Wrap up	Most important things Summary from counselor: "As we come to the end of our time today, there are a few things that stand out to me." "What will you take from this session?" "What action will you take as a result of our time together?"

Now that you have an understanding of the structure of a counseling session, let's look at we ways you may go deeper with your planning for your sessions. In the next section, both ideas and concrete ways to approach counseling may help you to prepare.

What Effective Counselors Do

Research into whether counseling works has demonstrated that it does indeed work. Prochaska and Norcross (2014) discuss the factors that have the strongest influence over the success of counseling. There are three overarching factors, which are described briefly next, followed by specific ways these factors are revealed in the counseling relationship.

THERAPEUTIC RELATIONSHIP. The **therapeutic relationship** or alliance is the **context for change**. This means that the relationship, unique in and of itself, establishes safety, trust, and anticipation that something different happens here (in this relationship) than what happens in other relationships. In other words, the therapeutic relationship creates something that goes beyond simply one client and one counselor: It creates a whole new entity, one in which change occurs. Without it, few, if anything, that follows will be effective.

HAWTHORNE EFFECT. The discovery of the Hawthorne effect makes for an interesting read, but for our purposes, here, the point is that a key to changing a person's behavior is to observe it. We'll say that again: Observation of a behavior is often a precursor to changing that behavior. Once you have established the foundation of the therapeutic relationship, clients may be more willing to look more closely at their behaviors. This is essential to be able to change.

POSITIVE EXPECTATIONS. Positive expectations from the counselor are transferred to the client positively affect outcomes. You may be familiar with the elementary school-based experiments that demonstrated what has come to be known as the Pygmalion effect. Essentially, when teachers expected more from their students, they behaved differently toward those students, and the students, in turn, worked to meet those higher expectations. In contrast, teachers who believed their students were flawed in some essential way and could not reach expectations, lowered their expectations of those students. Those students, in turn, met those low expectations through low performance. The catch in the experiments is that all the students in these studies were similarly capable but, unbeknownst to the teachers, were randomly assigned to the high aptitude and average or low aptitude groups, respectively. In counseling, you, the counselor, may be the last or only hope for a client to experience someone who believes in his or her capacity to change and grow, even if that growth is slow or seemingly minor.

Taken together, we have a therapeutic context (relationship) in which clients can safely observe their behaviors (Hawthorne effect), while experiencing the hope and expectation (Pygmalion effect) of change. As you read this, you might reflect on a recent time that you were able to experience this. What was the outcome? Or, have you ever experienced this? What might it be like?

In addition to the three overarching factors, Prochaska and Norcross (2014) also identify the following as valuable to maintaining the following factors:

- an emotionally charged environment (it's not just a casual conversation),

- a confiding relationship (important, personal material is held here),

- a healing setting (counseling environment),

- a rationale or conceptual scheme (your emerging theoretical perspective and theoretical approach),

- use of therapeutic ritual (e.g., greeting, start/stop time, checking in, takeaways),

- an inspired and socially sanctioned therapist (being in a graduate program, an intern, a license, a community or school-based facility),

- an opportunity for catharsis (time and space to release emotional energy without fear of being judged or ridiculed),

- the acquisition and practice of new behaviors (taking what they learn in session back to their life outside the session),

- exploration of the "inner world" (moving beyond behavior to what may underlie behavior),

- suggestion (a cautious offering of a new perspective on an old issue), and

- interpersonal learning (understanding the value and function of relationships with others).

The Working Alliance

As we continue to think about making and maintaining contact with clients, we will continue this chapter with the introduction of a concept, the therapeutic working alliance developed by Bordin (1979). This concept is referred to as the **working alliance**. According to Bordin, a strong working alliance supports the development of a strong counselor-client dyad and promotes positive outcomes from a therapeutic intervention. There exists a common focus to help the client alleviate pain and self-destructive behaviors. According to Bordin, there are three elements of the working alliance: agreement on goals; agreement on tasks; and the development of a bond. As these three elements evolve, they increase, on the part of the client, the development of a sense of collaboration and a sense of confidence in the therapeutic process (Ardito & Rabellino, 2011). Let's look at each of these and learn what they are and how they might influence the counseling process.

Agreement on Goals

Simply stated, **agreement on goals** means that you, the counselor, and the client have a mutual understanding of the purpose of your work together. This might refer to change as related to thoughts, feelings, or behaviors, or a combination of the three. The goal of the counseling work is dynamic and evolves as the therapeutic relationship grows and develops. A counselor who fosters direct communication with the client about these mutual goals supports the strength of the helping process. As you viewed in both Tables 4.1 and 4.2 that describe an initial and second session with a client, a discussion of goals is included. And of course, the value-based ethical principle of self-determination that we discuss in Chapter 5 reinforces respecting client goals in the counseling process.

We hear from Jose as he talks about establishing goals with his clients. His experiences are mixed. He is new with his work and has only three clients right now. And, he has met with two clients twice and is starting with a new client this week.

JOSE TALKS ABOUT AGREEMENT ON GOALS

Jose: I am working hard to understand how I can work with my clients with their goals. Right now, the agency has me using one of their forms to create my session plans. The treatment facility is very clear about the goals that they have for the clients they serve. And gaining client understanding of that goal setting is part of their intake and then the first counseling session. The facility has specific services and activities that all clients must participate in. So, I am, on my forms, trying to talk about goals in terms of two categories just to expand the client's participation. First, I read with the client a treatment center goal. For example, "Client will learn prosocial skills and use them appropriately in individual, group, and family settings." Then, I talk with the client about what that goal means to him or her. Finally, I ask the client, "What is a goal that you might have that relates to the pro social skills goal?" and we write that goal down. That personal goal serves as the basis for part of our individual counseling. In addition, I ask, "Now that you are in this facility, what do you want from being here?" "If you can imagine what you will be like when you are ready to leave, what do you see?"

The purpose of the element, **agreement on tasks**, is similar to agreement on goals, to develop a mutual understanding between the counselor and the client. It refers to any activities or exercises (theory-driven techniques) that the counselor and the client agree on to increase client development, awareness, and change. There will be times that the counselor brings material and activities that help the client focus on the agreed-on goals; or, the counselor provides the client with a choice of ways to participate in session; or, the client's activities drive the session. This agreement links with the agreement on goals, as the counselor and the client articulate the purpose of the activities. And at times because of the tasks, the goals, in response, may change.

Janice shares with us her experience with the element agreement on tasks.

JANICE TALKS ABOUT AGREEMENT ON TASKS

Janice: I really like this agreement. I like doing this and I see agreement on task as an activity that includes talking but also includes doing. Right now, I am working with sixth graders and, as they are in transition, this is just right for most of them. I have several students and they come with various issues. They all were referred by their teachers. I have lots of art material, music, sand trays, and young adult literature, including graphic novels. So far, the students are enthusiastic. I explain up front that they can set their own goals in their time with me. And I let them know this is their own special time. I let them choose or ask them if they want me to choose. My supervisor has not worked much with students in this way, so she is observing me. I am still finding my way. Just yesterday I had a student who wanted to listen to some really raunchy hip-hop! What to do? I swallowed hard and told the student that I needed to talk with my supervisor about this particular music because of its content. What helped me with this response was my age and life experience.

Development of the Bond

As you have learned in your studies, and are experiencing now with clients, forming a **bond** with them is important. For this bond to exist, feelings such as liking, caring, and trusting are reciprocal and develop over time. And, for clients with a limited or nonexistent social network and support, the formation of the bond becomes more important (Leibert, Smith, & Agaskar, 2011). Sam shares with us some of his thoughts about the development of the bond with his clients.

SAM TALKS ABOUT DEVELOPMENT OF THE BOND

Sam: You remember I am working in a clinic at my university. This means that there are always clients to see, and after I received a strong orientation from my site supervisor, I started seeing clients. When thinking about the development of a bond with my clients, I was so surprised about how different my reaction to each of my clients was. In some sense, it felt like real life. You know, you just like some people better than others. I am not sure that I am even supposed to feel this way as a counselor. I have been talking with my supervisor about my initial reactions to my clients. So, I am tracking my reactions to each client over time. We are then going to look at what happens to my feelings and orientation to each client throughout the term. We also talked about the difference between my initial reaction and how I work with a client. And how that initial reaction influences my work and my relationship with the client. My site supervisor explained to me that many counselors make up their mind about clients and their problems and then never alter them. So, we are going to track my developing impressions of clients. What a learning experience.

Let's work through Discussion Together 4.1 as a way of deepening your understand of the working alliance.

DISCUSSION TOGETHER 4.1
Developing a Working Alliance with Clients

What do you do in your counseling sessions to facilitate a working alliance with your clients? For each of your clients, what does your working alliance look like? How will you know when you have developed a strong working alliance? What seem to be the factors that strengthen your working alliance with your clients? What seem to be the barriers?

Trust

Trust becomes critical as the working alliance develops. What is it? How do you develop it? These are questions that can be addressed in very complex ways. Let's look at a definition of this term and then suggest some guidelines for developing trust between you and your clients. These guidelines integrate much of what you have learned thus far in your academic counseling program and in this text. In fact, the development of trust between the counselor and the client is embedded in learning to be a counselor and being a counselor. This way, the term "trust" moves from just a concept to an important element in your work with clients.

Trust, according to the Oxford English Dictionary (2018), is "a firm belief in the

> ### ETHICAL CONSIDERATION 4.1
>
> "Trust is the cornerstone of the counseling relationship, and counselors have the responsibility to respect and safeguard the client's right to privacy and confidentiality" (ACA Code of Ethics, 2014, p. 4). As you reflect on the role of trust in the counseling relationship, consider the ways professionals in your life have helped establish and maintain trust with you. Also, how have professionals violated your trust, either intentionally or inadvertently? How can these experiences inform the way you foster and protect trust with your clients?

reliability, truth, or ability of someone or something; confidence or faith in a person or thing." Ethics, like love, is hard to define, but you know it when you have it. Therefore, it can be more useful to think of behaviors that build trust. According to the American Counseling Association Code of Ethics (2014), justice, fidelity, and veracity are foundational to building the counseling relationship on a foundation of trust. Justice is defined as "treating individuals equitably and fostering fairness and equality" (ACA, 2014, p. 2); veracity more explicitly states, "honoring commitments and keeping promises, including fulfilling one's responsibilities of trust in professional relationships" (ACA, 2014, p. 2); and veracity is defined as "dealing truthfully with individuals with whom counselors come into professional contact" (ACA, 2014, p. 2). Here are some specific ways that you might enhance trust in your work with clients. Think about how you structure your sessions with clients and the basic skills that you use as a way to begin to establish this trust. Professional behaviors, helping behaviors, and client beliefs are linked to developing and maintaining trust.

Professional Behaviors

- You are on time for your sessions
- You provide counseling in a safe and private venue
- You explain your status as a practicum student, share your professional disclosure statement, and discuss your commitment to confidentiality and its exceptions
- You prepare for each session
- You demonstrate patience and flexibility with your clients

Helping Behaviors

- You help your clients be safe
- You show respect for your clients (unconditional positive regard)
- You tell your clients the truth
- You create a positive environment
- You support the building of client self-esteem
- You create an environment of hope
- You show your clients you are interested in them
- You show your clients you understand them (empathy)
- You allow clients to set the counseling agenda
- You help clients see their lives in new and less negative ways
- You show clients ways that their lives are better through counseling (skills, sharing fears, anxiety, pain, relationship building)
- You challenge clients in non-evaluative ways

Client Beliefs

- Your clients believe that you can help them grown and change
- Your clients believe that they can be themselves with you
- Your clients believe they are supported

The counselor and the client are present together during a counseling session. Counselors have an obligation to establish professional relationships that empower clients to accomplish a wide variety of goals related to wellness and positive mental health. Conducting a session requires a focus on both the counselor and the client, or more specifically the self and the other.

BEING PRESENT WITH THE CLIENT. First, as you prepare yourself as a counselor, we suggest a way of **being in the moment.** Buddhist philosophy underscores the importance of living in the present and maintaining an intentional attention to the present and maintaining a nonjudgmental approach to thoughts and actions (Banks, Burch, & Woodside, 2016; Luke, 2016). This attention to the present within the counseling session has a specific meaning for the counselor and, most especially, the counselor in training. It offers you a way to focus on the client. Clients come to counseling without knowledge of how to be a client and advocate for themselves while in this role. The ideas offered are related to helping clients both feel comfortable within the role and take advantage of the opportunities for growth and the change that it offers.

HERE-AND-NOW RESPONDING. Time is a curious thing in counseling sessions. During the first five minutes of a counseling session, you may freeze. Time may stop. You may forget every counseling skill that you learned and have practiced. Time may seem to be never ending and slow moving when you are disconnected from that confident and prepared counselor you pictured you would be. Or, you may feel that you and your client are seemingly disconnected. Then, time speeds up as you and your client work as one, "in the zone" or "in the flow," only to note that your time together is almost over and you must bring the session to an end.

Regardless of how you experience time in a session, the skill of learning to "quiet yourself and listen to your clients" (Sommers-Flanagan & Sommers-Flanagan, 2015, p. 5) helps you be present in the moment and use **here-and-now responding.** The term **mindfulness** captures this state of being, defined by the Oxford English Dictionary (2018) as the "meditative state of being both fully aware of the moment and of being self-conscious of and attentive to this awareness; a state of intense concentration on one's own thought process; self-awareness."

Often, being mindful in a counseling session will increase your ability to feel empathy, suspend your expectations for the past and/or hopes for the future, calm your internal dialogue, and project a sense of openness and acceptance (Banks, Burch, & Woodside, 2016). In turn, this attention to the moment will enhance your own self-awareness, the development of rapport, and a positive relationship with the client and it will increase your self-confidence as a professional helper (Wong, 2013).

There is a very simple way to gain mindfulness during a counseling session. Although it is simple and focused, it is not easy to achieve. Mindfulness requires a lifelong commitment and practice. Using mindfulness helps counselors achieve presence with the client in the here and now. There are a variety of contemplative practices (e.g., meditation, awareness, stretching, guided imagery) that may help you quiet yourself and listen.

In Discussion Together 4.2, we provide ways that you, your faculty, site supervisors, and peers can share with each other what it means to be in the moment with clients.

Think back over your experiences and describe a time when you believe you experienced being in the moment. What was that experience like for you? What are the concrete thoughts, feelings, and/or behaviors that help you define the experience as being in the moment?

Now, think back over your experiences helping others. What was the experience like for you? At any time, were you in the moment? Did have a time when you were out of the moment? What was being out of the moment like for you? How will you know if you achieve this state during the counseling session?

Sommers-Flanagan and Sommers-Flanagan (2015) offer one approach to develop the skill and the habit of being in the moment with their clients. They discuss "the perfect interviewer" using the following questions; these are useful to ask at any point during a session: What am I doing? Why am I doing what I am doing? What is the current role of my biases? What is my client's here-and-now response? (Sommers-Flanagan & Sommers-Flanagan, 2015, p. 18).

Common Terms for Talking About What You Do

When we are engaged with a client, we are doing *something*. There are three terms useful to know when talking about planning for and working with clients: skills, techniques, and theories. During your work in your academic program, you have learned to use each of these. Before turning our attention to the basic helping skills that will support your client work, let's clarify these three terms.

SKILLS. Skills training involves the *basic listening sequence* that exists across virtually all approaches. They coexist with common factors discussed earlier (Prochaksa & Norcross, 2014) that determine the extent to which a client will participate and be invested in counseling with you. Examples of such skills are listening, empathy, paraphrasing, and clarifying. Often, the use of basic helping skills is associated with specific theories. However, there are some basic helping skills that are useful to implement with most theories (Sommers-Flanagan & Sommers-Flanagan, 2018.

THEORY. Theory involves (ideally) an empirically derived way of viewing and understanding the human condition, whether from a health perspective (wellness) or a pathology-based perspective (medical). A theory is the set of guiding principles that direct a counselor's behavior in the clinical environment. Many times, associated with a theory are philosophic underpinnings, key concepts, goals of the therapy, role of the counselor or therapist, techniques useful to implement the theory, ways the theory can be applied, outcomes expected, broad contributions of the theory, and limitations of the approach (Corey, 2013; Sharf, 2016). There are over 400 theories today from which counselors can choose to guide their client work (Zarbo, Tasca, Cattafi, & Compare, 2016) and that number is growing rapidly. Seligman and Reichenberg (2014) organize theories according to five categories of treatment systems as a way of helping therapists seek commonalities among theories: treatment systems emphasizing background (e.g., Freudian, Adlerian); treatment systems emphasizing emotions and sensations (e.g., Rogerian, existential); treatment systems emphasizing thoughts (e.g., rational emotive behavior therapy, cognitive therapy); treatment systems emphasizing action (e.g., behavioral therapy, reality therapy, cognitive behavioral therapy); and other treatment approaches (e.g., family systems, integrative). Therapies can also be categorized by their format (e.g., individual, group) and time commitment (solution-focused brief therapy).

TECHNIQUES. Techniques are the theory-based, situation specific interventions used to address particular client concerns. While often used interchangeably, techniques are theory specific, whereas skills are more global. That said, counselors often practice from one theoretical perspective but use techniques from other therapies that belong to their same treatment system. For example, a counselor practicing cognitive behavioral therapy might "borrow" the reality therapy SAMIC3 planning tool to help a client establish goals (Wubblolding, 1991).

Table 4.3 contains samples of each: skills, theory, and techniques. Use this table to see if you can define each of the theories and describe how the skills and techniques relate to said theory.

TABLE 4.3. Relation between Theory, Skills, and Techniques

Skills	Theories	Techniques
• Empathy	• Person centered	• Modeling
• Listening	• Psychodynamic	• Roleplay
• Confronting	• Behaviorism	• Self-talk
• Paraphrasing	• CT/CBT	• Cognitive restructuring
• Clarifying	• Reality therapy	• Thought stopping
• Summarizing	• Solution focused	• Systematic desensitization
• Restating	• Gender aware	• Relaxation training

Basic Helping Skills

In this section, we describe three broad categories of basic skills that are essential to success in working with clients during practicum and beyond. You are already familiar with each of these from your work in your counseling classes. These include attending behaviors, clarifications, and redirections (see Erford, Hays, & Crockett, 2015, pp. 126–127). All these are predicated on stable, solid listening skills, which we summarize first.

When we encounter people who hear that we are counselors, a common response is, "Oh, I'll bet you are good at giving advice." In trying to clarify the work of a counselor, the reaction is usually one of disappointment: "So you just listen to people's problems all day? And that helps?" This is a major assumption about our work as counselors: that listening is so basic that anyone could do it and that it is hard to imagine that it is helpful. You may feel that way at times. In fact, Chad routinely hears from his practicum students that they are eager to get past the listening and get into the techniques and theories that do something. As it turns out, listening is both incredibly difficult to do and do well, and it is also very therapeutic (Sommers-Flanagan & Sommers-Flanagan, 2018. This will become clearer to you as you approach real clients in the context of practicum and after conducting roleplays in the classroom during a basic counseling skills course.

In transitioning to real-world clients, the following conceptualization of listening, drawn from Luke (2016, 2018) helps expand the concept of listening. Full-body listening involves (a) listening to clients' words, (b) listening to clients' absence of words, and (c) listening to clients' behaviors.

Attending

ATTENDING involves listening to the point that the client feels heard. Also, attending is managing your body language in a way that invites the clients to speak. Body language consists of **nonverbals** and **paraverbals**. Nonverbal body language is the use of head nods, open posture, and, in general, listening with one's whole body. Practicum is the place where you are able to practice sitting like a human and not a robot. Paraverbals are simply the vocalizations counselors use to acknowledge something a client has said without distracting them from their train of thought. Examples include "uh-huh," "hmmm," and "oh".

Question Categories

A second dimension of attending to the client is represented by **question categories**. Asking questions is a tricky component of attending, but we frame questions as learning about the individual as well as treating the individual. This is a precarious area for counselors and counselors in training, so we outline several considerations for asking questions. Information about these categories helps you view the complexity of questions and helps you decide, if you want to ask questions, the best way you can meet your and the client's needs.

MORBID CURIOSITY. **Morbid curiosity questions** are questions asked to meet the needs of the counselor: "When you say you were sexually abused, what happened?" (Alternative: "You don't need to say anything further. How important is it to you that I know more details?")

CARELESS CURIOSITY. **Careless curiosity questions** are questions asked that detract from therapeutic movement, if not result in a breach in trust: "You were assaulted … were you drinking?"

RESPECTFUL CURIOSITY. **Respectful curiosity questions** are questions that maintain the focus on the needs of the client: "I want you to feel comfortable in our relationship and confident that I understand more about your experience. Could I ask you a couple of questions about how you felt during your experience?"

OPEN AND CLOSED QUESTIONS. **Open questions** invite clients to explore by leaving room for them to respond in their own ways. For example, "What is it like for you to describe that to me?" versus a closed question that might ask, "Are you feeling anxious as you describe that to me?" **Closed questions**, as you saw in the previous example, are used to clarify something a client has expressed, or to close the conversation. For example, you might use a closed question such as, "Are you okay if we stop here?"

CLARIFYING QUESTIONS. **Clarifying questions** intend to clarify the meaning of a client comment and express the genuine desire a counselor has for understanding the client. These can be a little uncomfortable for clients, as it may be a rare thing for someone to listen until he or she understands. The following are examples of the ways clarifying questions may be used:

"When you said _____, I heard _____. It that accurate?"

"You feel _____. Is that correct?"

"I honestly did not track with what you just said. Will you repeat that last comment?"

IMPLIED QUESTIONS. **Implied questions** are questions to the client that don't necessarily end in a question mark. Counselors protect clients (and themselves) from question fatigue or from appearing to interrogate their clients, so statements that imply questions can be used. Here are a couple of examples:

"Sometimes I wonder if you are being transparent with me." (Explicit: "Are you being transparent?")

"I sense some hesitation …" ("Are you feeling hesitant?")

SWING QUESTIONS. **Swing questions**, described by Sommers-Flanagan and Sommers-Flanagan (2018), are questions that appear to be closed questions based on their structure but open the door for clients to say no while providing clarification. We use these with adolescents and clients who are mandated to counseling to ask their permission to explore issues with them. For example, we might ask, "Would you mind if we discuss this a little more?" or "Could I ask you about how it was for you in your family?" This explicit question is a yes-or-no response, but also invites elaboration.

Clarification

Clarification involves listening to the point that the client feels understood. The skills in this category overlap to some degree, but all share a common purpose: to manage the information in the session shared by the client and to ensure that the client feels heard and understood by the counselor. There are three types of clarification to consider. Sample responses are provided after the description of each type, based on a client statement such as, *"I have felt really bad for five years. No, I haven't told anyone about my depression."*

RESTATING. **Restating** involves reiterating a statement made by a client to assure accurate transfer of information. These are often verbatim, such as, "You've felt this bad for five years without telling anyone. Is that right?" A question follows, which is sometimes called a check-out, to make certain you understand the client's statement correctly.

PARAPHRASING. **Paraphrasing** involves a restatement using the counselor's own words to show understanding of what the client has said. For instance, a counselor might respond to the previous client statement example with, "You've been suffering in silence with your depression for a long time!"

SUMMARIZING. **Summarizing** is a way to clarify the most salient features of a large volume of information shared by the client. It helps both the counselor and the client to manage the information effectively. For example, the summary might result in the statement in the previous client statement only after the client has shared a 15-minute version of his or her story and the counselor has summarized.

Redirecting

REDIRECTING involves listening to the point where the client feels the need and subsequent motivation to change. To paraphrase Carl Rogers (1961), you might say to a client to redirect, "I respect you now ... and will continue to do so as you change. " The types of reflections characterize empathic redirection, along with pointing out incongruences.

REFLECTING THINKING (CONTENT). **Reflecting thinking (content)** is similar to clarifying, except that the purpose of reflecting thinking or content is to maintain focus on client cognition. It focuses the session on the facts of the client's situation, at least as the client experiences them. This type of reflection is particularly useful in working with clients who are especially emotive or awash with feelings about a particular issue. Reflecting thinking provides a cognitive anchor or safe harbor from which clients can more effectively explore their emotions. For example, in responding to the sample client statement, reflecting content might look like this: "You've been telling yourself for five years that it is not safe to share your painful experiences with anyone."

REFLECTING FEELING (AFFECT). **Reflecting feeling (affect)** involves highlighting a client's emotional experience in the session. Contrary to reflection of content, the purpose of reflecting feeling is to assist clients in moving beyond the facts and data of their situation and into the feelings that underlie their experience. This is used for supporting clients who struggle to make contact with their feelings about an issue they have brought to counseling. For example, consider this response to the client statement, "You've been feeling depressed and afraid, so you've created a place of emotional safety for yourself."

REFLECTING MEANING. **Reflecting meaning** is admittedly one of the more complex redirections in counseling. We frame reflection of meaning as **content plus affect in context** because it takes the reflection beyond the literal comments of the client and seeks to provide a reflection of his or her experience beyond which he or she may be aware. For example, "You have found purpose in suffering alone and in silence, until it stopped working and now you're unsure what to do next because you're hurting and isolated from sources of support. I wonder if you are afraid as well."

REFLECTING OR HIGHLIGHTING INCONGRUENCES AND DISCREPANCIES. **Reflecting or highlighting incongruences and discrepancies** is the final form of redirection discussed. This is a skill that is often described as confrontation, but we try to avoid such pejorative language. Counseling, by its very nature, is confrontational, but not in the ways most people picture when they think of one person yelling and talking down to another person. In contrast, highlighting incongruences or reflecting discrepancies must be done gently and respectfully, in a spirit of compassion and humility. Discrepancies can illuminate clients' ambivalence regarding change: They want to change and they want to stay the same, simultaneously! How very human of them (like the rest of us). Using this skill requires great care and might look something like this with our sample client: "Your depression leaves you feeling isolated and alone, but you find yourself withdrawn from those who would aid in preventing those feelings of isolation and aloneness. You seem to be a little caught between two opposing forces within you. I wonder if we could talk about this further?"

In Table 4.4 we present some prompts and a few questions to use when planning your sessions with your clients. These prompts are representative of the ways in which you can use these skills. In Reflection Question 4.1, you can use the description of each of the skills presented in Table 4.4 as you demonstrate the use of these skills.

TABLE 4.4. Basic Skills and Associated Prompts and Questions

Skills	Prompts or Questions
Attending	
Nonverbals and paraverbals	"Hmmm" and "oh"
Question categories	
Respectful curiosity	"I want you to feel comfortable. ... Could I ask you a question about ... ?"
Open questions	"What is it like for you ...?" "Tell me more about that."
Closed questions	"Are you alright today?"
Clarifying questions	"When you said _____, I heard _____. It that accurate?"
Implied questions	"It seems you are feeling angry today." "I sense you are happy with your family."
Swing questions	"Would you mind if we discuss this a little more?"
Clarification	
Restating	"This is what I heard you say. [Repeat] Is that right?
Paraphrasing	Put what the client says in your own words.
Summarizing	"This is what I heard you say about what happened last night between you and your father. First, ... second, ... third. ..."
Redirecting	
Reflecting thinking (content)	"You have been telling yourself 'I hurt my sister last week.'" "You have been thinking. ..."
Reflecting feeling (affect)	"You have been telling yourself 'I hurt my sister last week. I wonder if you are still angry.'"
Incongruent discrepancies	"On one hand, you say you want _____; yet, on the other hand, you're doing _____. Can you help me put those two things together?"

In Reflection Question 4.1 you will create a planning session document and include ways that you might use the basic helping skills described in this section.

How Do You Know If You're Doing It Right?

To end this chapter, you will hear from one our cast of characters, Kaisha, who shares her thoughts about early meetings with one of her clients. Kaisha's experience will help prepare you for reading and thinking about basic counseling skills that you will be using *today*.

Kaisha

My site supervisor had a list of students for me to work with the first day that I arrived for my practicum. I shadowed her for the first week. During that time, after each of her sessions, she would ask for my observations and talk through what the session goal was and we talked about what happened in session. During this second week, I met with four clients. Earlier (as described in Chapter 3), I talked about meeting with the student, his name is Daniel, who, describing his reactions to his parents fighting, blurted out, "I just wish they [his parents] would get a divorce." I had a tough time finishing the session. I was to see this client again, so I talked with my supervisor about my plans for the session, and the skills to keep in mind. I had the second session today. I wanted to hear more from Daniel today so, as my supervisor suggested, I spent 10 minutes before the session preparing. First, I wanted to read over the plan that I prepared. And then I was going to engage in a mindfulness activity. I planned a session that used a format introduced earlier in this chapter.

Kaisha concentrated on planning the beginning of the session and wanted to leave room for what her supervisor calls "flow" or the working part of the session. Kaisha's plan follows (see Table 4.5).

TABLE 4.5. Kaisha's Plan for her Second Session with Daniel

Minutes 1–8: Warm-up

-Two-minute connection: Kaisha decided she wanted to begin by referencing the previous session and asking the supervisor to join the session.

Daniel, I am so glad to see you this second time this week. As we talked about earlier this week, I am a practicum student here at the clinic. It is my job to provide you counseling services and support while I'm under supervision. Thanks for seeing me last session. What was that session like for you last week?

Daniel: I did not expect to feel so much intensity about my parents' conflict. I left a little shaken about expressing it. I'm okay now.

-One-minute emergent issues check: Tell me what is going on for you since we met.

-Three-minute linking to previous session:

Kaisha: I wonder if you could say a little more about the both the feelings you experienced in our last session, and about your experience of being surprised by all that emotion.

-Two-minute goals for session:

Kaisha: What seems important for you today, as you reflect on your emotions related to your situation?

Minutes 8–40: "Working"

-Gathering information

Daniel, as a way for us to proceed, I would like for you to take a few minutes and create a story based on what you said was important to you. Can you write a short story about what being with your parents in a good way would be?

[After Daniel has written, I say, "Daniel, thanks for working on this story. Would you like me to read it? And then I would like for you to read it to me aloud.]

-Offering feedback in the form of basic skills as discussed next

Minutes 40–50: Wrap-up

-Most important things

-Summary from counselor: "As we come to the end of our time today, there are a few things that stand out to me."

-"What will you take from this session?"

-"What action will you take as a result of our time together?"

Kaisha understands that her ideas about this session may not go exactly as planned, depending on what Daniel says and what he does. As she thought about the plan, although she was unclear of Daniel's goals, hers were to (a) discuss the presence of his intense emotions in an honest way without making Kaisha's issues prominent in the counseling session and (b) get to know Daniel better. She had time to do so, since he would be her client all term and they would meet every week. She made sure that Daniel had an opportunity to talk about last session and to help link the last session with this one. Kaisha wanted to use a narrative approach to get to know Daniel better, and she wanted to make sure that the focus of the session was on him. She also knows that he likes to both write and draw, so she wanted the session open enough to include the use of these two mediums of expression.

Summary

Counseling works. It works because of the relationship that is forged between the counselor and the client. This is a significant component of the work we perform as counselors: learning to make and maintain contact with clients. Practicum is the place to hone your relational skills through live practice and feedback. At this stage of your development, you may be uncertain how to utilize theory-based techniques. However, during practicum, it is paramount that you focus on learning to engage with clients as fellow humans. In this chapter, we have outlined a number of ways you can think about your work as a practicum student, along with basic skills applications with maintaining contact with your client. We also presented the working alliance as a concept that can help you enhance your relationship with your client and promote positive outcomes for the counseling process.

Key Terms

Agreement on goals   *Being in the moment*   *Clarification*

Agreement on tasks   *Bond*   *Clarifying questions*

Attending   *Careless curiosity*   *Closed questions*

Context for change	Nonverbals	Reflecting thinking (content)
Follow-up session outline	Open questions	Respectful curiosity
Hawthorne effect	Paraphrasing	Restating
Here-and-now responding	Paraverbals	Structure of the session
Implied questions	Pygmalion effect	Summarizing
Initial session outline	Redirecting	Swing questions
Maintaining contact	Reflecting feeling (affect)	Therapeutic relationship
Making contact	Reflecting meaning	Trust
Mindfulness	Reflecting or highlighting	Working alliance
Morbid curiosity	incongruence/discrepancies	

References

American Counseling Association. (2014). ACA 2014 Code of Ethics. Retrieved from https://www.counseling.org/resources/aca-code-of-ethics.pdf

Ardito, R. B., & Rabellino, D. (2011). Therapeutic alliance and outcome of psychotherapy: Historical excursus, measurement, and prospects for research. *Frontiers in Psychology, 2,* 270. Retrieved from https://www.ncbi.nlm.nih.gov/pmc/articles/PMC3198542/

Banks, B., Burch, T., & Woodside, M. (2016). "Introducing Mindfulness and Contemplative Pedagogy as an Approach to Building Helping Skills in Human Services Trainees. *Journal of Human Service, 36*(1), 47-60.

Bordin, E. S. (1979). The generalizability of the psychoanalytic concept of the working alliance. *Psychotherapy: Theory, Research, and Practice, 16*(3), 252–260.

CACREP Standards. (2018). *Section 5: Entry-level Specialty Areas—Clinical Mental Health.* Retrieved from https://www.cacrep.org/section-5-entry-level-specialty-areas-clinical-mental-health-counseling/

Corey, G. (2013). *Theory and practice of counseling and psychotherapy* (10th ed.). Pacific Grove, CA: Cengage.

Erford, B. T., Hays, D. G., & Crockett, S. (2015). *Mastering the national counselor examination and the counselor preparation comprehensive examination* (2nd ed.). Upper Saddle River, NJ: Pearson.

Leibert, T. W., Smith, J. B., & Agaskar, V. R. (2011). Relationship between the working alliance and social support on counseling outcome. *Journal of Clinical Psychology, 67*(7), 709–719. doi:10.1002/jclp.20800

Luke, C. (2018). *Career-focused counseling: Integrating theory, practice, and neuroscience.* San Diego, CA: Cognella.

Luke, C. (2016). *Neuroscience for counselors and therapist.* Thousand Oaks, CA: SAGE.

Oxford English Dictionary. (2018). Mindfulness. Retrieved from http://www.oed.com.proxy.lib.utk.edu:90/view/Entry/118742?redirectedFrom=minfulness#eid

Oxford English Dictionary. (2018). Trust. Retrieved from http://www.oed.com.proxy.lib.utk.edu:90/view/Entry/207004?rskey=kBjf4S&result=1#ed

Prochaska, J. O., & Norcross, J. C. (2014). *Systems of psychotherapy: A transtheoretical analysis* (8th ed.). Stamford, CT: Cengage.

Rogers, C. (1961). *On becoming a person.* London: Constable.

Seligman, L. W., & Reichenberg, L. W. (2014). *Theories of counseling and psychotherapy: Systems, strategies, and skills.* Boston, MA: Merrill. THIS IS IN CHAPTER

Sharf, R. S. (2016). *Theories of psychotherapy and counseling: Concepts and cases* (6th ed.). Pacific Grove, CA: Cengage.

Sommers-Flanagan, J., & Sommers-Flanagan, R. (2015). *Clinical interviewing* (5th ed.). Hoboken, NJ: John Wiley & Sons.

Sommers-Flanagan, J., & Sommers-Flanagan, R. (2018). *Clinical interviewing* (6th ed.). Hoboken, NJ: John Wiley & Sons.

Wong, Y. (2013). Returning to silence, connecting to wholeness: Contemplative pedagogy for critical social work education. *Journal of Religion & Spirituality in Social Work, 32*(3), 269–285.

Wubbolding, R. E. (1991). *Understanding reality therapy: A metaphorical approach.* New York, NY: Perennial.

Zarbo, C., Tasca, G. A., Cattafi, F., & Compare, A. (2016). Integrative psychotherapy works. *Frontiers in Psychology, 6,* 2021. Retrieved from https://www.ncbi.nlm.nih.gov/pmc/articles/PMC4707273/

Ethics in
PRACTICUM

INTRODUCTION

Depending on where you are in the course of your practicum experience, you may have already had "the dream." That is the dream that you forgot to sign a progress note, neglected to cover exceptions to confidentiality with your new client, or left your client file unsecured on your computer. Many, if not most, practicum students have the dream or some form of anxiety evoked from working with clients, especially as it relates to professional ethics. The first wave of this, of course, comes with your first course on professional ethics. Before engaging in the ethics course material, many new counseling students have no idea just how many ways there are to break rules (ethics and laws) or the breadth of specific guidelines for applying ethical and legal concepts and laws. And, just when some of that specific type of anxiety begins to find a place in CITs' thinking, they begin practicum, and many of those fears—and many news ones—come rushing back. The reality is, when considering professional ethics and legalities related to counseling, there are many things to keep in mind, and there are numerous rules to follow. These all come at a time when you are also expected to help clients and not just avoid hurting them. It can feel overwhelming. However, in this chapter you will develop a more refined ethical posture and learn specific ways you can help your clients. The goals of this chapter follow.

- Learn to use the 2014 American Counseling Association's Code of Ethics to guide your ethical stance and ethical behavior

- Identify many of challenging ethical issues that counselors in training (CITs) and counselors encounter

- Develop ways to approach ethical issues with humility, flexibility, and professionalism

- Learn how to use an ethical decision-making model

- Develop ways to consult with others about ethical issues

RELATED CACREP GOALS

Section 2: PROFESSIONAL COUNSELING IDENTITY COUNSELING CURRICULUM

- F. The eight common core areas represent the foundational knowledge required of all entry-level counselor education graduates. Therefore, counselor education programs must document where each of the lettered standards listed below is covered in the curriculum.

- 1. PROFESSIONAL COUNSELING ORIENTATION AND ETHICAL PRACTICE

- i. ethical standards of professional counseling organizations and credentialing bodies, and applications of ethical and legal considerations in professional counseling (CACREP, 2016a)

Section 5: ENTRY-LEVEL SPECIALTY AREAS

- C. CLINICAL MENTAL HEALTH COUNSELING

- 2. CONTEXTUAL DIMENSIONS

- l. legal and ethical considerations specific to clinical mental health counseling (2016b)

- G. SCHOOL COUNSELING

- 2. CONTEXTUAL DIMENSIONS

- n. legal and ethical considerations specific to school counseling (2016c)

Purposes of Ethical Behavior

Counseling is an aspirational enterprise, asking us to live up to ethical ideals such as unconditional positive regard for clients; it is also a developmental endeavor (Ametrano, 2014; Neukrug, Lovell, & Parker, 1996), that recognizes all of us—from the beginning CITs to the highly experienced clinician—are on a journey of self- and other acceptance. What supports the development of this unconditional positive regard of our clients is nonjudgmental mutual dialogue and consultation that we receive from others and that is also delivered to us within the context of nonjudgmental and accepting attitudes. Establishing this context represents stated ideals with which counselors would like to align themselves (Sommers-Flanagan & Sommers-Flanagan, 2017).

It is a challenge to actually live these standards of excellence. In fact, in order for individual counselors and the counseling profession as a whole to develop and grow, our internal debate about ethical and legal issues needs to be honest about two aspects of demonstrating professional behavior related to ethics. First, there exists the very real difficulty in conceptualizing our values in counseling (such as the directive to "bracket" one's personal beliefs) and, second, providing the kind of counseling experience that is mandated by our professional ethical code. For example, while most counselors, according to the 2014 ACA Code of Ethics, rightly endorse acceptance of all clients regardless of the lifestyles chosen by those same clients, most of us have likely encountered situations in which we've struggled to practice the very standards we endorse.

A recent example of this type of question is, "Should counselors refer based on strongly held beliefs?" which was raised in Tennessee in 2017. This question resulted in the first federal case of discrimination brought in response to state legislation permitting counselors to refer clients on the basis of the counselor's strongly held principles. This legal right is in conflict with ACA's stance on nondiscrimination but may be similar to a counselor's own values. CITs may have strong beliefs regarding a variety of issues (e.g., abortion, gay marriage, immigration), regardless of state statutes such as Tennessee's, but the 2014 ACA Code of Ethics requires counselors work with clients even if said client's values and goals are different than those of the counselor.

The dialogue around this issue evoked complex and nuanced dialogue and replies. A question such as this both demonstrates the challenges and complexities of ethical issues and underscores the need for the consideration of addressing ethical issues practicum students confront from a developmental perspective. This observation leads to the question, "Given what we know about the course of counselor development, how might a CIT or novice counselor determine how to think and act?"

Reflection Question 5.1 will help you view the 2014 American Counseling Association's Code of Ethics in a new light.

REFLECTION QUESTION 5.1

CONSIDERING ETHICAL ISSUES

Think back over your time in your counseling academic program. List the ethical issues that you have encountered both in and outside your classroom experiences. Choose one of these issues and answer the following prompts and questions: (a) Briefly describe the ethical issue you chose; (b) Why did you choose this issue? (c) What type of emotions do you attach to this issue? (d) How was the issue resolved or does the issue remain unresolved? (e) What did you learn from your encounter with this issue? (f) What feelings remain? (g) What emotions remain?

Many CITs and novice counselors tend to be more concrete in approaching ethical issues. This concrete approach is represented by an approach that asks, "What is the rule that I should follow?" and "What are the guidelines for following this rule?" Also, there is often anxiety, and perhaps fear, associated with encountering an ethical dilemma. Let's pause for a moment to return to your own responses to the questions and prompts in Reflection Question 5.1. and ask these questions:

- Do your responses reflect a concrete approach to the issue you chose and described?
- Did you wish for rules and guidelines to follow?

If you responded yes to these questions, your approach reflects your status as a novice. As a way of moving to another way of responding, you may want to ask yourself, "If this is the way I now consider ethical issues, where do I go from here?"

When considering ethical questions, an alternative way to reflect on them would be to use an integrated, holistic view of ethical behavior. But before attempting this holistic view, it is important to understand the rules. The American Counseling Association (2014) presents these ethical concepts.

American Counseling Association's Code of Ethics

The topic of ethics may be familiar to you since it has been covered in either a distinct course on professional ethics, a course on an introduction to the counseling profession, a professional identity course, or some combination of these courses. The reason for returning to the foundation of counselor professional ethics is two-fold. First and foremost, ethics is an ongoing process and the **ethical code is** a living document (Kaplan et al., 2017). It is not something a counselor in training can "cram" to know on a test and then move on (Bernard & Goodyear, 2009). Kaplan and colleagues (2017) describe **ethical practice** as being "a way of professional existence, not only a command of a body of knowledge" (p. 75). The second reason is related to the developmental process of professional CITs, as reflected in the approach in this text. Learning professional ethics in the context of a beginning skills course is (or should be) something of a different experience than revisiting ethics in the context of practicum. Professional ethics should move from hypothetical discussions of application to direct implementation of these concepts in practice with real-life clients. The reason for this, especially in practicum, is articulated best through the words of Perry Francis and Suzanne Duggar (2014), "Entry into and continued association with a profession requires all of its practitioners to make a commitment that they will abide by the profession's code of ethics and the profession's collective values as reflected in that code" (p. 131). The **American Counseling Association's 2014 Code of Ethics** and its preamble reflect these collective values.

As described in the preamble, there are six purposes to the Code of Ethics (American Counseling Association, 2014). As CITs develop their counseling skills, they have the responsibility to put on the mantle of professional responsibility as a counseling professional. The six purposes are listed in Table 5.1. This table highlights the multifaceted purpose of the Code. First, it provides guidance to counselors in practicing ethically—a hallmark of a profession. Second, the Code's purpose includes shifting from ethical obligations only to ethical considerations. Third, the Code is a unifying document, cementing the shared responsibilities across counselors in a variety of settings and roles. Fourth, the Code's purpose include **protection for clients** by outlining expectations for counseling in practice. Fifth, the Code is there as an extension of the American Counseling Association. Last, but not least, the Code provides a framework for addressing complaints and concerns regarding the behaviors of counselors.

TABLE 5.1. Purpose of the ACA Code of Ethics

1. The *Code* sets forth the ethical obligations of ACA members and provides guidance intended to inform the ethical practice of professional counselors.

2. The *Code* identifies ethical considerations relevant to professional counselors and counselors-in-training.

3. The *Code* enables the association to clarify for current and prospective members, and for those served by members, the nature of the ethical responsibilities held in common by its members.

4. The *Code* serves as an ethical guide designed to assist members in constructing a course of action that best serves those utilizing counseling services and establishes expectations of conduct with a primary emphasis on the role of the professional counselor.

5. The *Code* helps to support the mission of ACA.

6. The standards contained in this *Code* serve as the basis for processing inquiries and ethics complaints concerning ACA members. (ACA, 2014)

Source: American Counseling Association, 2014 ACA Code of Ethics. Copyright © 2014 by American Counseling Association. Reprinted with permission.

Preamble to ACA Code of Ethics

If you want to know what it means to be a professional counselor, the preamble conveys this (American Counseling Association, 2014). The preamble contains both the **professional values** as well as the **principles of ethical behavior**. You will find the preamble in Table 5.2. It is a great place to begin to develop an understanding the role of professional counselors and the behavioral expectations of the profession (Francis & Duggar, 2014).

TABLE 5.2. 2014 ACA Code of Ethics Preamble

The American Counseling Association (ACA) is an educational, scientific, and professional organization whose members work in a variety of settings and serve in multiple capacities. Counseling is a professional relationship that empowers diverse individuals, families, and groups to accomplish mental health, wellness, education, and career goals. Professional values are an important way of living out an ethical commitment. The following are core professional values of the counseling profession:

1. enhancing human development throughout the life span;

2. honoring diversity and embracing a multicultural approach in support of the worth, dignity, potential, and uniqueness of people within their social and cultural contexts;

3. promoting social justice;

4. safeguarding the integrity of the counselor–client relationship; and

5. practicing in a competent and ethical manner.

These professional values provide a conceptual basis for the ethical principles enumerated below. These principles are the foundation for ethical behavior and decision making. The fundamental principles of professional ethical behavior are

- *autonomy*, or fostering the right to control the direction of one's life;

- *nonmaleficence*, or avoiding actions that cause harm;

- *beneficence*, or working for the good of the individual and society by promoting mental health and well-being;

- *justice*, or treating individuals equitably and fostering fairness and equality;

- *fidelity*, or honoring commitments and keeping promises, including fulfilling one's responsibilities of trust in professional relationships; and

- *veracity*, or dealing truthfully with individuals with whom counselors come into professional contact. (ACA, 2014, p. 3)

Source: American Counseling Association, 2014 ACA Code of Ethics. Copyright © 2014 by American Counseling Association. Reprinted with permission.

You may have noticed in looking at the preamble the comment that counseling is a **professional relationship**. This is a signal that the relationships you will foster with clients will be unlike those relationships in your personal life. This relationship has established parameters that you, as the counselor, are duty- and role-bound to ensure adherence to. When we enter a counseling session, we take the profession with us, professionally speaking. We represent the thousands of counseling professionals across the country and around the world, past, present, and future. As long as we practice within the role assigned by our profession, we benefit from the support and to some degree the protection of the profession. Therefore, it is important to know the role and responsibilities associated with membership in the profession of counseling. One way to understand the role and responsibilities is by understanding the values of the profession as expressed in the preamble to the Code.

When you read about the values of the counseling profession, you may recall that much of the basic material presented is not new. What is new, however, is taking the information and moving from *what* to do, to *when, how* and *why* we do it (see Figure 5.1).

FIGURE 5.1. Moving Ethical Practice from the Concrete to the Complex and Reflective

Enhancing the development of counselors is an important aspect of the preamble. Remley and Herlihy (2016) identified three dimensions of this: taking a developmental view of client issues, possessing a wellness orientation to the client, and emphasizing prevention and early intervention over remediation and pathologizing. Most counseling students read these and agree whole-heartedly with the spirit of these values. However, it does not take long at a practicum site to be confronted with the stark reality that working in the world of practice (e.g., community mental health or schools) can bring. First, counselors cannot currently expect to be reimbursed by insurance and other third-party payers for "diagnosing" a client's strengths, or by summarizing a client's developmental trajectory. This can be quite a shock for CITs as they transition from classroom to clinic or school setting. Second, prevention and early intervention tend to work best prior to diagnosis and socio-emotional consequences, not after.

Third, whether in community mental health or schools, there are context realities that govern professional responsibility. At times it appears that the client does not always "come first." And, in many instances, practicum students experience the conflict between two very important ethical principles. These types of situations can cause dissonance for counselors and must be reconciled in order to grow successfully through these types of events. Supervision is one of the most effective settings to address the question, "What is ethical behavior in the context of the world of practice?"

A second component of the preamble involves the principle ethics associated with the profession. When we, as counselors, focus on the purpose of the material in the Code of Ethics, we establish for our practice the **ethical guidelines** that (a) protect our clients from harm, (b) open ourselves to the opportunity to do the most good possible, (c) harness the power of the individual in shaping his or her own life, (d) treat all clients equally, (e) keep our word, and (f) tell the truth. This statement presents the principle ethics embodied in the Code.

Discussion Together 5.1 allows faculty and site supervisors to share with you, as a practicum student, their personal experiences confronting ethical challenges and the behaviors, thoughts, and feelings these experiences evoked.

DISCUSSION TOGETHER 5.1
Living and Practicing Ethically

Ask your faculty supervisor and/or your site supervisor to share a memorable ethical challenge faced working with a client(s) in a clinical mental health or school setting. How did each of these aspects of ethical practice relate to the following: (a) protect our clients from harm; (b) open ourselves to the opportunity to do the most good possible; (c) harness the power of the individual in shaping his or her own life; (d) treat all clients equally; (e) keep our word; and (f) tell the truth.

Challenges of Ethical Practice

Ethical practice as a counselor can be challenging. These challenges may present what appear to be substantial issues or those of seemingly lesser importance, reflect the conflict among several professional values or ethical standards, or represent a personal struggle about how much time, energy, and emotion to invest. At times, confronting these ethical challenges represents a quandary about what to do, how to proceed. Other times, the ethical challenges aren't confronted; there is a lack of recognition that ethical dilemmas even exist. Counselors believe they know the right thing to do. Practicing ethically means, first, being able to recognize when an event, situation, context, or personal response indicates an ethical issue exists and then, second, being about to consult with others about issues with which we are aware and less aware. Neukrug's (2018) **ethical hotspots** alerts counselors to types of ethical issues they may confront in their work.

Ethical Hotspots

One of the ways to consider the challenges of ethical practice is to consider areas that practicing counselors face. Neukrug (2018) suggests that there are particular categories that represent ethical challenges (Table 5.3).

TABLE 5.3. Neukrug's (2018) Hotspots in Ethics for Counselors Aggregated by Logical Categories

The Counseling Relationship

- Bartering
- Using techniques that are not theory or research based
- Pressuring a client to receive needed services
- Working with a client in danger of harming self or others
- Trying to change your client's personally held beliefs or values
- Rather than working with a client, referring him or her due to value differences

Legal Issues

- Refraining from making a diagnosis to protect a client from a third party (e.g., employer who might demote a client)
- Breaking the law to protect your client's rights
- Reporting suspected child abuse, spousal abuse, or abuse of an older person

Social and Cultural Issues

- Based on personal values, choosing not to counsel and, instead referring an LGBTQ+ client to another helper
- Based on knowledge and interests, accepting clients who are only from specific cultural, ethnic, or gender groups
- Being competent in multicultural counseling
- Serving emerging populations with little knowledge of those groups

Boundary Issues

- Attending a client's wedding, graduation ceremony, or other formal ceremony
- Hugging a client
- Selling a counseling-related product to your client (e.g., book, audiotape, etc.)
- Having sex with a current or former client
- Self-disclosing your feelings to your clients
- Engaging in dual or multiple relationships with your clients (e.g., your client is also your child's teacher)

Confidentiality

- Guaranteeing confidentiality for groups, couples, and families
- Withholding information about a minor despite a parent's request for information
- Not allowing clients to view case notes about them
- Sharing confidential client information with a colleague who is not your clinical supervisor

Informed Consent

- Seeing a minor client without parental consent
- Not obtaining informed consent
- Not offering a professional disclosure statement to your client

Professional Issues

- Not being a member of a professional association in counseling
- Inappropriate fee assessment
- Reporting a colleague's unethical conduct without first consulting the colleague
- Not having malpractice coverage (on your own or through your agency/setting)
- Misrepresenting credentials
- Publicly advocating for a cause that is different from widely held views in your organization

Technology

- Supervision over the internet
- Counseling over the internet
- Security of client records on computers
- Viewing your client's social media without asking permission
- When conducting distance counseling or sending client information over the internet, using software without confirming it meets HIPAA regulations
- "Friending" clients on your personal social networking sites (e.g., Facebook)

Source: E. S. Neukrug, *Counseling Theory and Practice*, pp. 11-13. Copyright © 2018 by Cognella, Inc. Reprinted with permission.

Ethical Practice and Supervision

In practicum, you are engaged in supervision, both with your site supervisor and your faculty supervisor. Each has a unique role to fill and a perspective that will help you view and work through the ethical issues you encounter in practicum. There are several reasons that **ethical practice and supervision** are linked so powerfully; one relates to the responsibilities practicum supervisors assume, and the other represents an important component in ethical practice and ethical decision making. First, both faculty and site supervisors' responsibilities and commitments are two-fold: support the professional development of the CIT; protect the client's welfare (Bernard & Goodyear, 2014). With this responsibility, addressing ethical behavior is a critical part of the supervisory process. Second, supervision and consultation are aspects of ethical decision making. This process provides the practicum student with a course of action helpful to critically evaluating ethical challenges. In this course of action, seeking consultation is critical to developing more than one perspective to the dilemma and documenting that the practicum student and the supervisor were involved in the decision-making process.

Transcription 5.1 illustrates a discussion of an ethical issue during practicum supervision with a faculty supervisor and practicum peers.

> ## ETHICAL CONSIDERATION 5.1
>
> Consider examples of ethical challenges for five of Neukrug's ethical hotspots that you have seen thus far. If you need additional examples, ask your site supervisor for ideas. One thing you may find from this process is that the areas of most concern are the ones you will attend to the most, while those you are least concerned about will receive less of your attention. It turns out, the areas of least concern may represent blind spots that will deserve attention in your own self-reflection as well as in supervision. Take time to discuss this activity and what you learned with your site supervisor.

TRANSCRIPTION 5.1. PRACTICUM SUPERVISION ON CAMPUS #1

Our cast of characters is meeting for their weekly group supervision session led by their faculty member, Dr. Kim, the instructor for the course. After checking in on logistics and emergent issues, Dr. Kim invites topics for discussion related to practicum and based on the students' site experiences. Kaisha volunteers to discuss a situation that happened during a session at her site that week. The following is a transcription of the Kaisha's experience, along with her classmates' responses and her instructor's guidance of the class through an ethical decision-making process.

Dr. Kim: Kaisha, why don't you tell us what is happening at your site that has you concerned.

Kaisha: Well, this week I was co-leading an individual session with a client, Robin (pseudonym), for her fourth session. Robin, a 34-year old female, is in counseling for stress management and depression and struggles to manage her life effectively. My supervisor has spent the first few weeks building rapport, identifying concerns, and setting goals with Robin. I joined the counseling session with Robin after the second session. About halfway through this fourth session, Robin is describing a recent conflict with her daughter—one that occurs frequently. According to Robin, her daughter was yelling at her about what a bad mother she was. I interjected, saying, "Robin, you seem really upset about this interaction. We would like to hear more about this." Robin took and breath and related how earlier that week she was in the living room smoking a water bong, while her 14-year-old daughter was in the kitchen doing her homework. After Robin finished relating her story, the counselor—my site supervisor—stopped Robin and reminded her of the informed consent form that she had signed a few weeks back. She told Robin that smoking marijuana in the home with a minor represented an issue that she must report to Child Protective Services. Robin looked stunned, then got angry, then said she was too upset to continue the session and got up and left. It was my turn to be stunned. I could not believe all that had just happened. My supervisor had an emergency phone call at that time and had to leave, so I haven't really had a chance to debrief what happened.

Dr. Kim: Kaisha, I can see that you look a little shaken, even now. I'd like to ask you about your preliminary assessment of the situation, and then ask your classmates for their thoughts. Then, I'll lead you through a process of addressing ethical issues like this, both in practicum, and in your career.

Kaisha: That would be great! I've felt frustrated and confused, and maybe a little angry.

Dr. Kim: Okay, let's start with the frustration.

Kaisha: Well, I'm frustrated that we did not get to finish the session, that I could not debrief with my supervisor, and the look on Robin's face felt kind of upsetting.

Dr. Kim: What do you think you saw in your client's expression?

Kaisha: She looked shocked, but then she seemed to be hurt, like she had been betrayed.

Dr. Kim: At the very least, that's how you might have felt if you were in her shoes. Is that fair to say?

Kaisha: Definitely! I think that's where the anger is coming from. I felt like the client's rights were violated and I could not help her.

Dr. Kim: What about the confusion you feel?

Kaisha: I guess it would not have occurred to meet to stop the session and tell the client I had to call CPS. It makes me wonder if I am missing some big ethical insight piece; yet, I still don't know that I would have done that.

Dr. Kim: These are really great descriptions of your experience and your perspective, Kaisha. Thank you. This has made for a challenging week, I'll bet. Let's take a moment and go around the class for initial impressions of this situation.

Jose: This one is a no-brainer. Don't do drugs in your home and you won't get the cops called on you. If you can't do the time, don't do the crime.

Janice: It's not so clear for me. The kid wasn't reported to be using drugs with the mom, so I'm not sure she was in danger. I don't think I would have called and I'm wondering the same thing as Kaisha about my ethical compass.

Sam: Weed is not that bad. Some studies show that drinking alcohol is way more dangerous than the effects of smoking marijuana. I guess I don't see what the big deal is.

Dr. Kim: I'll jump in here and offer another perspective. What is one thing you notice about the nature of each person's "instinct" or initial impressions?

(silence)

Dr. Kim: What I noticed was that many perspectives seemed to be informed by personal opinion, moral perspectives on marijuana, and perhaps value judgments placed on the client/mother. This certainly reflects the diversity of perspectives on social issues we find in the wider community of humans. I wonder, then, how we are supposed to navigate this process when we all have strikingly different viewpoints?

(silence … waiting for "the answer")

Naturally, these students are awaiting the *answer* to the *problem* based on the *rule*. In this section, we describe an approach to the answer using an ethical decision-making model. But first, we need to reflect on this first statement in this paragraph and how it relates to counselor development in practicum. We can do this by briefly discussing the italicized terms.

ANSWER: It is to be expected that early on in counselor development, students will seek an answer to an ethical decision. One of the most notable assumptions here is that there is one right answer for a situation. "Right" is often a relative term when it comes to resolving ethical dilemmas. In fact, one of the primary reasons we as counselors use an ethical decision-making model is to identify potential answers to the situation (Scott, Boylan, & Jungers, 2015). Rather than looking for an answer, we seek to generate options and a rationale for taking the next step.

As CITs, this will feel uncomfortable at first, as you may want to have the answers to feel more secure. This is natural.

PROBLEM: The term "problem" is used often in counseling work that presumes to be wellness oriented, developmental, and solution focused. The first difficulty in using the term "problem" is that is sets us up for anxiety and opposition. Approaching an ethical dilemma using problem-based language creates a mind-set such as, "Uh-oh, here's another problem that needs to be fixed or solved." On the contrary, ethical decisions are opportunities to grow and to act in the best interest of the client and the profession. Note that substituting opportunity for problem is not merely semantics. It represents a shift in our orientation, reduces anxiety, and focuses our attention back on the process.

RULE: One of the first things you learned in your professional ethics course is that the 2014 ACA Code of Ethics (2014) is comprehensive but not exhaustive. You may also have noted that there are fewer rules than there are guidelines. These guidelines are built on the foundation of our counselor identity because there are so many permutations of client presentations and clinical scenarios that it would be impossible to generate enough rules to cover them all, much less learn them all (Scott, Boylan, & Jungers, 2015). Instead, CITs have the responsibility to learn what it is to have a counselor identity and orientation, learn the Code of Ethics, and utilize a decision-making model. You will find that this combination, in time, will make you more confident in making decisions.

Ethical Decision Making

There are many **ethical decision-making models** that may support your ethical decision making. The 2014 ACA Code of Ethics recommends using a model that addresses the components identified in the following standard:

> I.1.b. Ethical Decision Making
>
> When counselors are faced with an ethical dilemma, they use and document, as appropriate, an ethical decision-making model that may include, but is not limited to, consultation; consideration of relevant ethical standards, principles, and laws; generation of potential courses of action; deliberation of risks and benefits; and selection of an objective decision based on the circumstances and welfare of all involved (ACA, 2014, p. 19).

Corey, Corey, Corey, & Callanan (2017) present an eight-step model to help counselors work through their ethical decision-making process (see Figure 5.2).

FIGURE 5.2. Corey et al. Ethical Decision-Making Model

Source: Gerald Corey, Marianne Schneider Corey, Cindy Corey, and Patrick Callanan, *Issues and Ethics in the Helping Professions*. Copyright © 2015 by Cengage Learning.

The Corey and colleagues' model (Corey et al., 2017) is based on the 2014 ACA Code of Ethics and meets our standards of usefulness and ease of implementation (see Table 5.4).

TABLE 5.4. Summary of Corey, Corey, Corey, & Callanan (2015) Ethical Decision-making Model.

1. **Identify the problem or dilemma**. Gather information that will shed light on the nature of the problem. This will help you decide whether the problem is mainly ethical, legal, professional, clinical, or moral.

2. **Identify the potential issues**. Evaluate the right, responsibilities, and welfare of all those who are involved in the situation.

3. **Look at the relevant ethical codes for general guidance**. Consider whether your own values and ethics are consistent with or in conflict with the relevant guidelines.

4. **Consider the applicable laws and regulations** and determine how they may have a bearing on an ethical dilemma.

5. **Seek consultation** from more than one source to obtain various perspectives on the dilemma and document in the client's record the suggestions you received from this consultation.

6. **Brainstorm various possible courses of action**. Continue discussing options with other professionals. Include the client in this process of considering options for action. Again, document the nature of this discussion with the client.

7. **Enumerate the consequences of various decisions** and reflect on the implications of each course of action for your client.

8. **Decide on what appears to be the best possible course of action**. Once the course of action has been

implemented, follow up to evaluate the outcomes and to determine whether further action is necessary. Document the reasons for the actions you took as well as your evaluation measures.

Step 1: Identify the Problem

Mullen, Morris, and Lord (2017) normalized the experience of difficulty in navigating **ethical issues/dilemmas**, given their complexity and the fluidity of possible types of dilemmas. As simple as it may seem on the surface, identifying the dilemma to be resolved is quite challenging. This becomes apparent when, during a practicum supervision class, students work through this model together. For example, when considering the situation previously described, if you were the counselor, how would you frame the dilemma? To illustrate, we present Transcription 5.2 and then join our cast of characters as they discuss their various perspectives on the dilemma.

TRANSCRIPTION 5.2. PRACTICUM SUPERVISION ON CAMPUS #2

In this transcription, Dr. Kim, the faculty supervisor, and her practicum students continue their discussion of the ethical issue that Kaisha presented in Transcription 5.1.

Dr. Kim: So, what do you all think is the issue, here? We'll let Kaisha begin, since it is her client.

Kaisha: I've been thinking about this a lot. I think the issue is about client autonomy. Robin's power and control in the situation was taken away from her. She was helpless.

Dr. Kim: For you, this is an ethical issue regarding client autonomy.

Kaisha: Yes.

Dr. Kim: Okay. Jose?

Jose: It seems clear to me that it's a legal issue, both in terms of reporting illegal activity and duty to protect a minor.

Dr. Kim: Okay, for you it's legal issue involving protection of a vulnerable population.

Jose: Clearly.

Dr. Kim: Thank you. Janice?

Janice: It feels like an issue of confidentiality. I assume that this behavior is between the mother and her own conscience. The daughter does not appear to be directly harmed by the behavior, so I think we keep Robin's confidence.

Dr. Kim: Ah, so we have arrived at privileged or confidential communication. For Janice, this is a broader issue of client confidentiality, in that her behavior does not meet the threshold for an exception to confidentiality.

Janice: That's how I see it, yes.

Dr. Kim: Sam?

Sam: As I've listened to all these perspectives, my earlier response seems a little off base. I realize that my first opinion was based on my own values, not my clinical and ethical training. I guess I'm still stuck on how easy it was for me to look past a behavior based on my beliefs.

Dr. Kim: That's a pretty big step you've just taken, Sam. And it's a main reason that we use these types of models—they help us refine our thinking about such matters. Of the three perspectives you've just heard, which way are you leaning? Is it an issue based in principle ethics, the law, or informed consent? Or something else?

Sam: I recognize that marijuana use is illegal in our state, and that the adolescent's legal status is that of a minor. I also don't see Robin's daughter technically at risk; however, if the mom is free with disclosing smoking pot in the home when her 14-year-old daughter is there, what is she not telling? I think it's an issue of protecting a member of a vulnerable population. It's legal.

Dr. Kim: You look a little tired (smiles).

Sam: Yeah, I am.

One way to help us make sense of this complexity occurring in Transcription 5.2 is to categorize the areas of ethical concern. For example, Ed Neukrug's (2018) hotspots can be used as a quick reference guide to ethical issues (see Table 5.3). As you review the items in the table, consider each of the categories and make notes about which apply to the scenario that Kaisha describes during her practicum seminar.

Step 2: Identify Surrounding Issues

Few issues in counseling are stand-alone issues. A problem or issue identified in step one will rarely exist in isolation. One of the reasons is the presence of multiple **stakeholders** involved, both seen and unseen. A stakeholder is a person, group, organization, or institution that maintains an interest in or a concern for a plan, decision, or, perhaps, outcome. In the case of the client described, most notably is the mother, her 14-year-old daughter, other children potentially living in the home, the school, local law enforcement, and others, perhaps. When exploring the ethical steps to take, it is vital to recognize the context and connective tissue that extends to others. Additionally, there are other factors to consider besides the primary problem. For instance, we might begin to wonder where our client obtains marijuana, how she pays for it, and whether this is the only drug she uses—all we know at this point is what she has told us. We might also inquire whether there are younger children living in the home or whether there are other vulnerable individuals (e g., elderly, informed). Unfortunately, this step can serve to complicate what we thought had been clarified in the first step. Nevertheless, this step is crucial to identify potential blind spots in determining a course of action.

Step 3: Examine Ethics and Values

One factor that complicates ethical decision making during practicum is moving from the clarity of the classroom to the cloudiness or ambiguity of the world of practice. In the classroom, client confidentiality can feel clear; yet, exceptions to confidentiality intrude on that clarity in cases like the one discussed in this chapter.

It is beyond the scope (or space) in this chapter to discuss every ethical variation related to any ethical decision. To illustrate step 3, we have provided a brief ethical exchange using only the ethical code. When moving through this ethical decision-making step, consider the following questions:

CAN I AND HOW WOULD I? Can I justify my disclosure of my client's information? How would I justify not disclosing?

LIMITS OF CONFIDENTIALITY. Does my client understand the limits of confidentiality, especially how it works in my relationship with them?

DISCLOSURE OF INFORMATION. How does the Code address disclosure of confidential information my client shares with me when the disclosure is related to a minor? How can I determine the severity of the threat to a vulnerable population?

INFORMED CONSENT. Is informed consent in my work with this client an ongoing, a living document?

A second component of this step is recognizing the place and role of one's own values and how they may be in concert or conflict with ethical mandates of the profession. For example, as we discussed earlier in this chapter, in Tennessee in late 2017, the first federal case of discrimination was brought in response to state legislation permitting counselors from referring clients on the basis of the counselor's strongly held principles. This legal right is in conflict with ACA's stance on nondiscrimination but may be similar to a counselor's own values. In the instance in Tennessee, the client was a gay male whose belief was that he had been discriminated against specifically due to his affectional orientation. A CIT may have strong beliefs regarding this issue, and while, at the time of this writing, it is legally permissible in a state such as Tennessee, it violates the 2014 ACA Code of Ethics by referring a gay client to another counselor because the client's values and goals are different than those of the counselor.

The position of this text is to follow the ACA in training counselors to identify the difference between a counselor's role as a citizen and his or her role as a counselor. Citizens may object to anything they choose; counselors, in contrast, don the robes of the profession and their attitudes and behaviors must be consistent with those professional values. And, it is in practicum where these personal values and the values of the profession are highlighted most strongly. Unfortunately, one of the most effective ways to scrutinize your decision is to picture yourself on the witness stand in a court of law, sitting in front of state and federal law, your professional ethics, and the alleged victim of a behavior. When asked to justify your action (or inaction), what will you say? If this sounds intimidating, it is. Our professional ethics are designed to protect clients, whom the profession recognizes as vulnerable, in that they are seeking help from you/us, the provider. That imbues the counselor with unequal power and requires that we proceed with all caution.

Step 4: Law vs. Ethics

In most, if not all cases, a counselor's obligation to uphold the law supersedes his or her ethical obligations. Fortunately, the ACA Code offers guidance on this deceptively tricky standard.

TABLE 5.5. Counselor's Obligation to Uphold the Law

I.1. Standards and the Law

I.1.a. Knowledge

Counselors know and understand the ACA Code of Ethics and other applicable ethics codes from professional organizations or certification and licensure bodies of which they are members. Lack of knowledge or misunderstanding of an ethical responsibility is not a defense against a charge of unethical conduct.

I.1.b. Ethical Decision Making

When counselors are faced with an ethical dilemma, they use and document, as appropriate, an ethical decision-making model that may include, but is not limited to, consultation; consideration of relevant ethical standards, principles, and laws; generation of potential courses of action; deliberation of risks and benefits; and selection of an objective decision based on the circumstances and welfare of all involved.

I.1.c. Conflicts Between Ethics and Laws

If ethical responsibilities conflict with the law, regulations, and/or other governing legal authority, counselors make known their commitment to the ACA Code of Ethics and take steps to resolve the conflict. If the conflict cannot be resolved using this approach, counselors, acting in the best interest of the client, may adhere to the requirements of the law, regulations, and/or other governing legal authority (ACA, 2014, p. 19).

Following a decision-making model and documenting your work in each step is critical. This sounds easy enough, but once again, in the real-world of counseling practicum, it is easy to overlook, forget, and outright ignore doing your **due diligence**. Due diligence means that you, as a practicum student, or as a professional counselor for that matter, have undertaken your work with care, according to proper standards. As a counselor, this means that you approach client work and client care according to established professional standards and that you follow ethical guidelines and legal laws and regulations. Furthermore, as we indicated earlier, you must document your professional behavior and care of the client. Documenting the ways in which you follow an ethical decision-making model helps describe your practice of due diligence.

As a practicum student, there are numerous places to keep records of your work. You will want to record the issues you encounter in your daily and weekly reflections, your site and faculty supervision, and in your client case notes. A useful practice is, when confronted with what you identify as an ethical dilemma, you combine your notes into a special file by issue or incident—and that you share this file with your site and faculty supervisor.

A common mistake that students and CITs, hoping to feel and appear competent, make is attempting to resolve a complicated issue on their own. Even though you may be experiencing feelings of inferiority, fear, and uncertainty, which accompany the practicum experience, making decisions in isolation makes you, your client, and possibly the agency, vulnerable. It is accepted—expected—in practice to consult with clinical, administrative, ethical, and legal experts and other colleagues to proceed appropriately. This need for **consultation** continues throughout your professional counseling career. It is integrated with your professional identity and your professional development.

Step 6: Brainstorm Options and Include the Client

One of the traps our clients fall into, and one in which we mimic early on in our training, is polarizing decision options. Rarely is there one right answer or a choice between two opposite extremes. Returning to our example, our practicum student could feel reduced to "report or ignore." However, there may be other options available. One option includes the second—and perhaps most critical—component of this step. Present the dilemma to the client and engage him or her in the decision-making process. Here is how the dilemma might be roleplayed in class (see Transcription 5.3).

TRANSCRIPTION 5.3. USING ROLEPLAY TO EXPLORE ETHICAL ISSUES

Dr. Kim: Kaisha, I'd like you to play the role of your client instead of yourself. You can select a peer to play your role. The others will be consultants in the process. "Counselor," why don't you begin by describing the situation as you see it.

Kaisha selects Jose to roleplay her, and she will play Robin.

Jose as Kaisha: Robin, I want to return to something you said a moment ago; it really caught my attention.

Kaisha as Robin: Okay (turns head slightly, as if expecting something).

Jose as Kaisha: You look as if you might have an idea of what I have in mind.

Kaisha as Robin: Was it about the weed? You're not going to report me, are you? (looks panicked).

Jose as Kaisha: Well, you are correct that your comment about smoking marijuana with your 14-year-old upstairs raises some concerns for me.

Kaisha as Robin: And now you have to report it! (begins to simulate crying).

Jose as Kaisha: You seem to be feeling strong emotion right now. I hope we can talk about what you're feeling. Honestly, I have not made any decisions about what comes next except to talk with you. Can you tell me what you are feeling?

Kaisha as Robin: I'm scared I'm going to lose my kids! It would not be the first time I've been reported.

Jose as Kaisha: I guessed you were feeling upset, but I had no idea how this was playing out in your mind. It means a lot that you've shared this with me. It sounds like this would not be the first time you have been afraid of losing your kids.

Kaisha as Robin: The school reported me a couple of years ago because both my kids were missing school. A social worker came out to the house and warned me to keep them in school … or else.

Jose as Kaisha: They really said, "or else"?

Kaisha as Robin: Well … no, but that's what it felt like.

Jose as Kaisha: That makes sense. Thank you for clarifying. And now you're afraid it is happening again?

Kaisha as Robin: Yes. Please don't tell anyone. Don't you have to keep our sessions private?

Jose as Kaisha: That's one of the things I'd like to talk about. You may remember a few weeks ago that we talked more about confidentiality and its limits, right? One of those limits involves kids being harmed or being at risk of being harmed.

Kaisha as Robin: Yes, I know. I should have never said anything.

Jose as Kaisha: Actually, my guess is that you meant to say what you said.

Kaisha as Robin: What do you mean? Why would I do that?

Jose as Kaisha: That's what I wanted to ask you (smiles).

Kaisha as Robin: Because I need help parenting my kids and that's terrifying to admit?

Jose as Kaisha: It certainly sounds like a terrifying thing to be going through. Can we talk further about the help you feel you need, and how we might go about doing that? Even if that means making a call to social services to let them know you need the help and asking where we might find the support you need?

Step 7: Identify Potential Consequences of Decisions

Step seven involves "if, then" thinking and is a recognition that our action or inaction has consequences—whether we want them or not. Counselors make decisions and accept responsibility for both the decisions and the potential consequences of those decisions. Practicum is a place and time where this orientation is really put to the test. It is important to recognize that each of the possible approaches to resolving an ethical dilemma carries with it associated outcomes. It can also be instructive to recognize and highlight that this parallels decision making in the lives of clients.

Step 8: Act and Evaluate

Up to this point, the whole process is fairly cerebral—it mostly takes places in our heads. This step underscores that decision making is and culminates in some action or behavior (recall that inaction is also a form of behavior!). As counselors, we commit to a course of action, but it does not stop there. After acting, we evaluate the action and its consequences. We document the action and the evaluation thereof. No one expects perfection and 100% accuracy in making decisions. What is required is documentation of a transparent process for making decisions, taking action, and assessing those actions and their consequences; then, as necessary, correcting or modifying those actions.

In Discussion Together 5.2, trace your use of the decision-making model to address an ethical issue you encountered in practicum. This activity will help you and your supervisor integrate supervision, action, and recordkeeping.

DISCUSSION TOGETHER 5.2
Using the Ethical Decision-Making Model

Identify an ethical decision you have encountered in your practicum experience. Trace the ways in which you follow the decision-making steps described in this text. Review the decision making using standards by answering the following questions (Woodside, 2017): Was this decision consistent with other decisions I have made? If one of my classmates faced a similar situation, would I recommend the action I took? What was my motivation for making this decision (self, other, agency or school, supervisor influence)? Am I willing to share my decision-making process with others? Did I have to compromise my own beliefs? Why or why not?

CULTURAL CONSIDERATION 5.1

In reflecting on Corey and colleagues' (2015) ethical decision-making model, what nuances do you anticipate in the process relative to cultural differences? In other words, how might a counselor of an underrepresented cultural identity status respond to and perhaps modify this model? What implications are there of using this model related to clients of underrepresented cultural identity status?

Summary

Few counselors, or people in general, for that matter, wake in the morning seeking to violate the right of others, put clients in jeopardy, or otherwise behave unethically. There may be a few notable exceptions, but, in general, humans tend to do try to do the right thing. Unfortunately, intending to do the right thing is often insufficient for doing the right thing. Rather than waking up and deciding to be unethical in their professional practice, it is more likely that they engaged in mildly questionable practices over time. This is an insidious process of "fudging" here and there until they find themselves in the midst of an ethical quagmire. For instance, you may read in the 2014 ACA Code of Ethics not to have sexual relations with your clients for five years after terminating the clinical relationship and think, "That is absurd; who would sleep with their clients?" The blurring of ethical and moral lines can occur almost imperceptibly. For example, a new counselor may feel that completing a graduate degree in counseling gave them sufficient preparation for making ethical decisions, so he or she does not need to look closely at his or her behavior or continue his or her reading and education. This same counselor may also turn a blind eye to ethical standards, making rationalizations that "while that standard may apply to most counselors, it is different for me." Eventually, he or she contracts with a client that he or she—wittingly or unwittingly—find attractive. Because he or she does not seem him- or herself as vulnerable "like other counselors," he or she permits playful flirtations, personal disclosures, and receipt of phone calls and texts outside the clinical context, to further cloud his or her judgment. Eventually, a sexual relationship develops to accompany the intimate emotional relationship that has been allowed to develop. When the client complains to the board after the counselor breaks off the relationship, the counselor says, "it just happened." As you can see from this discussion, it clearly did not "just happen." This example can feel terrifying, but it should also feel liberating. Ethical violations do not happen out of nowhere; they follow a fairly apparent trajectory. While not a call to analysis paralysis, it is a call to trust what thousands of counselors and counselor educators who have gone before you know, and follow their direction in planning to practice ethically instead of merely hoping you won't mess up.

Key Terms

American counseling association's 2014 code of ethics

Consultation

Due diligence

Ethical code

Ethical decision-making model

Ethical guidelines

Ethical hotspots

Ethical issues/dilemmas

Ethical practice

Ethical practice and supervision

Principles of ethical behavior

Professional relationship

Professional values

Protection for clients

Stakeholders

References

American Counseling Association (ACA). (2014). *2014 ACA Code of Ethics*. Alexandria, VA: Author.

Ametrano, I. M. (2014). Teaching ethical decision making: Helping students reconcile personal and professional values. *Journal of Counseling & Development, 92*(2), 154–161. doi:10.1002/j.1556-6676.2014.00143.x

Bernard, J. B., & Goodyear, R. K. (2014). *Fundamentals of clinical supervision* (5th ed.). Boston, MA: Pearson.

Corey, G. (2017). *Theory and practice of counseling and psychotherapy* (10th ed.). Pacific Grove, CA: Cengage.

Corey, G., Corey, M. S., Corey, C., & Callanan, P. (2015). *Issues and ethics in the helping professions,* (9th ed.). Belmont, CA: Brooks/Cole.

Council for Accreditation of Counseling and Related Programs. (2016a). Section 2: Professional Counseling Identity. Retrieved from https://www.cacrep.org/section-2-professional-counseling-identity/

Council for Accreditation of Counseling and Related Programs. (2016b). *Section 5: Entry-level specialty areas—Clinical mental health*. Retrieved from https://www.cacrep.org/section-5-entry-level-specialty-areas-clinical-mental-health-counseling/

Council for Accreditation of Counseling and Related Programs. (2016c). *2016 CACREP Standards. Section 5: Entry-level specialty areas—School counseling*. Retrieved from https://www.cacrep.org/section-5-entry-level-specialty-areas-school-counseling/

Francis, P. C., & Dugger, S. M. (2014). Professionalism, ethics, and value-based conflicts in counseling: An introduction to the special section. *Journal of Counseling & Development, 92*(2), 131–134.

Hodges, S. (2016). *The counseling practicum and internship manual: A resource for graduate counseling students*. New York, NY: Springer.

Kaplan, D. M., Francis, P. C., Hermann, M. A., Baca, J. V., Goodnough, G. E., Hodges, S., ... & Wade, M. E. (2017). New concepts in the 2014 ACA Code of Ethics. *Journal of Counseling & Development, 95*(1), 110–120.

Mullen, P. R., Morris, C., & Lord, M. (2017). The experience of ethical dilemmas, burnout, and stress among practicing counselors. *Counseling and Values, 62*(1), 37–56.

Neukrug, E. S. (2018). *Counseling theory and practice*, (2nd ed.). San Diego, CA: Cognella.

Neukrug, E. S., Lovell C., & Parker, R. J. (1996). Employing ethical codes and decision-making models: A developmental process. *Counseling and Values, 40*(2), 98–106.

Remley & Herlihy (2016). Ethical, legal, and professional issues in counseling (5th ed.). Boston, MA: Pearson.

Scott, J., Boylan, J. C., & Jungers, C. M. (2015). *Practicum and internship: Textbook and resource guide for counseling and psychotherapy*. New York, NY: Routledge.

Sommers-Flanagan, J., & Sommers-Flanagan, R. (2017). *Clinical interviewing* (6th ed.). Hoboken, NJ: John Wiley & Sons.

Woodside, M. (2017). *The human services internship experience: Helping students find their way*. Thousand Oaks, CA: SAGE.

CHAPTER 6

Diversity in
PRACTICUM

INTRODUCTION

Bringing a sensitivity to diversity in the practicum requires knowing and understanding our cultural selves as well as knowing and understanding our cultural clients. This seems self-evident, but it is more easily considered than achieved. Take a moment and pause to reflect: Quickly list the top five characteristics that define you. Try not to overthink it; just write. Once you have done so, answer the following questions:

- What do you notice about your list?
- What categories do you see?

For instance, the most common, major categories of diversity include (a) race, (b) ethnicity, (c) nationality or national origin, (d) gender, (e) sexual orientation (affectional orientation), and (f) religion. Compare your list of characteristics to the six presented. To what extent to does your list match up?

Often, members of marginalized groups or statuses identify these categories as core to their identity much more readily than do their majority peers. In contrast, many members of the majority, for example, white, heterosexual, cisgender males may be less likely to list these six characteristics as core to their identity. As you read this and reflect on what you have observed, is this true of you to some extent? Why do you believe this is the case? Why is this relevant to your work as a counselor? This chapter addresses these and many other questions related to the cross-cultural experiences you have as you work to provide multicultural counseling to all of your clients. The chapter goals follow.

GOALS OF THE CHAPTER

- **Understand the role and value of cultural considerations in practicum**
- **Learn the ways in which our individual biases and perceptions influence the counseling relationship**
- **Understand the importance of empathy in promoting cross-cultural relationships**
- **Identify and plan to implement multicultural counseling competencies, relative to the developmental stage of practicum**

RELATED CACREP GOALS

Section 5. Entry-Level Specialty Areas, C. Clinical Mental Health Counseling; 2. Contextual Dimensions:

- j. cultural factors relevant to clinical mental health counseling (CACREP, 2016a)

Section 2: Professional Counseling Identity Counseling Curriculum; Professional Counseling Orientation And Ethical Practice

- d. the role and process of the professional counselor advocating on behalf of the profession
- b. advocacy processes needed to address institutional and social barriers that impede access, equity, and success for clients (CACREP, 2016b)

Practicum as a Cross-Cultural Experience

By the time you read this chapter, you have likely begun your practicum work and work with clients. For many, if not most of you, Dorothy's comment to her dog, Toto, when a tornado transports them from Kansas to the Land of Oz, "Toto, we're not in Kansas anymore!" has already hit you. Regardless of your particular site, you have entered an environment that is likely very different than the classroom environment to which you may have grown accustomed. Your practicum site is also likely very different than other work environments you may have been in, unless you have worked in a mental health or school setting previously. In fact, your experience in this new environment is a **cross-cultural experience**. What exactly is a cross-cultural experience?

Cross-cultural refers to communications or exchanges that are "pertaining to or involving different cultures or comparisons between them" (Oxford English Dictionary, 2018a). The basis for helping is interacting with clients and establishing meaningful relationships. Since each individual represents a unique set of cultural influences, a helper's communication and interaction with a client represents an exchange across at least two cultures. This experience can lead to the growth of the novice counselor, and by extension benefit the client, but it can also stultify the counselor, possibility resulting in harm to clients.

Culture shock is one response that practicum students may have when they enter the culture of their practicum site and begin working with clients who represent cultures very different from their own. Let's look at culture shock within the context of entering a practicum site and counseling clients for the first time.

Culture Shock

Culture shock for practicum students is a fairly common experience, though perhaps not for the reasons you might at first think. In formal terms, culture shock is "a state of distress or disorientation brought about by sudden immersion in or subjection to an unfamiliar culture" (Oxford English Dictionary, 2018b).

To understand what culture shock may mean during practicum, let's listen in as our cast of characters (practicum students), Janice, Jose, Kaisha, and Sam, share their experiences of their own culture shock as they entered their practicum sites.

TRANSCRIPTION 6.1 STUDENTS RESPOND TO CULTURE SHOCK

Janice: As a parent of high school-aged students, I thought that a practicum at a middle school would be a pretty easy transition, even though I'm an anxious person in general. The school I was assigned was near the inner city of a mid-size city. I went in thinking, "Okay, I know the stereotypes of inner city life, but these are middle-schoolers; I've raised three of my own. I can do this." This first shock was having to enter a fenced-in property, not unlike a prison yard, and then entering the building through metal detectors while being watched by the SRO (student resource officer). As I started to get my bearings, I noted two things; the first was the smell. It was not the smell of children or of institutional cafeteria food. It smelled a little like dirt and urine and mold. Then I saw the children—sorry, adolescents—and the signs of poverty assaulted my senses. I could not believe the amount of insufficient and damaged clothing (I was there in January, so it was freezing outside) that I saw. By the end of that week, rather than providing counseling for relational problems, I was a mediator between various state and local agencies, from the Department of Child Welfare to Truant Officers. I recall thinking back during that first week in practicum class when Dr. Kim warned that practicum is often a cross-cultural experience, "I don't have a problem with Black and Hispanic kids, so I'm fine." I really had little appreciation for what that would mean.

Jose: To be honest, I was a little concerned about entering my site (residential alcohol and drug center for youth) for the first time. Even though my heritage is blended, I can "pass" for White, and often I can pass for straight. I know I should not have to even think about such things, but I do think about them, a lot. I am aware of how cruel kids can be to those who are different, whether ethnically or affectionally. To my surprise, these have not really been issues for me. However, what I was not prepared for were stories of physical and sexual abuse, neglect, and lack of family involvement. I imagined entering the site and using my skills to provide a rationale for not using drugs and alcohol. Instead, I found clients from these families that ranged from intense control and over-involvement to mild neglect, to gang-like families that were manufacturing and distributing substances. And, I thought I would have an easier time connecting with racial and ethnic minorities because, you know, I can relate. I had no idea how different my experience of family and culture and poverty was from many of them. Some families wanted their kid "fixed" and to move on, while others called to make sure their kid kept his mouth shut about family matters. Other families just never visited, called, or responded to requests for family sessions. I'll tell you this, since that first week, I've called my own mother probably twice as often as I did before.

Kaisha: For the first year of the program, I felt strongly that I wanted to try working in an outpatient mental health clinic. As a teen, I had struggled with anxiety and depression, and my family did not have access to these services. I was excited to meet my new colleagues and potential clients that first week of practicum at the community mental health clinic. I was not prepared for what mental health looks like in a community setting. I had assumed that I would encounter many clients who, like myself, had difficulties with general mental health issues such as anxiety and depression. And I did, except that instead of the majority of clients being there for growth-focused therapy, I saw the vast majority of people using community mental health as a lifeline. What I mean is, this clinic primarily treats clients who have severe and persistent mental illness, such as schizophrenia, bipolar disorder, intellectual disabilities, and suicidal ideation and attempts, all inhabited by many people with physically broken bodies, due either to their behaviors, the behaviors of others, or genetics. I thought I would be writing treatment goals and plans around confronting dysfunctional thinking, examining unrealistic expectations; instead, I have been working to help people not die or self-destruct between their appointments which, by the way, are not every week, but every three weeks because the center does not have funding to meets the needs of the community.

Sam: I feel really lucky be able to work as a practicum student at the campus counseling center. I like the idea of using person-centered counseling to address adjustment and phase-of-life issues with clients. Since I was recently an undergrad, I could really relate to the students—or that's what I thought. I'm only 26, so undergrad was not that long ago for me, but I guess a lot has changed. Or, more importantly, I found that having been through the college experience myself recently was not sufficient to help me understand what my clients were going through. One example involved my being a Black male with some experience playing high school sports. When my first Black male athlete came to see me I thought, "Alright, I've got this." It did not take long to realize that this 19-year-old's experience was vastly different than mine. We could connect somewhat as African Americans, but his orientation to education and life itself was so different from mine. I realized that what I thought I understood about person-centered approaches was academic, book based. I have had to work really hard to bracket my assumptions about my client's experiences based on shared characteristics. This experience has made me humble about my abilities as a counselor, but probably not as humbling as my second experience of culture shock. I was shadowing a counseling at the center as she met with a 20-year-old female student. The student disclosed having been sexually assaulted on campus two weeks prior. I remember thinking how glad I was to be shadowing. I would not know what to tell this young woman. It was then that I realized, again, that what I thought I knew about counseling and the experiences of others was radically different than reality. It hit me that I did not understand the college experience for Black athletes and women; who else was I misunderstanding?

Sam's concluding, somewhat rhetorical question ("Who else was I misunderstanding?") is an important one. We are often unaware of those things that we do not know. Cultural Consideration 6.1 will help you begin to explore the culture shock you have experienced in practicum thus far. It will help you explore your current awareness of you, your clients, and culture.

Considering Diversity

The importance of understanding the breadth of diversity is critical to developing multicultural awareness, knowledge, and skills. The term "diversity" refers to multiple aspects of culture including those beyond race, ethnicity, and nationality. Those may include "the way of life of a particular people, esp. as shown in their ordinary behavior and habits, their attitudes toward each other, and their moral and religious beliefs" (Cambridge Dictionary, 2018). These may also encompass "beliefs, customs, arts, etc., of a particular society, group, place, or time" (Merriam-Webster, 2018a). And even the terms "race," "ethnicity," and "nationality" are complicated as we as counselors think about individuals who are multi-racial, multi-ethnic, and/or multi-national (Livingston, 2017).

When considering diversity, what are some of the various aspects to acknowledge? To begin, let's add to the list of cultural cat-

> ### CULTURAL CONSIDERATION 6.1
>
> As you can see from reading about Janice, Jose, Kaisha, and Sam's reaction to culture and their practicum experiences, the experience of culture shock in practicum differs from student to student. When you encountered a client who appeared to be like you, what was that like for you? Describe that client. How did you denote the similarities? The differences? Did your sense of similarity or difference change during the counseling process? When you encountered a client who appeared to be different from you, what was that like for you? Describe that client. How did you denote the differences? The similarities? Did your sense of difference or similarity change during the counseling process?

egories presented in the first paragraph of this chapter. Reviewing the quotes from Janice, Jose, Kaisha, and Sam related to their cross-cultural experiences in practicum, they added the following categories: ableness or (dis)ability, generational, mental health issues, trauma, socioeconomic status, and educational background/orientation. You may be able to think of others as well. You ask, "Once I recognize such cultural categories as these, how can I use this information to work with my clients in a more culturally sensitive way?"

Fouad and Kantamneni's model of cultural dimensions (2008) provides a way of looking at the multiple aspects of cultural perspectives, and Swanson and Fouad (2015) offered this model in the context of career counseling. An adaptation of Fouad and Kantamneni's model that describes the role of culture factors on vocational interests and career choice is useful for thinking about clients. Their model provides three dimensions of characteristics or variables, from the narrowest to the most broad: individual level, group level, societal level. Reversing the order of the three dimensions of Fouad and Kantamneni's model of cultural dimensions, these dimensions of the client are viewed first through the broadest lens. This first perspective captures the context in which the client lives. The second and third perspectives narrow to the group and then to the individual.

DIMENSION 3: SOCIETAL-LEVEL CHARACTERISTICS OR VARIABLES. The broadest level of **societal-level characteristics or variables** involves the social-level characteristics. This dimension includes factors such as issues of acculturation, cultural values, opportunity structure, discrimination, schooling/education level, barriers or systemic oppression, and labor market (Swanson & Fouad, 2015).

DIMENSION 2: GROUP-LEVEL CHARACTERISTICS OR VARIABLES. The **group-level characteristics or variables** is the set of characteristics most often associated with culture. It contains variables such as gender, race, ethnicity, family and relationships, role models, social class, religion, and sexual orientation (Swanson & Fouad, 2015).

DIMENSION 1: INDIVIDUAL CHARACTERISTICS OR VARIABLES. The **individual characteristics or variables** relate to the culture of one, wherein the individual has traits that are independent from the other two dimensions, though they may be influenced by those dimensions. This dimension includes interests, needs, personality, and self-efficacy (Swanson & Fouad, 2015). Other elements to add to the list are experiences, environments (early and current), biology, and genetics (Luke, 2016, 2017), as well as mental health status (see Figure 6.1).

FIGURE 6.1. Adaptation of Fouad and Kantamneni's model of cultural dimensions

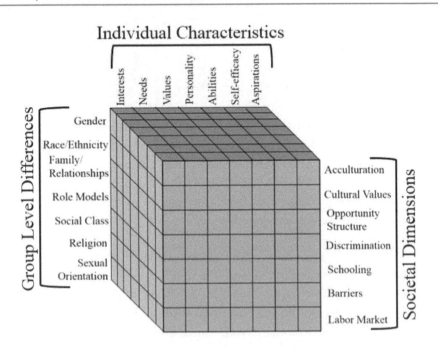

To illustrate how to use this model when meeting clients, picture viewing them through a three-lens kaleidoscope. Figure 6.2 illustrates this perspective. When we meet a client, we view that client through the larger societal lens, and then the lens of group characteristics, and then the lens of individual characteristics.

FIGURE 6.2. Developing a Multicultural View of the Client

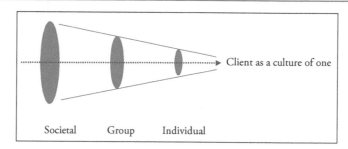

Each of these lenses is vital to understanding and connecting with the person, and it is complicated. Yet, we can all move toward greater competence in this area. One point is critical when considering the various client-related dimensions: *Counselors can never presume to "know" the client in front of them based on any single characteristic or group membership.* For instance, you may have read about the cultural characteristics of African Americans. While that information is critical in developing cultural awareness, it is to the client's and the profession's detriment for a counselor to "know" an African American client feels a certain way because of a generalized characteristic of a particular race. This type of generalizing or stereotyping is inaccurate at each dimension of Fouad and Kantamneni's model of cultural dimensions. Marianne presents her practicum students with a description of a client, an African American male, to illustrate the cultural dimensions in terms of Fouad and Kantamneni's model of cultural dimensions, and to describe an individual who denies a stereotype of the African American male.

DIMENSION 3: SOCIETAL-LEVEL CHARACTERISTICS OR VARIABLES. He lived in Hawaii and Indonesia in his early years. In his late elementary school, junior high, and high school years, he lived in Hawaii. He attended school with few African Americans and is self-reported to have experienced racism. He had educational opportunities. For college, he lived in California and then in New York City, attending the prestigious Columbia University. He worked in the business sector in New York and then as a community organizer in Chicago.

DIMENSION 2: GROUP-LEVEL CHARACTERISTICS OR VARIABLES. As previously identified, this individual identifies as African American, although his mother is White and his father is African (Kenyan). He is male, American (roots in Hawaii), raised by his mother and his grandparents. His mother and father divorced when he was two. His father returned to Harvard for a PhD and then returned to his home country, Kenya. His mother remarried an Indonesian man. The family moved to Indonesia. His mother and his step-father had a daughter, his half-sister. This male self-reports feeling the lack of and the loss of his father. He only saw him once during his formative years. His role models included, but are not limited to, his maternal grandparents and a law professor at Harvard. This African male's family is committed to education. His mother and father met in college at the University of Hawaii, his mother and step-father also met there. His maternal grandparents emphasized the importance of education and set high educational expectations for him.

DIMENSION 1: INDIVIDUAL CHARACTERISTICS OR VARIABLES. This African American male is interested in sports, politics, and fighting for the rights of others. He wants to succeed and is driven to excel in his work. He entered the political arena. After assuming several high-profile political offices, researchers published several personality assessments that attributed him the following characteristics: ambitious, accommodating, conscientious, retiring, dominant, and dauntless (Unit for the Study of Personality in Politics, 2012).

As you read the description of this African American male with such a unique background, many of you might have recognized the profile of former president Barack Obama. Remember each of your clients represents a unique amalgamation of cultural dimensions that resist stereotypes and generalizations. And remember that a person can never fully be known based on one characteristic (e.g., status as a client) or another (e.g., race).

Reflection Question 6.1 provides an opportunity for you to view one of your clients from Fouad and Kantamneni's multicultural lens.

REFLECTION QUESTION 6.1

WHAT A CLIENT'S CULTURE LOOKS LIKE

Describe a client, in terms of Fouad and Kantamneni's model of cultural dimensions: Dimension 3: Societal-level characteristics or variables; dimension 2: Group-level characteristics or variables; dimension 1: Individual characteristics or variables. What additional information do you believe you need about the cultural dimension of your client? What do you believe to be the most salient dimensions of the client's world? How would these determine your work with this client? What would the client say are the most salient dimensions?

What Is Multicultural Counseling?

Multicultural counseling remains a critical dimension of offering counseling services and working with clients. In the 1990s, Paul Pederson (1998) suggested that multicultural counseling was the fourth force in counseling, joining the other three forces: psychodynamic, humanistic, or behavioral perspectives. The counseling profession and professional counselors and educators recognize this fourth force as essential to recognizing the cultural context in which services are delivered and the cultural identity of the client. Using a culture-centered approach to counseling helps professional counselors build empathy and develop relationships, conduct assessment, plan interventions and then implement them, and conduct evaluations of outcomes (Hays & Erford, 2018).

Today the American Counseling Association (ACA) promotes their professionally approved **multicultural and social justice counseling competencies** (MSJCC; Ratts, Singh, Nasser-McMillian, Butler, & McCullough, 2015) to support the development of and use of a multicultural approach to counseling. Awareness of these competencies (Ratts et al., 2015) adopted by ACA, will both help you understand the breadth of multicultural counseling and the more specific aspects of it. An abbreviated form is presented in Table 6.1. Reading the entire 14-page document provides you with more in-depth information (see Ratts et al., 2015 reference). Ratts, Singh, Nasser-McMillian, Butler, and McCullough (2016) provides an additional explication of the competencies.

TABLE 6.1. Multicultural and Social Justice Counseling Competencies

I. COUNSELOR SELF-AWARENESS

Privileged and marginalized counselors develop self-awareness, so that they may explore their attitudes and beliefs, develop knowledge, skills, and action relative to their self-awareness and worldview.

1. **Attitudes and beliefs**: Privileged and marginalized counselors are aware of their social identities, social group statuses, power, privilege, oppression, strengths, limitations, assumptions, attitudes, values, beliefs, and biases.

2. **Knowledge**: Privileged and marginalized counselors possess an understanding of their social identities, social group statuses, power, privilege, oppression, strengths, limitations, assumptions, attitudes, values, beliefs, and biases.

3. **Skills**: Privileged and marginalized counselors possess skills that enrich their understanding of their social identities, social group statuses, power, privilege, oppression, limitations, assumptions, attitudes, values, beliefs, and biases.

4. **Action**: Privileged and marginalized counselors take action to increase self-awareness of their social identities, social group statuses, power, privilege, oppression, strengths, limitations, assumptions, attitudes, values, beliefs, and biases.

II. CLIENT WORLDVIEW

Privileged and marginalized counselors are aware, knowledgeable, skilled, and action-oriented in understanding clients' worldview.

1. **Attitudes and beliefs**: Privileged and marginalized counselors are aware of clients' worldview, assumptions, attitudes, values, beliefs, biases, social identities, social group statuses, and experiences with power, privilege, and oppression.

2. **Knowledge**: Privileged and marginalized counselors possess knowledge of clients' worldview, assumptions, attitudes, values, beliefs, biases, social identities, social group statuses, and experiences with power, privilege, and oppression.

3. **Skills:** Privileged and marginalized counselors possess skills that enrich their understanding of clients' worldview, assumptions, attitudes, values, beliefs, biases, social identities, social group statuses, and experiences with power, privilege, and oppression.

4. **Action**: Privileged and marginalized counselors take action to increase self-awareness of clients' worldview, assumptions, attitudes, values, beliefs, biases, social identities, social group statuses, and experiences with power, privilege, and oppression.

III. COUNSELING RELATIONSHIP

Privileged and marginalized counselors are aware, knowledgeable, skilled, and action-oriented in understanding how client and counselor privileged and marginalized statuses influence the counseling relationship.

1. **Attitudes and beliefs**: Privileged and marginalized counselors are aware of how client and counselor worldviews, assumptions, attitudes, values, beliefs, biases, social identities, social group statuses, and experiences with power, privilege, and oppression influence the counseling relationship.

2. **Knowledge**: Privileged and marginalized counselors possess knowledge of how client and counselor worldviews, assumptions, attitudes, values, beliefs, biases, social identities, social group statuses, and experiences with power, privilege, and oppression influence the counseling relationship.

Source: M. J. Ratts, A. A. Singh, S. Nassar-McMillan, S.K. Butler, and J.R. McCullough, *Multicultural and Social Justice Counseling Competencies*, pp. 5-14. Copyright © 2015 by American Counseling Association. Reprinted with permission.

3. **Skills**: Privileged and marginalized counselors possess skills to engage in discussions with clients about how client and counselor worldviews, assumptions, attitudes, values, beliefs, biases, social identities, social group statuses, power, privilege, and oppression influence the counseling relationship.

4. **Action**: Privileged and marginalized counselors take action to increase their understanding of how client and counselor worldviews, assumptions, attitudes, values, beliefs, biases, social identities, social group statuses, and experiences with power, privilege, and oppression influence the counseling relationship.

IV. Counseling and Advocacy Interventions

Privileged and marginalized counselors intervene with, and on behalf, of clients at the intrapersonal, interpersonal, institutional, community, public policy, and international/global levels.

a. **Intrapersonal:** The individual characteristics of a person such as knowledge, attitudes, behavior, self-concept, skills, and developmental history.

   Intrapersonal interventions: Privileged and marginalized counselors address the intrapersonal processes that impact privileged and marginalized clients.

b. **Interpersonal**: The interpersonal processes and/or groups that provide individuals with identity and support (i.e., family, friends, and peers).

   Interpersonal interventions: Privileged and marginalized counselors address the interpersonal processes that affect privileged and marginalized clients.

c. **Institutional**: Represents the social institutions in society such as schools, churches, community organizations.

   Institutional interventions: Privileged and marginalized counselors address inequities at the institutional level.

d. **Community**: The community as a whole represents the spoken and unspoken norms, value, and regulations that are embedded in society. The norms, values, and regulations of a community may either be empowering or oppressive to human growth and development.

   Community interventions: Privileged and marginalized counselors address community norms, values, and regulations that impede on the development of individuals, groups, and communities.

e. **Public policy**: Public policy reflects the local, state, and federal laws and policies that regulate or influence client human growth and development.

   Public policy interventions: Privileged and marginalized counselors address public policy issues that impede on client development with, and on behalf of, clients.

f. **International and global affairs**: International and global concerns reflect the events, affairs, and policies that influence psychological health and well-being.

   International and global affairs interventions: Privileged and marginalized counselors address international and global events, affairs, and polices that impede on client development with, and on behalf of, clients.

   Adapted from Ratts et al. (2015)

Reflection Question 6.2 supports your thinking about the challenges you face related to multicultural counseling and social justice and establishing a counseling relationship with your clients.

REFLECTION QUESTION 6.2

MSJCC AND COUNSELING RELATIONSHIP

In reflection of the counseling relationship, which area do you anticipate might present the greatest challenge for you in building a relationship with your client: attitudes and beliefs, knowledge, skills, or action?

As you consider these multicultural and social justice counseling competencies, there are two concepts that require a deeper understanding: privilege and empathy. Both have an important part in approaching counseling from a multicultural perspective.

Privilege and Empathy in Multicultural Counseling

Aspects of Privilege

You will note that embedded in the multicultural and social justice counseling competencies (Ratts et al., 2015, 2016) are commitments to advocacy and **social justice** as well as recognizing **privilege** and eliminating or limiting its harm. As counselors, committing to social justice means upholding the rights of others and confronting unfair treatment of others. The need for this emphasis on social justice results from both unfair treatment to many marginalized populations and the power one dominant group holds over other less dominant group. Understanding and addressing privilege is one way to understand how power influences unfair treatment and oppression.

Privilege, a term used frequently in the multicultural and social justice counseling competencies, means the right and ability to not have to think about certain attributes. Understanding the absence of "something" creates difficulties for us; we are accustomed to viewing what exists, rather than what is hidden. Let's look at three examples.

EXAMPLE ONE. **White privilege** is defined by the benefits or the power that non-Hispanic Whites have because they belong to a dominant group in power in society. The majority of the institutions (education, business, culture), controlled by non-Hispanic Whites, allow access and grant benefits and favors to those individuals who are Caucasians. Others not a part of this dominant group, such as people of color, Asians, and those from the Middle East, are granted fewer benefits. Implicit in the concept of privilege, and for this example White privilege, is that those in this dominant group do not recognize their power and that the benefits they accrue may be, in essence, unearned.

EXAMPLE TWO. Another example relates to gender. For example, females are significantly more likely to be sexually assaulted (NCADV, 2018) than males (Conley et al., 2017; Mitchell, MacLeod, & Cassisi, 2016). This leads to women's increased awareness of their femaleness, particularly for safety reasons. Males, on the other hand, do not require the same awareness, and may, therefore, not attend to this specific dimension of their identity. For males, it is their privilege to allow this dimension of their identity to fade into the back of their mind. Being male becomes an unconscious part of their awareness; at least in relation to safety, it is a place where unchallenged assumptions live.

EXAMPLE THREE. Counselors, and even counselors in training or entering practicum also experience privilege as they work with clients. For instance, the counselor is the one who asks the questions, while the client is the one with the problem. The privilege is embedded in the roles of counselor and client.

The Centrality of Empathy in Multicultural Counseling

When considering diversity and counseling, it is important to consider the **empathy** a counselor has for it is directly related to effective counseling within a multicultural framework (Hays & Erford, 2018). However, considering the nature of empathy and its impact on cross-cultural work adds additional complexity to the practice of multicultural counseling. Empathy grounds multicultural counseling, as represented by the concepts introduced thus far: (a) multicultural awareness, knowledge, and skills; (b) Fouad and Kantamneni's model of cultural dimensions; (c) multicultural and social justice counseling competencies; and (d) the concept of privilege (see Figure 6.3).

FIGURE 6.3. The centrality of empathy in multicultural counseling

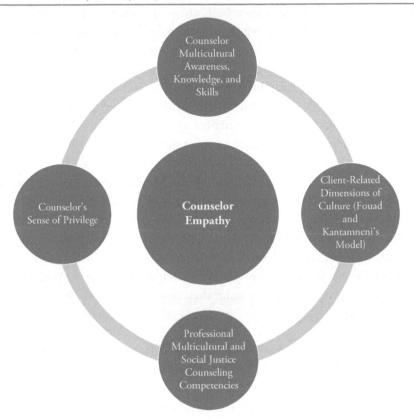

A discussion of empathy includes both culture of the client as well as the culture of the counselor (and the interaction with the culture of the client) (Ratts et al., 2015, 2016). The need to understand both is embedded in the multicultural and social justice competencies (Ratts et al., 2015, 2016).

COUNSELOR SELF-AWARENESS. **Counselor self-awareness** occurs when "privileged and marginalized counselors take action to increase self-awareness of their social identities, social group statuses, power, privilege, oppression, strengths, limitations, assumptions, attitudes, values, beliefs, and biases ..." (Ratts et al., 6)

CLIENT WORLDVIEW. Understanding the **client worldview** occurs when privileged and marginalized counselors take action to increase self-awareness of "clients' worldview, assumptions, attitudes, values, beliefs, biases, social identities, social group statuses, and experiences with power, privilege, and oppression ..." (Ratts et al., p. 6)

COUNSELING RELATIONSHIP. A focus on the **counseling relationship** means that privileged and marginalized counselors take action to increase their understanding of how "client and counselor worldviews, assumptions, attitudes, values, beliefs, biases, social identities, social group statuses, and experiences with power, privilege, and oppression influence the counseling relationship" (Ratts et al., 2015, p. 6).

Slattery and Park (2012) provide a description of counselor empathy that helps integrate it into the equation of multicultural counseling competence. They describe three facets of building empathy for others, especially clients.

CLIENT FACTORS. **Client factors** related to empathy include the client's age, race, size, gender, presenting problems and diagnosis, history of abuse, and social skills.

CLINICIAN FACTORS. **Clinician factors** related to empathy include the clinician's age, race, size, gender, interactional style, and clinical skill.

CONTEXT FACTORS. **Context factors** include the setting, time of day, nature of the therapeutic relationship, and stressors in the life of the client or clinician.

A Closer Look at Empathy

Luke, Redekop, and Moralejo (in press) have conceptualized empathy in the context of its counterfeits. Three types of empathy-related concepts are presented by Luke and colleagues, **sympathy**, empathy, and **projective sympathy,** to lay the foundation for the multicultural and social justice competencies (Ratts et al., 2015). Fundamental to both respect for differences and also humility about our own experiences is the ability to understand, judgment free, the experience of another person.

SYMPATHY. Simply put, sympathy involves feeling the emotion of the other person. There are few emotional or psychological boundaries between the two, allowing the emotion of one to permeate the emotion of the second person. This is antithetical in counseling. Sympathy is a poor substitute for the skill of empathy and leads to additional boundary violations and counselor burnout (Stebnicki, 2008).

EMPATHY. Empathy, in contrast to sympathy, is the process of viewing the world through the experience of the other person (Rogers, 1961). It is not devoid of emotion in the counselor; instead, it is a recognition of and compassion for the emotion of the other person, while recognizing that the emotion belongs to the client. Understanding and caring do not require taking on the emotion of the other person.

PROJECTIVE SYMPATHY. Projective sympathy is the process of assuming what you would feel in a given situation described by another person and then responding with concomitant advice (Luke, Redekop, and Moralejo, in press). In counseling, when counselors assume they know what their client feels because of how they [counselors] would feel in the same situation, these counselors may make erroneous assumptions about what clients are experiencing and what they need.

For example, in a cultural context, imagine a female describing to her male friend how a male coworker smacked her "behind" in the breakroom at work and laughed when she flushed saying, "I figured you'd like that." The male friend, seeking to be helpful, imagines how he would have felt in that moment, assumes that is how his female friend feels, and responds with, "You should have kneed him in the groin." Despite being well-meaning, this male friend can scarcely understand from a cultural or empathic perspective the female's experience of the systemic oppression against which this behavior occurs. If the female friend responds negatively to her coworker, she is likely to be labeled as a gender-based epithet. If she expresses gratification or a neutral response, the assumption is that she has given her permission for this type of behavior, resulting in the use of some invective.

ETHICAL CONSIDERATION 6.1

Consider the types of connecting with clients described—sympathy, empathy, and projective sympathy. How might these different experiences impact your ability to connect with your client (or not) and then how they might lead you to impose your values on your client?

Professional Aspects of Empathy

There are two components of empathy related to skills in the art of connecting. The first might be called **empathy experienced**, and it is the phenomenon of sensing the world from another person's perspective. The second component can be called **empathy expressed**, and involves communicating this attempt at understanding to the client. It is arguable whether a counselor can express something he or she has not ex-

perienced, but it seems clear to us that regardless of the depth of the empathic experience, if it is not communicated (expressed) clearly to the client, it has very little therapeutic benefit. Returning to the conundrum regarding expressing something you have not experienced, it is our view that this tends to spark meaningful dialogue among students and counselors alike. Spending time in class together talking this through, not necessarily to resolution, but toward illumination, may help these ways of expression become clearer. Discussion Together 6.1 helps focus your thinking.

DISCUSSION TOGETHER 6.1
What is the Nature of Empathy?
Is empathy best conceived as a propensity toward seeing the world from the perspective of another person, or is it a learned skill?

There are two primary reasons personal experience need not be the basis of empathy: First, one's own limited experiences need not—and should not—limit the number and type of clients that can be worked with; and, second, similar experience is not the same experience. The idea that understanding must equal experience is a prominent theme in substance use disorder counseling on an almost daily basis. The client in treatment asks the counselor if the counselor is "in recovery." One of the main reasons for this question is the assumption on the part of the client that if the counselor is in recovery, he or she (the counselor) will be more likely to understand the client's experience. This somehow reassures the client that he or she won't be judged in the same way as someone who is not in recovery. This is faulty logic. Having similar experiences is not sufficient to create judgment-free understanding (Luke, Redekop, & Jones, 2018). In fact, the opposite is often true. For these providers in recovery, there is an overwhelming temptation to make assumptions regarding the client's experience and to attempt to implement what worked for them, and judge the client when it does not work from them as well. Experiential Activity 6.1 will help you understand this point.

EXPERIENTIAL ACTIVITY 6.1
A Discussion about Empathy

As you think about your multicultural competence at this stage of practicum, and based on your encounters with your clients and colleagues thus far, what meaning might this symbol in Figure 6.4, which has been identified as the symbol for empathy, hold for you?

FIGURE 6.4.

You may be relieved to know that developing multicultural competence is a matter of leaning in to the role and identity of a counselor. It might help to hold in your mind that multicultural counseling competence is not about political correctness; it is not about merely using the right term in front of certain people. It involves human factors such as verbal and nonverbal communication, emotional expression, empathy, and general communication patterns (Hays & Erford, 2009). The work of Hays and Erford (2017) describes, in concrete terms, the basic multicultural competencies you develop and refine during practicum. The competencies articulated by Hays and Erford (2009, 2017) are presented in Table 6.2 for ease of reading and reflection. See Reflection Question 6.3 for a suggested way to use the adapted Hays and Erford list of multicultural counseling competencies.

TABLE 6.2. Counseling Considerations for MCC (Adapted from Hays and Erford, 2009, 2017)

Verbal communication

- Primary tool used in counseling
- Power is embedded in language; those who do not speak the majority language are marginalized
- Language barriers
- Feelings of frustration/invalidation
- Use of metaphors from the client's culture to deepen levels of understanding
- Preferences for expression in native languages
- Awareness of resources in the community (by counselors)
- Employment of interpreters or the learning of a second language (by counselors)

Nonverbal communication

- Facial expressions
- Proxemics—use of personal physical distance
- Kinesics—body movements, positions, postures
- Paralanguage—verbal cues other than words
- Operation often outside of conscious awareness; difficult to falsify
- Key to understanding a client's genuine feelings
- Often ambiguous and culturally bound
  - Interpersonal space and eye contact
  - Interpretation within client's culture
- Awareness of counselors' own nonverbal behaviors

Emotional expression

- Universal experiences: anger, sadness, gladness, fright, surprise, disgust
- Expression and causes of emotions vary among and within culture
- Socialization influences the way emotions are experienced
- Use of norms from within the client's culture to determine if expression is pathological
- Inclusion of the client's beliefs regarding the origin of emotions in the counseling process

- Characterized by openness and honesty (between counselor and client)
- Counselor does the following:
  - Consistently check with the client to ensure accurate interpretation and understanding
  - Engage in a self-reflective process
  - Respond based on the client's frame of reference
  - Self-disclose appropriately to promote trust

REFLECTION QUESTION 6.3

COUNSELING CONSIDERATIONS FOR MCC

In considering Table 6.2, in what areas do you feel you have strong skills and limited skills?

Observe and Infer

The phenomenon of jumping to conclusions—making assumptions based on incomplete information—is one that counselors know well. Even though this is a common human behavior, it works against multicultural competence. One way that to conceptualize this in terms of intervening and promoting genuineness in diverse and multicultural interactions involves the distinguishing between **observations** and **inferences** (Slattery and Park, 2012). According to Merriam-Webster (2018b), to observe is "to see and notice (someone or something)" or "a: to watch carefully especially with attention to details or behavior for the purpose of arriving at a judgment." This observation is not to be conflated or confused with the subsequent step of judging—in this case judging means to arrive at a conclusion or judgment, rather than being simply a pejorative act. To infer is "4.b. to derive as a conclusion from facts or premises <we see smoke and infer fire> (Merriam-Webster (2018b).

The challenge for humans and counselors in training is to remain vigilant regarding which is being implemented at any given time, an observation, a judgement, or an inference. For example, an all-too-common comment from some counselors involves addressing clients by their diagnosis rather than their name: "I have my borderline at 10:00 today (sighs)." If questioned, the counselor may explain that he or she is merely being descriptive of the client. Unfortunately, many epithets have been used to "describe" underrepresented and otherwise oppressed individuals. In spite of the best intentions of these counselors, the disposition toward "the borderline" leaks through the positive attending behaviors and communicates a lack of acceptance. The observation would be that the client has behaviors that evoke a negative reaction from the counselor. And this reinforces the stereotypes that abound of the borderline client. The inference, then, is that the counselor needs to seek supervision or consultation about possible counter-transference or burnout risks. The following two interventions may help you understand the concepts of inference and observation in a clearer way.

Intervention One

Chad regularly runs an intervention in a multicultural counseling course. He uses images from popular news outlets covering the aftermath of Hurricane Katrina. In one image from one news source is a young African American male carrying items in his arms and in a bag through chest-high water. The caption comments about "looting." Around the same time, another news source has an image of a White couple carrying items through chest-high water that they "found." In both cases, the inferences were presented as observations, both critical errors leading to bias. It's not hard to image Black readers seeing these and feeling quite visceral emotions about these characterizations. One might further imagine White readers with conscious and unconscious biases clicking their teeth in agreement with the characterizations and shaking their heads at the state of the world. The point here is not to make claims about the media, White or Black disaster victims, or the readers. The point is that observations and inferences are not interchangeable and must be dealt with cautiously as counselors approach clients who represent the other. Even their behaviors in session reveal their implicit views. Nonverbal and paraverbal communications are powerful influences, as they correspond to or contradict verbal messages, in life, as in therapy and supervision. These behaviors often occur outside of conscious awareness, such as **microaggressions**—"subtle and often automatic put-downs" (Sue & Sue, 2015).

Intervention Two

Another intervention is based on acceptance and commitment therapy (ACT) (Hayes, 2004) and is supported in clinical applications of neuroscience integration with counseling (Badenoch, 2008; Luke, 2015). ACT challenges the notion in traditional CBT that negative, dysfunctional thoughts should be confronted; rather, these thoughts should be observed as fleeting, like passing scenery viewed from the window of a speeding train: They are only as real as the attention given them. Hayes cites research on depression, that when clients can provide a rationale for their depression (a proxy for grasping thoughts and feelings), they are more treatment resistant. Badenoch parallels this with depression from a neurobiological perspective. Clients who embrace their depression as the totality of their experience struggle more to free themselves from it; in contrast, when they accept their depression as arising from brain-based phenomena, they are free to behave outside those neural experiences. Similarly, when bias is experienced as a real, natural, brain-based phenomenon, counselors are able to move forward in freedom and congruence.

The intervention, based on this research, involves assisting counselors in differentiating between observation and inference (Slattery & Park, 2012). For example, when viewing a Web photo of an African American male steadily gazing at the camera and wearing a white tank top, students are asked to make observations and later inferences. When a student makes the observation that this is a "mug shot," the class catches their collective breath. This is clearly an inference from the observation, but more than that, it may be a view to a bias. Rather than excusing or justifying, it is important to create a safe space to recognize that this is a neural based, in-group reaction to an out-group member. When accepted as such, and separated from an observation, the student is invited into a new personal insight. Rather than a shaming exercise, it is one that illuminates. The source of the error may not be character based as much as it is neural based.

John and Rita Sommers-Flanagan (2018) offer recommendations for working with clients in multiculturally competent ways. See Table 6.3. The table has been adapted from their book, *Clinical Interviewing.*

TABLE 6.3. Recommendations for Working with Clients in Multiculturally Competent Ways

Open inquiry	
Do ask about tribal, ethnic, or background differences that are obvious or are made obvious by information provided by the client	Don't insist on a more thorough exploration of these differences than is offered
Do realize that acculturation and cultural identity are fluid and developmental	Don't assume all members of a given family group or couple have the same levels of cultural identity or the same experiences interfacing with the dominant culture

Family	
Do recognize that for many or most nondominant cultures in the US, the role of family is central. The concept of family is often broader, more inclusive, and more definitive in a given individual's sense of identity. Therefore, be attuned to matters of family with heightened awareness and sensitivity, whether you are a member of the dominant culture or from a minority culture	Don't impose either your own definition of family or the definition of family you've read about with regard to the client's culture. Simply be open to the client's sense of family
Do graciously allow family members to attend to some part of an initial interview if they request to do so	Don't define family along biological lines

Communication styles	
Do remember that patterns of eye contact, direct verbalization of problem areas, storytelling, and note taking all have culturally determined norms that vary widely	Don't assume a chatty or overly familiar style, even if that is your predominant style. Strive to demonstrate respect
Do ask for clarification if something is not clear	Don't ask for clarification in a manner that suggests your lack of clarity is the client's problem

Religious and spiritual matters	
Do accept the client's beliefs regarding the sources of distress: ancestral disapproval, the evil eye, God's wrath, or trouble because of misbehavior in another life. A strong relationship of trust must be established before one can determine the adaptive and maladaptive aspects of such beliefs and thereby work within the frame toward healing and growth	Don't assume you are being told the whole story regarding faith or belief systems early on. Most are powerful and quite private and will not be easily or fully shared
Do take advantage of any possible link to meaningful spiritual or religious beliefs or connections that may help address the current distress	Don't hesitate to allow input into the problem from religious or spiritual persons respected by the client

These recommendations for working with clients in multiculturally competent ways are intended to help you develop more effective relationships with clients.

Summary

In this chapter, we have covered the gamut of multicultural counseling issues. One area that is conspicuously absent from this chapter is descriptions of and advice for counseling specific racial, ethnic, religious, gender, and other numerous cultural groups. This is intentional. For one thing, you will cover these in great detail in a multicultural counseling course, but perhaps more importantly, we have demonstrated how, as a practicum student—a counselor in training—you can think like a multiculturally competent counselor. The purpose of this chapter has been to promote your reflection and skill development in encountering the other. This is no small task, as it asks you to think beyond cultural categories and group characteristics and then to know yourself and how to learn about the personhood of your client. We believe this is best accomplished through a thorough understanding and application of empathy. As you move toward mastery in this area, you will observe the recognition of it in the face of your client, even if they cannot label it as such.

Key Terms

Client factors

Client self-awareness

Client worldview

Clinician factors

Context factors

Counseling relationship

Cross-cultural

Cross cultural experience

Culture shock

Diversity

Empathy

Empathy experienced

Empathy expressed

Fouad and kantamneni's three-dimensional model of cultural dimensions

Group-level characteristics or variables

Individual characteristics or variables

Inferences

Microaggressions

Multicultural and social justice competencies

Multicultural counseling

Multicultural counseling competencies

Observations

Privilege

Projective sympathy

Social justice

Societal level characteristics or variables

References

Badenoch, B. (2008). *Being a brain-wise therapist: A practical guide to interpersonal neurobiology.* New York, NY: Norton.

Campbell, A., Vance, S. R., & Dong, S. (2017). Examining the relationship between mindfulness and multicultural counseling competencies in counselor trainees. *Mindfulness, 9*(1), 79–87. doi:10.1007/s12671-017-0746-6

Council for Accreditation of Counseling and Related Education Programs. (2016a). *CACREP Standards: Section 2: Professional Counseling Identity.* Retrieved from https://www.cacrep.org/section-2-professional-counseling-identity/

Council for Accreditation of Counseling and Related Education Programs. (2016b). *CACREP Standards: Section 5: Entry-level Specialty Areas—Clinical Mental Health.* Retrieved from https://www.cacrep.org/section-5-entry-level-specialty-areas-clinical-mental-health-counseling/

Cambridge Dictionary. (2018). Culture. Retrieved from https://dictionary.cambridge.org/us/dictionary/english/culture

Conley, A. H., Overstreet, C. M., Hawn, S. E., Kendler, K. S., Dick, D. M., & Amstadter, A. B. (2017). *Journal of American College Health, 65*(1), 41–49. doi:10.1080/074481.2016.1235578

Fouad, N., & Kantamneni, N. (2008). Contextual factors in vocational psychology: Intersections of individual, group, and societal dimensions. In S. D. Brown & R. W. Lent (Eds.). *Handbook of counseling psychology* (4th ed.) (pp. 408–425). Hoboken, NJ: John Wiley & Sons.

Hayes, S. C. (2004). Acceptance and commitment therapy and the new behavior therapies: Mindfulness, acceptance, and relationship. In S. C. Hayes, V. M. Follette. & M. M. Linehan (Eds.), *Mindfulness and acceptance: Expanding the cognitive-behavioral tradition* (pp. 1–29). New York, NY: Guilford Press.

Hays, D. G., & Erford, B. T. (2017). *Developing multicultural counseling competence: A systems approach* (3rd ed.). New York, NY: Pearson.

Livingston, G. (2017). *The rise of multiracial and multiethnic babies in the U. S. Pew Research Center.* Retrieved from http://www.pewresearch.org/fact-tank/2017/06/06/the-rise-of-multiracial-and-multiethnic-babies-in-the-u-s/

Luke, C. (2016). *Neuroscience for counselors and therapists: Integrating the sciences of mind and brain.* Thousand Oaks, CA: SAGE.

Luke, C. Redekop, F. & Moralejo, J. (in press). From microaggressions to neural-aggressions: A neuro-informed counseling perspective. *Journal of Multicultural Counseling and Development.*

Luke, C., Redekop, F., & Jones, L. K. (2018). Addiction, Stress, and Relational Disorder: A Neuro-Informed Approach to Intervention. *Journal of Mental Health Counseling*, 40(2), 172-186.

Merriam-Webster. (2018a). Culture. Retrieved from https://www.merriamwebster.com/dictionary/culture

Merriam-Webster. (2018b).Observe. Retrieved from https://www.merriamwebster.com/dictionary/observe

Mitchell, J. C., MacLeod, B. P., & Cassisi, J. E. (2016). Modeling sexual assault risk perception among heterosexual college females: The impact of previous victimization, alcohol use, and coping style. *Violence Against Women, 23*(2), 143–162. doi:10.1177/1077801216638767

NCADV. (2018). National statistics. Retreived from https://ncadv.org/statistics

Oxford English Dictionary. (2018a). Cross-cultural. Retrieved from http://www.oed.com.proxy.lib.utk.edu:90/view/Entry/44812?redirectedFrom=crosscultural#eid7853478

Oxford English Dictionary. (2018b). Culture shock. Retrieved from http://www.oed.com.proxy.lib.utk.edu:90/search?searchType=dictionary&q=culture+shck&_searchBtn=Search

Pederson, P. (1998). *Multiculturalism as a 4th force.* Philadelphia, PA: Taylor and Francis.

Ratts, M. J., Singh, A. A., Nassar-McMillan, S., Butler, S. K., & McCullough, J. R. (2016). Multicultural and social justice competencies: Guidelines for the counseling profession. *Multicultural Counseling and Development, 44*(1), 28–48. doi:10.1002/jmcd.12035

Ratts, M. J., Singh, A. A., Nassar-McMillan, S., Butler, S. K., & McCullough, J. R. (2015). *Multicultural and social justice competencies.* Retrieved from https://www.counseling.org/docs/default-source/competencies/multicultural-and-social-justice-counseling-competencies.pdf?sfvrsn=8573422c_20

Rogers, C. (1961). *On becoming a person: A therapist's view of psychotherapy.* London, UK: Constable.

Slattery, J. M., & Park, C. L. (2012). *Empathic counseling: Meaning, context, ethics, and skills.* Pacific Grove, CA: Brooks Cole.

Sommers-Flanagan, J., & Sommers-Flanagan, R. (2017). *Clinical interviewing* (6th ed.). Hoboken, NJ: Wiley.

Stebnicki, M. A. (2008). *Empathy fatigue: Healing the mind, body, and spirit of professional counselors.* New York, NY: Springer.

Sue, D. W., & Sue, D. (2015). Counseling the culturally diverse: Theory and practice (7th ed.). Hoboken, NJ: John Wiley & Sons.

Swanson, J. L., & Fouad, N. A. (2015). *Career theory and practice: Learning through case studies* (3rd ed.). Thousand Oaks, CA: SAGE.

Unit for the Study of Personality in Politics. (2012). *Barack Obama's leadership style.* Retrieved from http://personality-politics.org/barack-obama-2012

CHAPTER 7

Critical Incidents
IN PRACTICUM

INTRODUCTION

Imagine yourself sitting in a practicum class, reviewing your video of session four during the seventh week of the term. Your instructor stops the video and asks you, "What was going on for you during this moment?" At first your mind goes blank, trying in the moment to recall what you might have been thinking at that time, which was two weeks prior. You also sense that something must have happened for your instructor to stop the video, and your mind thinks the worst. Almost by instinct, you feel your defenses rising, preparing yourself for an attack. As this happens, you hear yourself saying something to your instructor like, "What do you mean?" "What would you ask me that?" In support of your fears, your instructor highlights that, in the video, you suddenly stopped using basic listening skills and began giving your client advice, and in such a way that it appears judgmental. You're stunned. The instructor is right. Your classmates are leaning in, attentively. What happens next? This interaction in supervision illustrates the area of focus for this chapter: **critical incidents** in practicum and the importance of supervision. The goals for the chapter follow.

- Define and describe critical incidents in practicum
- Normalize the experience of critical incidents in practicum
- Describe the important part that supervision plays during critical incidents occurring in practicum
- Recognize and manage critical incidents to facilitate maximum growth potential

RELATED CACREP GOALS

Although there are no explicit connection to CACREP Standards, the study of critical incidents reflects standards related to skill development, multicultural and social justice issues, and the importance of site and faculty supervision.

Defining Crisis and Critical Incidents

A crisis, in developmental terms, is a situation in which the resources of the individual are stretched as a new challenge tests the limits of his or her abilities. Newman and Newman (2015) describe a **developmental crisis** in this way, "[It] refers to a period of role experimentation, exploration, and active decision making among alternative choices" (p. 411).

The crises referred to here can be biological (sweaty palms, heart palpitations, or breathing changes), environmental (lock down of site due to bomb threat), experiential (client describes in detail experience of self-harm), or social (rupture in relationship with client; rupture in relationship with supervisor), or various combinations of these. In the context of the practicum experience, these symptoms might be similar. For example, the first time a practicum student experiences sweaty palms, heart palpitations, or breathing changes in reaction to a client, it can signal a developmental crisis.

From the definition of developmental crisis emerges what is termed a **critical incident**, or the point in time when a crisis presents an opportunity for growth. Critical incidents are challenging, and at times uncomfortable or even painful. In other words, critical incidents during practicum, even though challenging, are opportunities to grow and develop. Reflection 7.1 helps you consider critical incidents from the perspective of your current experiences.

REFLECTION QUESTION 7.1

CRITICAL INCIDENTS AND YOUR CURRENT EXPERIENCES

Have you had experiences and instances that you might label a critical incident or crisis? What was each incident like for you? How was it resolved, or are there lingering issues?

Now that you have reflected on your own experiences of critical incidents, let's look at scholarly definitions. Howard, Inman, and Altman (2006) define critical incidents as "significant learning moments, turning points, or moments of realization that were identified by the trainees as making a significant contribution to their professional growth" (p. 88). Several authors describe critical incidents in a variety of ways (see Table 7.1).

TABLE 7.1. Scholarly Descriptions of Critical Incidents

Howard, Inman, and Altman (2006)	**Professional identity.** These include "role identification, newness, career choice, and limitations" (p. 93). **Personal reactions.** These include "self-insight and self-awareness; competence, supervision, and philosophy of counseling" (p. 93).
Morrissette	"[E]motional over-involvement and sexual attraction in counseling, countertransference, competency-based anxiety, conflicts with supervisors and clients, and vicarious traumatization" (1996, p. 32, as cited in Howard et al., 2006).
Heppner and Roehlke	"[S]elf-awareness, professional development, competency, and personal issues" (1984, p. 32, as cited in Howard et al., 2006)
Furr and Carroll	"[V]alue conflicts, cognitive development, competency beliefs, professional development, perceived support and obstacles, personal growth in and outside of the program, and skill development" (2003, p. 90 as cited in Howard et al)
Furr and Carroll	**Categories of critical incidents.** Beliefs, cognitions, affect, and behavior (2003, p. 90, as cited in Howard et al.)

An integration the information related to critical incidents is presented in Figure 7.1. This figure provides you with a visual for what critical incidents in practicum might look like. When you think about a critical incident you or your peers have experienced, it may be helpful to use one or more of these aspects: professional development; the nature of the critical incident; the type of the critical incident; and the values and skills you may need to address the incident.

FIGURE 7.1. Concept and experience of the aspects of critical incidents in practicum

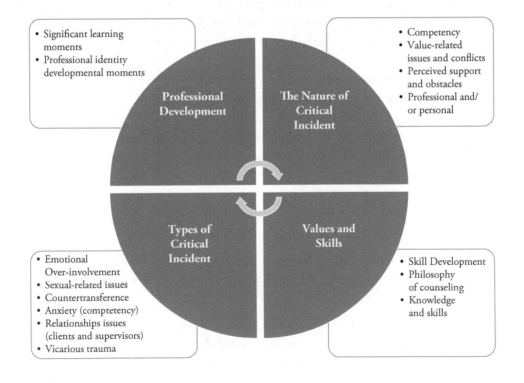

Now, let's look at critical incidents in practicum. This will help you and your supervisor develop a common understanding of critical incidents and gain a common language with which to discuss them.

Critical Incidents in Practicum

As you know from your own experience, practicum students encounter myriad challenges as they work with real clients for the first time. In addition, this is likely the first time that work is closely scrutinized by the site and faculty supervisors. And, in fact, after graduation and as a new employee as a professional counselor, more than likely, the supervision you will receive will be limited. Given these conditions, it is natural that your awareness (and anxiety) is heightened, creating the critical part of incidents that feel like crises. The most prevalent ones are **skill-based events, diversity-based events, role-based events, personal-based events, attraction-based events, gender-based events**, and **attitude/behavior-based events**. These categories of critical events are developmentally expected; in fact, the majority of practicum students can expect to experience some form of these. In some sense, they are developmental rites of passage. Figure 7.2 presents a visual for these seven categories of crises incidents.

FIGURE 7.2. Categories of Crises Incidents

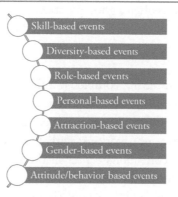

To describe specific examples of critical incidents related to practicum that represent each of these categories, our four practicum students, Janice, Jose, Kaisha, and Sam, reflect on their own experiences and share their most memorable ones.

Skills-Based Events

Jose: "I was working with a group and during check-in a client remarked, "I am evil." This comment was so unexpected. I was sure that this was a crisis moment for the client and that all sorts of 'psychotic' behaviors were going to follow. I completely forgot that I could follow up with a reflection statement, asking for clarification of what that meant to the client.

In supervision, Jose said, "I realized that sometimes I don't know how to respond to clients in the moment."

As it turns out, Jose did have the requisite skills; those skills just disappeared when he needed them in the context of practicum with real clients. When asked what he would like to have said, based on basic relationship, helping, and group process skills, he said, "I can't imagine what that is like for you. Could you say a little more about what being evil means for you?" [Pause] an then, "Has anyone else in the group felt evil or like you had done such bad things in your life that there was no way to recover? I see some heads nodding; could you tell all of us and Jose about that?"

During review of Jose's video in group supervision, another classmate noted that Jose's body language reflected what he was feeling. The deficit appeared to be located in Jose's physical recoil when the client said "I am evil." This recoil communicated Jose's skill deficit was not located in basic skills but in his body language. The video shows his judgment of the client. The supervisor then redirected the focus of the discussion toward self-regulation and transmission of feelings through facial expression and body language.

Note to practicum students: Practicum is often the first time a CIT will encounter a client in the clinical setting, with the expectation that he or she has to do something with client information or about client behavior. The skills required during a counseling session feel very different from those used in roleplays in the relative safety of the classroom. The first few times you, as a practicum student, encounter a client's unexpected statements or experiences, it is natural to momentarily forget the skills you have learned and been practicing.

Note to supervisors: Students often say that they felt like they needed to go back through their skills and theories courses because now the material seems far more relevant. However, while review of previous material is often a good practice, the reality is most students can remember what they have learned in prior classes—they just need to be reminded that they remember.

Diversity-Based Events

Janice: Janice entered practicum having completed a Diversity Issues in Counseling course in her program. Through that class, she became highly sensitized to her own privilege as a White, adult, educated, female, and to the language she used in referring to different demographic groups. During practicum, Janice was working with Darius, an African American teen who had just returned from a youth corrections center in the western part of the state. He was on probation for a number of misdemeanor crimes. Counseling is a condition of Darius's probation, so he is meeting with Janice in the middle school setting. During the fourth session together, Janice challenges Darius's "excuse-making" relative to his school performance (not turning in his homework and not completing in class assignments), citing that he seems to be blaming others for his lack of success rather than taking any responsibility himself.

Note to practicum students: Privilege is a complex topic to teach, learn, and experience during counseling practicum. The first time that you, as a practicum student, become aware of your privilege while with a client can be jarring. It may be the first time you realized your position of privilege or the influence poverty had in your own life. It may be that during a session you first experience that your race has never been something you had to think about until you sat with a person of color and had to walk with them through their experience of racism. It may be an experience like what happened in the classroom, wherein during a conversation about race, students were asked if they were walking down a sidewalk and a Black man was on one side of the sidewalk and a White man was on the other, which side they would prefer to walk on.

Female students remarked that both sides represented equal threats because both people were male, and for women, maleness is a greater threat than race.

Note to supervisors: The consummate struggle for humans is to authentically encounter another person, recognize the gulf of individual experiences that separate us, and respectfully connect both as unique individuals and as humans. Practicum is a place where biases tend to leak out and are often captured on video. These can—and should—be somewhat painful to experience, because they offer the opportunity to be turning points in our thinking and behaviors toward others. As a supervisor, you will want to help students address the issues of privilege that students experience.

Role-Based Events

Ladany, Friedlander, and Nelson (2005) note the difference between what is referred to in the counseling literature as **role ambiguity** and **role conflict**. Role ambiguity refers to the uncertainty of what to do and how to act in practicum and other clinical supervision. Ideally, supervisors must teach students how to be practicum students and how to receive supervision. However, this may not always occur, so it is then the practicum student's responsibility to ask for what he or she needs—even when he or she is not sure what it is precisely that he or she needs.

Sam: Sam is in his weekly meeting for triad supervision (he is one of four students placed at the campus clinic). For the third week in a row, the site supervisor has narrowly focused on clinical documentation. Along the way, the supervisor seemed to forget to affirm Sam's progress and commitment, instead focusing on the "billable" component of treatment necessary to document for their grants and contracts report.

As it became clear to Sam, at the end of the session, that no affirmation was forthcoming, he asked, "Do you think that I am making satisfactory progress?" The supervisor responded, "Yes, you're doing fine."

> ### CULTURAL CONSIDERATION 7.1
>
> Students often say to us that they understand the concepts of increasing self and other awareness, learning about other cultures, and challenging attitudes. But they also ask about the specific skills (outside of basic counseling skills) referred to in the Multicultural and Social Justice Counseling Competencies (MSJCC) regarding working toward cultural counseling competence. In light of the discussion of diversity-based critical events, reflect on the skills you might need to refine or develop to increase your competency in this area.

Note to practicum students and supervisors: In this case, role ambiguity led to the supervisor missing Sam's need for concrete affirmation of skills. At the same time, Sam did not know that he needed to ask explicitly for what he needed.

Another role-based event in supervision involves role conflict, in which the supervisor and supervisee disagree about a case or issue in supervision. One of the most common ones for practicum students involves times when practicum students feel caught between the site supervisor's and the faculty supervisor's perspectives. Role conflicts also occur when practicum students feel that their supervisor's feedback is biased, unethical, or mismatches their own theoretical perspective. Let's look at Kaisha's experience related to role conflict.

Kaisha: Kaisha learns during a treatment team meeting that there are times when a client's diagnosis does not fit the medication needed to manage her symptoms, so the diagnosis is modified. During one case, a client was diagnosed with Borderline Personality Disorder and was struggling to manage her moods and be able to rest. Because there is currently no medication approved for BPD, the prescriber changed the diagnosis to Bipolar I disorder to better manage the client's symptoms. Kaisha is alarmed to hear this and approaches her site supervisor about this "obviously unethical" practice, to which the site supervisor responds, "This is community mental health and we do what it takes to best help our clients."

Note to practicum students: Role conflict during practicum is common. In fact, the conflict may occur because of conflicts between your role as a student and as an employee of the practicum site. There may be a conflict between what you are learning about professional counseling in your academic program and what is happening in the world of practice. A third conflict may occur between differing perspectives between your two supervisors. Direct communication requesting clarification of the discrepant behavior is the most ethical, reasonable course. For instance, Kaisha might ask her site supervisor for additional information to help her resolve her conflict of competing ethical standards (integrity versus beneficence), recognizing that no satisfactory resolution may be forthcoming.

Note to supervisors: Role conflict is common in the practice of professional counseling. And, practicum students, operating as the bridge between the academic world and the world of practice, are bound to encounter this type of conflict. The first step in addressing role conflict is recognizing it when it occurs. One aspect of effective supervision includes helping students understand that these conflicts are to be expected and by providing students with a platform for addressing them. Consultation with her faculty supervisor may lead to Kaisha exploring more about what has been called **moral distress** or **moral injury** in the helping fields: the conflict between one's own understanding of and orientation to ethical behavior and that practiced in one's place of business.

Personal-Based Events

The terms **transference** and **countertransference** can trigger visions of psychoanalytic theory and evoke negative reactions from you as a practicum student. While inaugurated through the lens of Freudian theory development, these concepts have been recognized as legitimate, atheoretical constructs that affect the counselor-client relationship (Redekop, Luke, & Malone, 2017). Transference occurs when a client treats the counselor as if the counselor was someone from the client's life with whom he or she has unresolved conflict. For example, a client may view a female counselor as a mother figure for whom he or she has feelings of unaddressed anger. In session, the client may accuse the counselor of being judgmental and critical. The counselor (practicum student) may have no idea this accusation comes from the client's prior relationship with a parent.

These times are striking examples of how much is going on for clients that may have little to nothing to do with the counselor. In fact, practicum students are susceptible to thinking that clients are thinking about the practicum student as much as the practicum student is thinking of him- or herself. These critical events of transference offer opportunities for the student to reflect on his or her behavior while exploring the client's response in non-defensive ways.

Countertransference is essentially transference experienced by the counselor toward the client. Janice's experience provides an example.

Janice: Janice, in her work as practicum student/counselor at a middle school, sees Cletus, a 16-year-old male with behavior issues, twice a week. Cletus is using marijuana and regularly skips school. Cletus is having an impact on Janice that is outside of her current awareness. Review of the session video shows Janice giving what look like disapproving looks, making statements about being available via text or e-mail to Cletus between sessions, and giving parent-like advice. During group supervision, it becomes clear that Cletus reminds Janice of her son, who overdosed and almost died. Her son also dropped out of high school. Janice acknowledges that Cletus is triggering her, as if she is trying to help her son by forcing Cletus to change.

Note to practicum students: Both transference and countertransference are completely natural. As you know from studying these phenomena in class, they can also be incredibly useful in counseling. Both are also, at times, difficult to identify and work through. Asking for help during supervision to both discover possible aspects of transference and countertransference in your work with clients can be a routine part of supervision. Through this process of discovery, you can gain insights that support your work with clients and promote your professional development.

Note to supervisors: The experience of both transference and countertransference are completely natural, and you will want both aspects of the counseling process to be a regular part of supervision. For instance, both transference and countertransference can be seen as valuable data. You might say to your practicum students, "Your clients' reactions to you, and your reactions to them, can provide valuable information about both your biases, as well as how clients affect those in their environment." This clinical utility is, of course, contingent on the counselor being aware of his or her reactions, whether the issue is located within, or is something that the client evokes from others as well. Let's look at Jose's experience in supervision as an example.

Jose: In practicum supervision last week, Jose shares that his client, Bre, makes him angry. Jose's supervisor, Dr. Kim, helped Jose take an objective, reflective look at the Bre's case file, along with the video highlights from a tape that illustrated the behavior evoking these feelings. Dr. Kim and Jose explored what specifics of Bre's behavior may be pushing buttons in Jose. Then, Dr. Kim was able to direct the conversation back to understanding the client: "What if Bre is evoking these reactions from other primary figures in her life? How might she be using these behaviors to protect herself, or to otherwise get some payoff? How might we use your personal reaction to explore this with her, without making it about you?"

Attraction-Based Events

In your life, you will experience an attraction to another person without your consent. This is the nature of attraction: We are drawn to the people we are drawn to. A variety of factors affect attraction, including, but not limited to physical attributes. Physical attraction can develop from emotional and psychological connection, and this is often the case with attraction in the context of counseling in general and practicum in particular. Physical attraction is one thing: It is fairly easy to spot and feels concrete. Some individuals have physical attributes that may be deemed objectively attractive, while there are also those physical-behavioral features that are attractive in more subjective ways (e.g., height, weight, hair color, freckles, etc.). Then, there is attraction based on the relationship. Cognitive and emotional intimacy over time can create powerful attraction. This can be the type of attraction that sneaks up on counselors.

When addressing attraction, the counseling literature addresses several dyads and directions for attraction, as illustrated in Figure 7.3.

FIGURE 7.3. Dyads and directions for attraction

Client ← → Counselor ← → Supervisor → Client

Many times, CITs are caught off guard by feelings of attraction that they experience or by the attractions others feel for them, even though they may be clear that acting on these feelings, especially those related to clients, are prohibited by the American Counseling Association's 2014 Code of Ethics (American Counseling Association, 2014). "Sexual and/or romantic counselor–client interactions or relationships with current clients, their romantic partners, or their family members are prohibited. This prohibition applies to both in- person and electronic interactions or relationships" (A.5.a).

Equally prohibited are sexual relationships between a supervisor and a supervisee (Bernard & Goodyear, 2014). Sexual relationships between a supervisor and a supervisee fall into the category of a "multiple relationship" (Gottlieb, Robinson, & Younggren, 2007) and represent a misuse of power present in a supervisory relationship. Issues that exist include a loss of boundaries between professional and personal relationships, a threat to open and honest communication, a skewing of feedback and evaluation, and the presence of predatory seduction and exploitation of a nonconsensual relationship.

Note to practicum students: At times, the most difficult issues to confront are those that are prohibited by a professional code of ethics. Sexual attraction is one of those issues. Compounding the difficulty to confront your own feelings of sexual attraction or the feelings of others is our society's messages that topics of a sexual nature should not be discussed. And, in fact, sexual activity represents our basest nature and its expression evokes guilt and shame (Weiten, Dunn, & Hammer, 2017). You will want to explore issues of sexual attraction with your supervisors and be alert to the attractions that may exist in the relationships in which you engage during practicum (see Figure 7.3). Often the temptation to enter a sexual relationship with a client or supervisor catches students unaware. The term "slippery slope" is used to describe the process that that leads to inappropriate and unethical relationships. For example, these relationships begin with benign personal characteristics, behaviors, and situations that escalate to sexual encounters over time (Hamilton & Spruill, 1999). Reflection Question 7.2 helps you look at some aspects of vulnerability to may lead to attraction-related events.

THINKING ABOUT YOUR VULNERABILITY TO ATTRACTION-RELATED EVENTS

Hamilton and Spruill (1999; see pp.318-327) provide risk factors that may lead to attraction-related events. We present several of these risk factors for you to consider.

CIT or therapist responses to clients:

- Do you find it difficult to set limits on the demands your client makes of you?

- Do you accept phone calls from your client at home or your office when the client needs you to (a) help with a "crisis," (b) deal with minor problems, or (c) alleviate his or her loneliness or meet his or her need to talk to someone who "understands"?

- Do you make statements such as "This is not my usual practice; I ordinarily don't do this, but, in your case ..." or "Under the circumstances, it seems OK to ..."?

- Do you take care to dress or look more attractive than usual for a particular client? Do you find yourself wondering what the client thinks about you?

CIT or therapist needs:

- Do you find it difficult to set limits on the demands your client makes of you?

- Do you accept phone calls from your client at home or your office when the client needs you to (a) help with a "crisis," (b) deal with minor problems, or (c) alleviate his or her loneliness or meet his or her need to talk to someone who "understands"?

- Do you make statements such as "This is not my usual practice; I ordinarily don't do this, but, in your case ..." or "Under the circumstances, it seems OK to ..."?

- Do you take care to dress or look more attractive than usual for a particular client? Do you find yourself wondering what the client thinks about you?

Session characteristics:

- Do you find it difficult to set limits on the demands your client makes of you?

- Do you accept phone calls from your client at home or your office when the client needs you to (a) help with a "crisis," (b) deal with minor problems, or (c) alleviate his or her loneliness or meet his or her need to talk to someone who "understands"?

- Do you make statements such as "This is not my usual practice; I ordinarily don't do this, but, in your case ..." or "Under the circumstances, it seems OK to ... "?

- Do you take care to dress or look more attractive than usual for a particular client? Do you find yourself wondering what the client thinks about you?

- Are you reluctant to talk about transference or boundary issues, particularly feelings related to sexual attraction by or to the client?

- Do you find it difficult to tell your treatment team or supervisor some details related to your client?

Other:

- Have you offered to do such things as give the client a ride home, give tutoring in a difficult class, or arrange a meeting outside the therapy hour or place?

Note to supervisors: Supervisors who assume the initiative regarding multiple relationships between supervisors and clients can create an opportunity for open discussion of these issues in practicum dyadic or triadic supervision and in group discussions. CITs are particularly vulnerable, some because they are lonely, others are less confident in their abilities, and still others may not recognize ethical conflicts. Students in practicum need special care and support related to issues related to sexual attraction (Hamilton & Spruill, 1999; Ladany, Friedlander, & Nelson, 2005). Hamilton and Spruill (1999) provide concrete suggestions for beginning forthright discussions about multiple relationships and boundary crossings. These include the following:

1. Helping CITs understand the influence of aspects of the therapeutic relationship (e.g., self-disclosure, feelings of closeness, familiarity, physical proximity)

2. Disclosing examples or incidents related to their own feelings of sexual attraction (or as the recipient of sex attraction) during the counseling process

3. Presenting case studies that illustrate CITs talking about their own experiences related to multiple relationships. (This normalizes the issues and models the ability to discuss issues sexual in nature)

4. Distinguishing between feelings of sexual attraction and unethical actions

5. Understanding boundary violations and linking these to initiating or encouraging sexual misconduct

6. Understanding the role of clear case conceptualization as a way to monitor ethical behavior

7. Modeling clear boundaries with students and clients

Gender-Based Events

"Walker, Ladany, and Pate-Carolan (2007) defined a Gender-Related Event (GRE) as an 'interaction, process, or event in supervision that the trainee felt was directly or indirectly related to or influenced by: (a) the trainee's sex or the client's sex, (b) the social construction of gender, or (c) stereotypes and assumptions of gender roles'" (as cited in Bertsch et al., 2014, p. 12). In other words, gender-related events in practicum are those situations in which your sex or gender interacts with the gender or sex of your client and/or that of your supervisor in ways that negatively affect you or your client. An interaction that Kaisha experienced at her practicum site, an outpatient mental health clinic, helps clarify this category of crisis event.

Kaisha: Kaisha, 23 years old, meets her client, Roy, for the first time. Roy is a 43-year-old male who greets Kaisha with a, "Wow, I did not expect to get such a pretty counselor. I feel better already!" Kaisha feels immediately uncomfortable and unsure what to say in response. Her default in social situations is to say "thank you," so that's what she does with Roy. As she says it, she regrets it right away, believing she has sent the wrong message to Roy. She wonders if she should have confronted this statement from the beginning to let Roy know that therapy is unrelated to her physical attributes.

As you think about this situation, we offer Reflection Question 7.3.

REFLECTION QUESTION 7.3

THINKING ABOUT GENDER-RELATED EVENTS

Do you believe Roy's comment was inappropriate? Was it a gender-related event in practicum? Can you think of other situations that might illustrate a gender-related event? Based on our discussion of other crisis events, how might you have handled Roy's situation or other situations that you suggested earlier.

Attitude/Behavior-Based Events

Defensive. Guarded. Self-protective. All three of these responses represent ways practicum students may react during an attitude/behavior-based event. Ladany and colleagues (2005) describe three types of critical events in this type of event: crisis in confidence, emotional exhaustion, and characterological difficulties. Since counselor development is an iterative, recursive process, this means that success or confidence during one iteration does not mean that success or confidence will immediately occur during the next. For example, you may have had the best roleplay video session in a basic skills course, only to find yourself struggling to connect with a client in practicum. Somehow you managed to forget how to speak, listen, and feel like you know what you are doing.

ETHICAL CONSIDERATION 7.1

While simplistic to claim, it is accurate to say that ethical dilemmas are best managed when there is time for preparation. However, many critical events and incidents are emergent—they appear out of nowhere (or at least we often did not seem them coming). It is in these times that we (CITs and experienced counselors and counselor educators alike) are most vulnerable for ethical violations. Consider a recent time when you were caught off guard and how you responded. In what ways can these experiences inform the ways in which you may fall prey to ethical violations in the context of a critical incident?

Disruptive Critical Incidents

A critical incident is not necessarily a crisis: a crisis does not have to result in trauma. In fact, during a critical incident, we are most susceptible to growth, uncomfortable as that may seem. Beyond the seven categories of critical events that are developmentally expected and can be considered as developmental rites of passage, there are four additional critical incidents that may or may not occur during your practicum, but if/when they do, they can be fairly disruptive. These are termed **disruptive critical events**. These include working with **clients in crisis, confronting client symptoms, encountering client sexualized behaviors,** and responding to **the personal question**. Each of these has its own impact and challenges.

Clients in Crisis

Many clients come to counseling either because they are in crisis or they are experiencing the lingering effects of a past crisis. Crises for clients can reflect issues that are developmental in nature (Baruth & Manning, 2016), such as those that occur during the aging process. Other crises, linked to a specific time and/or place, represent situational issues and can include those related to violent crime, geopolitical struggles, or weather-related disasters (Miller, 2012). Crises can include those brought about as human needs go unmet (Maslow, 1971), such as safety or security needs. In addition, environmental influences may provoke crises responses. These range from global-related, social institution-related, and family-related issues, all of which impact the individual and stretch his or her coping mechanism (Jackson-Cherry & Ertford, 2017). Environmental issues may also be related to power, privilege, and discrimination, reflecting oppressive environmental influences.

In addition to the clients in crises, practicum students may be involved in crises within the workplace. These types of crises represent a variety of categories: disaster or trauma occurring within the community (e.g., natural disasters or fire), violence within the community or the workplace (e.g., active shooter and subsequent deaths, bomb threats), or client-related violence (e.g., threatened or actual harm to self or harm to others).

Regardless of the type of crisis, CITs are expected to respond in at least two ways. First, professional responses require practicum students to act in ways that address and ameliorate the crisis at hand. Second, practicum students also must attend to their own reactions after the fact, request supervision, and support and confront the possibilities of burnout, compassion fatigue, and vicarious trauma.

One example of a crisis that practicum students may encounter is that of confronting the challenge of controlling an out-of-control client. This type of crisis may be site dependent. It is likely to happen in outreach settings such as homes or public facilities and mental health out- and in-patient facilities. Client violence also is likely to occur in addiction treatment facilities.

The first time a professional, whether a staff member or a practicum student, witnesses a client engaged in violent behavior, the impact can be palpable. This was, indeed, Jose's experience. He had been at his practicum site for three weeks, learning the ropes and acclimating to the residential treatment setting. On a Tuesday morning of his fourth week, Jose was conducting a group when he heard a noise, looked into the hallway and saw several of the staff surrounding a client, placing him in a therapeutic hold while attempting to shuttle him into the "quiet room." Jose was stunned. He felt paralyzed and unsure what to do, think, or feel. Afterward, he described his experience like this:

Jose: "Today I left our facility quite shaken. I have seen lots of work with adolescents. But I have never seen a client so violent, enraged, and uncontrollable. As a part of my orientation, I was trained in **restraint reduction** and crisis prevention. This is a class, something that all employees have to take. It was much more in depth than the training I received in my previous work with kids. I heard a ruckus out in the hall while I was leading an anger management group. I peered out the door, rather than opening it. All my clients rushed to the door to see. They tried to open the door so they could be in the hallway. I blocked their movements and asked them to return to their seats.

What I saw and then what I heard about the incident was frightening. And I don't frighten easily. I have to admit, it caused me so much stress to think about restraining one of our clients. I had trouble sleeping. I think that it was the violence involved that preyed on my imagination. I am going to need some help processing this."

This type of client crisis results in a client being physically and/or chemically restrained by a physician, subdued by a law enforcement officer, or other involuntary physical incapacitation. Physical restraint in a treatment facility can range from locking the door behind a client to limit access to his or her room or another part of the facility to interventions designed to immobilize a client to inhibit the ability to act out aggressively to staff and other clients, and go all the way up to four-point restraints and chemical restraints. Four-point restraints are considered physical or mechanical, in that straps are used to restrict the movement of all four limbs. Chemical restraint involves using a psychotropic medication—usually a sedative, often in the form of an injection in the case of emergencies—to calm and slow an aggressive or manic client. Seclusion is another form of restraint that, while involuntary, is low contact/impact. Additionally, some clients being transported to a treatment facility by law enforcement are very likely to arrive in handcuffs and ankle shackles. The sight of these images and incidents can be quite unnerving to anyone, but especially to practicum students. The feelings one experiences can create doubt, fear, and confusion. It is as if all training leaves in that moment as the assault on the senses becomes overwhelming.

Client Symptoms

Prior to practicum, and, depending on the experience of each individual in practicum, symptoms of mental health issues can seem quite abstract, even cerebral. In contrast, experiencing a client's symptoms firsthand can be a jarring experience. Clients enter treatment intoxicated, in withdrawal from substances, and/or experiencing hallucinations, delusions, or thought distortions. They can be depressed and suicidal, manic and impulsive, or coldly distant and homicidal. Children and adolescents in schools can be withdrawn, aggressive to their peers and teachers, hyperactive, or depressed. While these experiences will be more or less common depending on the site, being confronted with a client's fully florid symptoms can result in a practicum student's experience of disequilibrium.

Two examples of practicum students confronting difficult client symptoms for the first time illustrate the challenges involved. Kaisha provides us a description of this experience. One of her responsibilities at the outpatient community health clinic was to conduct intake interviews. Early on in her practicum, her site supervisor observed her work. Kaisha remembers those early intake experiences. She describes one that took her by surprise. Then, Sam describes his first encounter with a suicidal client and shares his reactions.

Kaisha: "I was completing an intake interview during my first weeks in practicum. One intake I remember most was with a client; his name was John [pseudonym]. My supervisor observed my first intakes and then provided me feedback right after the intakes were over. Having supervision was really helpful early in my practicum.

One component of the intake interview was a psychosocial assessment. During post-interview supervision, my supervisor asked me what I had learned about John. I admitted to feeling overwhelmed by John's experiences and lost during the interview process. John described his drug use and abuse history. Then he talked about his abduction by a rival gang. And he described his history of abuse in very dramatic language. I admitted that I was mesmerized by the recounting of these events; it was like reading a novel or watching a movie. I knew I should focus on John and the assessment form, but I had never encountered someone with such a story.

Then my supervisor reminded me that she had an easier time with her view of John. She has five years of experience and she also said, 'and I was in the interview room to observe.' She told me that she could both hear John's words and observe his body language. My supervisor spoke to me in a very gentle tone of voice as she walked me back through the intake processes. She used a notepad and then outlined John's story and indicated all the places that John was fabricating his story. In fact, he made up a majority of this account. As it turned out, John was withdrawing from methamphetamine and was experiencing persecution-themed delusions."

Kaisha explained her reaction to this situation: "Even though I was aware of the withdrawal, I had never seen delusional behavior firsthand. First, I was astounded. I couldn't believe that I had missed the entire reason for John's entry into our clinic. How could I help him, if I couldn't see what his issues might look like? Second, I got so caught up in John's tale, I totally left the counseling role. I was surely 'in the moment with John,' but I didn't have that outside voice that was observing what was happening.

Later I reflected; I was so thankful for my supervisor. And she was so easy with the way we reviewed what had happened. She made me feel we were in the work together. I learned so much from this situation."

Sam: "As part of my practicum experience, I am working with a group of college students who had mental health issues prior to their enrollment in school. These students are registered with the Disabilities Services Office. They volunteered to participate in the campus clinic group counseling program focused on depression and is aptly named, 'Living with Depression.'

My group meets once a week. Last week I was very worried about one of my clients, thinking she might be at risk for suicide. When I played the tape of my group session for my supervisor, my supervisor concurred with my concern for Mara. My supervisor suggested that I follow-up with Mara after today's group session. Last week Mara had made several comments during the group regarding hopelessness that may have indicated suicidal thoughts, yet she denied them when probed during group. She continued to make these comments today. I followed my supervisor's recommendation to ask Mara to stay after group and meet with me to address concerns for her safety.

During the debrief, Mara told me that she intended to take her own life last week. She said she still felt that way but did not want to share this in group, for fear that the group might talk her out of it. I was ready for this and my supervisor and I had made preparations together to implement the standard protocol for formal suicide risk assessment. Once I made the formal assessment, I told Mara that I would need to call in my supervisor.

I was really calm during my group and when I talked with Mara. No one knew what turmoil I had been in. What if Mara had committed suicide before we met again? It would be my fault. What if Mara wouldn't meet with me after group? What if she didn't confirm her suicidal thoughts? Could I really conduct a suicide risk assessment? Was I a good enough counselor to handle this issue? Did I really want to deal with issues such as suicide where life and death are on the line? My supervisor trusts me, is that trust misplaced?"

Client Sexualized Behaviors

Clients, like most humans, can struggle to appreciate physical and emotional boundaries between people. In everyday life, there are social taboos that circumscribe appropriate interactions. For example, it is generally not appropriate to ask a person who is not an intimate acquaintance how much money they make or whom they voted for in the last election. There are implicit and explicit rules for social behavior. Other social rules are more ambiguous. For instance, is complimenting a person on their physical attractiveness a compliment or a come-on? Usually, the answer resides in the context of the relationship, the feeling one gets from the interaction and the perceived intention of the person giving the compliment. In other words, it is ambiguous. This becomes even more complex in the context of the counseling relationship. Should we expect, and therefore accept, that clients will violate social taboos because they are "sick," or is it fair to expect, and therefore hold them accountable, to follow cultural norms for social behavior? Often practicum students, and counselors as well, are confronted with issues related to sexuality, and professionals are often uncomfortable and unsure of how to address the challenges client sexuality brings. Let's look at this through the lens of the following scenario:

Kaisha: "As you all know, my practicum is in an outpatient community mental health clinic. We serve clients from all walks of life. Most of our clients are older than I am. My age, 23, I feel is often an issue or draws questions from our clients. I am working with a client, Steven, who is 60-something, male, and in treatment for a mood disorder. One source of this mood disorder is an early-life trauma.

Many of our clients spend much of the day at our center. During the break between the first and second segments of the treatment day, Steven approaches me and asks if he can take a picture of me. He says, 'I think you are so beautiful.' I was shocked by this request and comment. I snapped abruptly, "That comment is inappropriate. You need to focus on your work here and not my looks.' Steven immediately left the center. The following week, Steven returned to the center. At one point in the day, he appeared to be taking a picture of me while my back was turned. I think he was photographing my ass."

Here is the way that Kaisha is processing these two events with Steven: "I am really confused about how to handle this situation. I know that Steven should not be making sexualized comments to me. But I also know that I responded the way I would to a person who I knew or even a person who I didn't know. Yet I didn't respond as a counselor to a person who is in treatment. I was caught off-guard with Steven's comments. I have had heard these types of comments before here at the center. I think it is because of my age. I need help with this!"

There are three critical incidents described that can cause a disruption in a CIT's professional work and shake his or her confidence. Each of the three, working with clients in crisis, confronting client symptoms, and encountering client sexualized behaviors, represents the realities of a professional counselor's work. These examples serve to underscore the potential that clients have to surprise, dismay, astound, and stymy us during the helping process. In fact, client interaction has the potential to shatter a novice counselor's equilibrium. It is important to face our strong reactions and ask for help through supervision and consultation. Remember, practicum is a learning experience. Let's end this the discussion of disruptive incidents with Reflection Question 7.4. This reflection will help you identify critical incidents that you and your peers have encountered during practicum and that have disrupted your work.

REFLECTION QUESTION 7.4

CONSIDERING CLIENT-RELATED CRITICAL INCIDENTS

What client-related critical incidents have you experienced in your practicum? How do you determine when an incident is critical? What did/do you need when you encounter a critical event? How did you get what you needed?

A fourth disruptive event is the personal question that clients ask a counselor during the counseling session. Let's look at these questions and consider how counselors might respond to them.

Have You Ever ... ? The Personal Question

Perhaps one of the most common, yet unsettling critical incidents that also highlights the cross-cultural nature of counseling occurs the first time a client asks you a personal question. Often, clients will assume a more familiar posture toward a CIT than is appropriate for the relationship. This is not something to judge the client about; it is an opportunity to invite discussion about the nature of the therapeutic relationship. Nevertheless, client questions can unnerve us. Here are some of the more common ones and recommendations for addressing them:

1. Are you in recovery/Have you ever used drugs?

2. Are you married?

3. Do you have children?

THE ICEBREAKER. Most students find themselves stultified when clients ask personal questions. One of the first steps in responding to these questions is understanding the motivation for the question. Many times, as indicated, clients are being conversational because of their own anxiety or uncertainty about what to do or how to act in a counseling situation. Social interaction often revolves around asking questions, so clients, like CITs, have been socialized to ask questions. For example, a client's question, "Are you married?" is not intended as a threat to your marital status as much as it is an icebreaker. In a different context, the question might instead be, "Where do you work?" This would be absurd in the counseling context, so they ask a question about a familiar human experience.

The key to responding to all these questions, but a personal relationship question in particular, is to be non-defensive. One strategy is to answer the question briefly and shift the focus back to the client. Another approach is to *lean in* to the question and invite questions about yourself, noting the types of questions you are more and less comfortable answering, as a way to frame the relationship going forward. Either way, it is important to attend to your internal response to the question and to seek supervision for responses that seem an overreaction to the question.

LEVELING THE PLAYING FIELD. Clients also ask personal questions about the counselor to level the playing field. They may reason that if you are going to ask them personal questions, it is only fair that they be able to ask personal questions of you. For example, they may ask if you have children. This often happens with clients who are seeking counselor for family disruptions related to their children. Parents tend to be fiercely protective of their children, but to a greater extent, they are defensive about their own parenting. For counselors or students without children who are asked this, the initial response can be crisp no or not yet, but the message has been delivered: "If you are going to question my parenting, I'm going to question you about your lack of parenting." In these cases, the question may indicate the client is feeling guarded, so the response needs to be reflective. For example, "Parenting can be an isolating experience. I hope you will sense that this is a judgment-free zone, regardless of my own parenting status." Another approach is to answer the question and follow up immediately with an invitation for the client to express any concerns he or she may have about counseling. If he or she declines, but there is a continued sense of guardedness, you might, once again, lean in to the issue: "Some parents are actually uncomfortable talking with a counselor who does not have children. It would be understandable if you felt like that; I just hope we could talk a little about that."

At other times—most commonly occurring in the context of treatment of substance use disorders—the question is intended to deflect responsibility from the client. Clients will ask, "Are you in recovery, too?" and the look on their face shows their evaluation of the response. Some clinicians take a direct approach, saying, "Treatment is about you, not me." This approach can appear defensive and become a setback in building the therapeutic alliance. Using a reflective approach provides another option. Regardless of the type of response, this question from clients can catch CITs off guard.

Empathy serves us well here, first by imagining the experiences clients with substance use disorders have experienced: judgment, rejection, disappointment, confusion. Second, empathy is enhanced by asking the client about his or her concerns that exist behind the question. For instance, Chad typically responds with something like this: "I wonder what the answer to your question will do for you in your treatment. I hope that regardless of my history, you will feel accepted and also challenged to meet your goals." At other times, a more oblique approach can be effective: "I'll make a deal with you. At the end of our work together, if you still want to know, ask me again and I'll tell you." When done relationally, empathically, clients tend to lose interest in the counselor's history. This is because their implicit question is, "Will you be able to understand my experience and treat me differently than others have (e.g., with judgment, rejection, disappointment, confusion?)"

Summary

Critical incidents can be positive or negative events, and they can result in a student's growth or decline. The purpose of this chapter has been to assist you in identifying some of the more common critical incidents that occur in the context of counseling practicum, and to guide you in responding reflectively. There are seven categories of critical incidents: skill-based events, diversity-based events, role-based events, personal-based events, attraction-based events, gender-based events, and attitude-behavior-based events—all help you understand the range of critical incidents. The experience of a critical incident may also be disruptive to your understanding of and work with clients. Incidents such as seeing clients in crisis, confronting the realities of client symptoms, and encountering client sexualized behaviors may upset your equilibrium and require support from consultation and supervision. Disruptions can also occur when clients ask counselors personal questions. Understanding the purpose of the questions and non-defensive responses can enhance the counseling relationship.

Critical incidents are part of the work of a professional counselor, and they represent both opportunities and challenges for your professional growth. Supervision is critical to the understanding and managing of critical incidents. To enhance your experience of supervision, be transparent with your supervisors regarding the experiences you are having related to practicum, as critical events can be transformative in the lives of CITs.

Key Terms

Attitude/behavior-based events

Attraction-based events

Clients in crisis

Confronting client symptoms

Countertransference

Crisis

Critical incident

Developmental crisis

Disruptive critical events

Diversity-based events

Encountering client sexualized behaviors

Gender-based events

Moral distress/injury

Personal based-events

Restraint reduction

Role ambiguity

Role conflict

Role-based events

Skill-based events

The personal question

Transference

References

American Counseling Association (ACA). (2014). *2014 ACA Code of Ethics*. Alexandria, VA: Author.

Baruth, L. G., & Manning, M. I. (2016*). Multicultural counseling and psychotherapy: A lifespan approach*. New York, NY: Routledge.

Bernard, J. M., & Goodyear, R. K. (2014). *Fundamentals of clinical supervision* (5th ed.). Boston, MA: Pearson.

Bertsch, K. N., Bremer-Landau, J. D., Inman, A. G., DeBoer Kreider, E. R., Price, T. A., & DeCarlo, A. L. (2014). Evaluation of the critical events in supervision model using gender related events. *Training and Education in Professional Psychology, 8*(3), 174–181.

Caldwell, J. C., & Vera, E. M. (2010). Critical incidents in counseling psychology professionals' and trainees' social justice orientation development. *Training and Education in Professional Psychology, 4*(3), 163–176. doi:10.1037/a0019093

Gottlieb, M. C., Robinson, K., & Younggren, J. N. (2007). Multiple relations in supervision: Guidance for administrators, supervisors, and students. *Professional Psychology: Research & Practice, 38*(3), 241–247.

Hamilton, J. C., & Spruill, J. (1999). Identifying and reducing risk factors related to trainee-client sexual misconduct. *Professional Psychology: Research & Practice, 30*(3), 318–327.

Howard, E. E., Inman, A. G., & Altman, A. N. (2006). Critical incidents among novice counselor trainees. *Counselor Education and Supervision, 46*(2), 88–102. doi:10.1002/j.1556-6978.2006.tb00015.x

Jackson-Cherry, L. R., & Ertford, B. T. (2017). *Crises assessment, intervention, and prevention* (3rd ed.). Boston: Pearson.

Ladany, N., Friedlander, M. L., & Nelson, M. L. (2005). *Critical events in psychotherapy, supervision: An interpersonal approach*. Washington DC: American Psychological Association.

Maslow, A. (1971). *The further reaches of human nature*. New York, NY: Viking.

Miller, G. (2012). *Fundamentals of crisis counseling*. Hoboken, NJ: John Wiley & Sons.

Newman, B. M., & Newman, P. R. (2015). *Development through life: A psychosocial approach* (12th ed.). Stamford, CT: Cengage.

Redekop, F., Luke, C., & Malone, F. (2017). From the couch to the chair: Applying psychoanalytic theory and practice in counseling. *Journal of Counseling & Development, 95*(1), 100-109.

Weiten, W., Dunn, D. S., & Hammer, E. Y. (2017). *Psychology applied to modern life: Adjustment in the 21st century* (12th ed.). Pacific Grove, CA: Cengage.

CHAPTER 8

Developing Your
PROFESSIONAL IDENTITY

INTRODUCTION

Prosopagnosia is the inability to recognize the faces of others. In some cases, it includes not recognizing one's own face. Imagine walking past a mirror and not recognizing the person in the reflection. The ability to look at ourselves and to recognize the person we see looking back is fundamental to our identity. Prosopagnosia is a rare neurological condition; however, a more common phenomenon among new counselors in training (CITs) is the absence of a professional reflection—counselor identity. This identity does not develop overnight, nor does it develop merely as the result of obtaining a master's degree in counseling. It is a process that requires focused effort and attention, as well as intention. It is so important that this chapter is devoted to discussing it, so that one day, when you walk past a mirror of counselor identity, you will clearly recognize the counselor looking back at you.

You may already be asking questions related to counselor identity. The search for this identity may begin as early as submitting your application to the program, writing your professional biography, describing why you want to become a counselor, and speaking of your career hopes and dreams in your applicant interview. And, for most students, this search continues throughout the program. Both Chad and Marianne remember the application process for their master's programs. Chad recounts,

"I had very little concept of what it meant or would mean to be a counselor. I figured it involved helping others, but understood little beyond that. The application process was nominal for me and I made the decision somewhat out of desperation, since I struggled to find a job with some semblance of meaning once I had my bachelor's degree. I certainly had a lot of self-doubt about entering a master's program, but a false confidence in my skills based on a lack of understanding of the profession. Actually, it was not until my doctoral program that the professional identity pieces began to fall into place (sigh)."

When Marianne interviewed as part of the application for her master's in counseling program, Marianne was terrified that someone would ask her, "Well, tell me how you view counseling; exactly what is it?" Although she prepared for the interview, she describes this experience and her response.

"I kept hoping that I would gain some information from the faculty and students I talked with. I had read about counseling, but reading is not the same thing as actually knowing what it is. I made some notes and kept my responses simple. For instance, I explained that counseling was establishing a special relationship, a professional relationship, where I could help someone help him- or herself. Please don't think that I was especially smart or insightful. Even though this sounds good, I had no idea what it meant."

If your experiences are similar to most students, you have had many friends and family ask you about your area of study and your choice of career. "What exactly is counseling?" "Why did you choose to be a counselor?" "How is counseling different from being a social worker or a psychologist?" may be some of the questions you were asked. These are difficult questions to answer, aren't they?—especially when you are early in your study of counseling and just beginning your professional development. In fact, you may feel inadequate to the task of providing an answer.

On the other hand, you may know people who respond in a supportive way by stating, "I always knew you were going to be a counselor." "I am not a bit surprised since you were so good at helping others and providing advice." "You are a perfect match for this profession!" At first glance, these comments make you feel good. But on further consideration, there is an unspoken assumption that you and the speaker understand exactly what counseling is and you already have the knowledge, skills, and values to be the "perfect" professional. While you wish this were true, you are patently aware of your deficits. In fact, even in your first counseling courses, many of your beliefs and skills required critical reflection (e.g., counseling does not equal advice giving; professionals do not counsel their family members). The goals of the chapter follow.

- Increase your understanding of and appreciation for counselor development
- Learn about counseling professional identity development
- Explore your own counselor identity development

SECTION 2: PROFESSIONAL COUNSELING IDENTITY

- k. strategies for personal and professional self-evaluation and implications for practice
- l. self-care strategies appropriate to the counselor role (CACREP, 2016)

Professional Counseling Identity

Across professions, researchers and educators acknowledge there exists a trajectory in the development of most professionals. Many times, early professional work begins with education, skill building, and related field experience, which leads to graduation, licensure, and/or employment as a beginning professional. For those who remain within the same said employment or related field, these professionals mature to mid-career as they gain the necessary experience to be categorized as an expert (Ronnestad & Skovholt, 2003). The concept of professional counseling identity aids our understanding of this professional growth and development over time. In Figure 8.1, you view an illustration of this progression of experience.

FIGURE 8.1. Progression of professional counseling experiences

Lived experiences

Coursework and graduate experiences

Professional self

How might you recognize a professional counselor out in the real world? Would you know if you passed one on the street? Likely not. Unlike our mirror analogy at the beginning of the chapter, a counselor's identity is more of a set of internal characteristics that reveal themselves through certain behaviors. Defining the identity of professional counselors is an important area of focus in the counseling literature. Spurgeon (2012) confirmed the importance of this activity and affirmed the American Counseling Association's (ACA, 2014) consensus of the **definition of professional counseling**: "Counseling is a professional relationship that empowers diverse individuals, families, and groups to accomplish mental health, wellness, education, and career goals" (p. 4, col.1, para 2). Spurgeon commended the American Counseling Association's development of **20/20: A Vision for the Future of Counseling,** created for the expressed purpose of establishing standards for the profession and making public the profession's achievements. Those principles are as follows:

- Sharing a common professional identity is critical for counselors.

- Presenting ourselves as a unified profession has multiple benefits.

- Working together to improve the public perception of counseling and to advocate for professional issues will strengthen the profession.

- Creating a portability system for licensure will benefit counselors and strengthen the counseling profession.

- Expanding and promoting our research base is essential to the efficacy of professional counselors and to the public perception of the profession.

- Focusing on students and prospective students is necessary to ensure the ongoing health of the counseling profession.

- Promoting client welfare and advocating for the populations we serve is a primary focus of the counseling profession. (Spurgeon, 2012, p. 5).

The 20/20 principles were retrieved from https://www.counseling.org/about-us/about-aca/20-20-a-vision-for-the-future-of-counseling/statement-of-principles

Aspects of Professional Identity

Counselor educators and researchers suggest there exist multiple aspects of **counselor professional identity**. Nugent and Jones (2009) indicated that **professional identity** emanates both from personal attributes and professional training. These two aspects of a professional's experience, together, express a professional identity within a context in which the work takes place. This context might be a counseling private practice, agency, or school, to name a few. Other researchers suggest that professional identity includes a view of the self as a professional counselor (Brott & Myers, 1999; Gibson, Dollarhide, & Moss, 2010; Reisetter et al., 2004), a sense of competence (Moss, Gibson, & Dollarhide, 2014; Reisetter et al., 2004), acting ethically (Hendricks, 2008) or "doing what is right" (Henderson, Cook, Libby, & Zambrano, 2007), and a connection to the broader community and the professional community (Gibson et al., 2010). Janice, Jose, Kaisha, and Sam describe their counseling professional identity as they begin the second half of their practicum experience. Here is what they said. See if anything they describe resonates with you.

Janice: Although I learned a lot from my classes about what counseling is, I think a lot of my identity is being formed by watching my site supervisor. She really focuses on two parts of the job. She works with kids and establishes relationships and gains their trust. And she is constantly teaching and reteaching the school staff and teachers the role of the counselor in a school setting.

Jose: I am learning so much about my identity as it relates to my own race/ethnicity and sexual/affectional self. I don't know if this is a standard answer, but right now I see the focus switching from me to my clients and then back to me and then back to my clients. My clients see me and treat me as a counseling professional. They see me more as that professional than I see myself. Does that make any sense?

Kaisha: In our community mental health setting, there doesn't seem like a time to even consider what being a counseling professional really means. By the time I get into the building, there are a million demands on my time and I am seeing clients all day. I meet with my supervisor at the end of the day some days, or even get the supervision-in-the-hallway approach. I am just part of the counseling staff.

Sam: In our clinic, I am always able to talk with my supervisor at the end of the day. I am learning about my skills and how my background and biases influence the way I work with clients. I am also learning about licensure, and my supervisor talks with me about my future as a counselor. I am learning about different states and different settings and all the possibilities out there. My supervisor is an officer in the state counseling organization and I am helping plan a state conference.

As professional identity exists both within the individual and the professional's work context, detailed descriptions of these two aspects of professional

> ## ETHICAL CONSIDERATION 8.1
>
> Sometimes ethical practice is embedded in what counselors do. Other times, it is clearly stated, especially when issues arise. Describe some of the ethical behaviors that you see in the practicum students' descriptions of their professional identities and those embedded and explicit.

identity help describe it (Woodside, 2017) (see Figure 8.2). You saw both these reflected in the comments provided by Janice, Jose, Kaisha, and Sam.

FIGURE 8.2. Aspects of professional identity

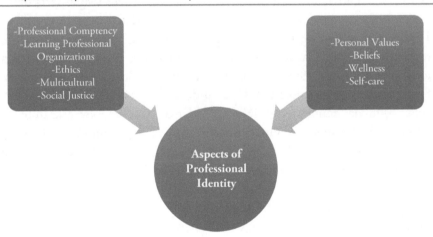

Personal Context

The **personal context** for the professional counselor constitutes the values and beliefs and wellness and self-care for said professionals.

VALUES AND BELIEFS. The **values and beliefs** that help define an individual are the basis for an individual's thoughts, feelings, and behaviors. These values and beliefs provide the foundation for personal dispositions such as commitment, openness, responsibility, integrity, self-awareness (Spurgeon, Gibbons, & Cochran, 2012), and flexibility (Luke, 2016). Translated into professional counseling practice, these are related to the "use of self" (Woodside, 2017).

WELLNESS AND SELF-CARE. These two aspects of the personal context, **wellness and self-care,** reflect an individual counselor's value of self and a willingness to devote time and energy to meeting personal needs as well as client and other work-related needs (Myers, Sweeney, and Witmer, 2000). Maintaining a lifestyle that balances work with other personal commitments such as health, family and relationships, and spirituality, contributes to positive work attitudes and protects the counselor from burnout, compassion fatigue, and vicarious trauma (Painter & Woodside, 2016).

Professional or Work-Related Context

PROFESSIONAL OR WORK-RELATED CONTEXT. Professional or work-related context represents knowledge and skills, continuing education and lifelong learning, organizational definitions, professional ethical orientation, and social justice orientation—all of which guide professional practice.

PROFESSIONAL COMPETENCY: KNOWLEDGE AND SKILLS. The essential **knowledge and skills** necessary to the work of the professional counselor are established by the Council for Accreditation of Counseling and Related Programs (CACREP), regulatory bodies, such as the National Board for Certified Counselors (NBCC), and state licensure boards, and academic programs (Practicum in Counseling Handbook and Practicum Syllabus). Related to professional competency, the 2014 ACA Code of Ethics states, "Counselors practice only within the boundaries of their competence, based on their education, training, supervised experience, state and national professional credentials, and appropriate professional experience" (American Counseling Association, 2014, Section C.2.a.).

CONTINUING EDUCATION AND LIFELONG LEARNING. Professional counselors commit to seeking ways to enhance their professional growth and development (American Counseling Association, 2014) through **continuing education and lifelong learning.** In fact, professional identity reflects a dynamic process that moves novices from the boundary to full participation in the counseling community (Luke & Goodrich, 2010; Woodside, Paulus, & Ziegler, 2009). It is also continuous and lifelong. Continuing education comprises activities and education that extend the counselor's professional growth and development. These can include conference programs, workshops, courses, supervision, reading programs, teaching, and scholarship and research.

ORGANIZATIONAL DEFINITIONS. Organizational definitions help us better define counseling and the counseling professional. For example, the American Counseling Association, the Council for Accreditation of Counseling and Related Programs (CACREP), the National Board for Certified Counselors (NBCC), and state licensing boards help define counseling. These definitions define and describe the framework that guides the work and the ethical principles of counseling, the curriculum for education and training of counselors, and the responsibilities counselors have to themselves, their clients, their colleagues, their work context, and the community (local and broad) in which they live and work.

PROFESSIONAL ETHICAL ORIENTATION. Professions offer to their members ethical guidelines that serve as a **professional ethical orientation**. Members of the profession are expected to support and utilize these in their day-to-day practice. The 2014 ACA Code of Ethics defines the values and principles by which professional counselors work and presents nine major aspects of ethical dimensions of counseling ethics. In the Code of Ethics preamble, this code articulates core professional values:

> Professional values are an important way of living out an ethical commitment.
> The following are core professional values of the counseling profession:
>
> 1. Enhancing human development throughout the life span;
> 2. Honoring diversity and embracing a multicultural approach in support of the worth, dignity, potential, and uniqueness of people within their social and cultural contexts;
> 3. Promoting social justice;
> 4. Safeguarding the integrity of the counselor-client relationship; and
> 5. Practicing in a competent and ethical manner. (American Counseling Association, 2014, p. 3, para. 2)

SOCIAL JUSTICE ORIENTATION Although the practice of social justice represents a fundamental value of the counseling professions' ethical orientation, within the framework of the professional identity of a counselor, its importance demands special attention. Using a social justice orientation, professional counselors commit to the recognition and understanding that power and privilege are inherent in social, economic, and political environments. Thus, counselors' advocacy and attention to social justice provide a counter to the destructive practices of oppression and provide counseling and counseling-related work that is founded on the principles of social justice.

A way to understand these aspects of professional identity is to apply them to your own development. In Reflection Question 8.1, you can begin to assess the learning opportunities and experiences with which you have engaged thus far and how those have helped you understand what it means to be a professional counselor.

REFLECTION QUESTION 8.1

MY INTERACTIONS WITH THE ASPECTS OF PROFESSIONAL IDENTITY

Which of the following have you experienced thus far in your training: explored your own personal values and beliefs; discussed and/or engaged in wellness and/or self-care activities; participated in building counseling competencies and skills; learned about or participated in professional organizations; learned about or engaged in ethical decision making and ethical practice; learned about or engaged in multicultural-related thoughts, feelings, and behaviors; learned about or engaged in advocacy and social justice?

One of the goals of Reflection Question 8.1 is to help you link the concept of professional identity to more concrete thoughts, feelings, and behaviors of the professional counselor. From the stories that you told, could you tell when you were in the middle of a change in your own development? The following questions in Cultural Consideration 8.1 and Ethical Consideration 8.2 may help you articulate this change.

Professional identity manifests itself in the world of practice and may occur while counseling clients, working with colleagues, and working in the community. Because professional identity is dynamic, your own professional identity is changing and will continue to do so while you are in your academic program, and throughout your entire career as a professional counselor. Understanding the process of professional identity development raises your own your awareness of it and may help you anticipate the ways in which your professional identity development may occur.

CULTURAL CONSIDERATION 8.1

AND ETHICAL CONSIDERATION 8.2

Review how you answered the question in Reflection Question 8.1. Based on your responses, answer the following:

Where you were making a shift in how you saw yourself and saw your development as a professional? Talk about how ethics and cultural diversity play a part of this development.

How Counseling Professional Identity Develops

Researchers in counselor education and counseling psychology suggest several ways that professional identity development unfolds. For example, conducting a longitudinal study of counselors and therapists, Ronnestad and Skovholt (2003) identified six phases of professional development: lay helper, beginning student, advanced student, novice professional, experienced professional, and senior professional. From their results, they suggested several themes of professional development including (a) shifts in focus of attention, (b) changes in emotional functioning, (c) the critical nature of professional reflection for continuous development, and (d) the influences of professional development. In agreement in their discussion of a study of school counselors, Brott and Meyers (1999) stated that the initial professional development begins with the counselor education program, continues during the early professional years, and persists throughout the professional career. They described **professional counselor identity development** as "a process rather than an outcome" (Brott & Meyers, 1999, p. 339) where, over time, practicing counselors, personally and professionally, view themselves as such. It is key for understanding your own development that you look closely at the ways in which you have changed during your involvement in your academic program.

In fact, as you ready yourself for your practicum experience, you may be asking, "What is my current professional identity? How do I think my practicum experience will influence that identity? What part will my faculty supervisor, site supervisor, site colleagues, and practicum peers play how I think about myself as a counselor? How will I intentionally or inadvertently affect my own development?" The **process view of professional counselor identity development,** developed by Gibson and colleagues (2010), is useful as a way of viewing your own development. It focuses on the professional identity development that CITs experience during their academic program.

Process View of Professional Counselor Identity Development

Gibson and colleagues (2010) process view of professional counselor identity development, resulted from their research of four groups of CITs. Specifically, the four groups of counseling students included (a) those CITs just accepted into a counselor education program, (b) CITs prior to beginning practicum, (c) CITs prior to internship, and (d) CITs after internship and prior to graduation. The purpose of their research was to describe a theory of professional counselor identity development for counseling students across the span of their involvement in the counselor education academic program. The researchers were looking for the tasks required of students that engaged in what the authors called **identity transformation**. Gibson and colleagues (2010) labeled these three tasks transformational tasks. According to the Oxford English Dictionary (2017), the definition of transform is "the act of changing in form, shape, appearance; metamorphosis." Look back at the descriptions that Janice, Jose, Kaisha, and Sam provided related to their early practicum experience; each talked about transformations or changes they were experiencing.

Janice recounted learning about counseling identity from her site supervisor, watching her focus on gaining trust and establishing relationships with the students with whom she works and helping administrators and staff understand the work of the professional school counselor. Jose's focus is more personal as he struggles to view his own race, ethnicity, and sexual preference and those of his clients. He is also learning that his clients see him as a counseling professional; Jose's clients have a stronger sense of his professionalism than he does. Kaisha's professional development is grounded in her participation in the day-to-day activities of her agency. She identifies with the work and being part of a team or staff. Sam is learning about counseling professional development in two ways: first in his discussion with his supervisor about his own biases and how they influence his work with clients. He is also learning about licensure and portability issues. Each of these four practicum students are involved with counseling professional identity development; they focus on different aspects of the personal context and the professional and work-related context (see Figure 8.2).

Three Transformational Tasks

The three transformational tasks that, according to Gibson and colleagues (2010), relate and support counseling professional identity are (a) **definition of counseling**, (b) **responsibility for professional growth**, and (c) **transformation to systemic identity**. Each of these three tasks represents an important part of a counselor's growth and development (see Figure 8.3).

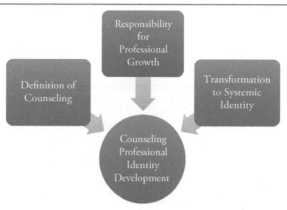

Descriptions of each of the three transformational tasks and concrete ways to relate these tasks to the experiences you are having in practicum help clarify your own professional identity development.

Transformational Task 1: Definition of Counseling

This task represents a CIT's understanding of the work and work-related tasks of the profession and those who work as counselors (Gibson et al., 2010). This type of understanding, related to professional definitions, is similar to those suggested by the ACA's consensus definition described earlier and ACA's 20/20: A Vision for the Future of Counseling. All levels of CITs, from those joining the counselor education program through pre-graduation, agree that the public is unaware of what professional counselors do in their work, may not see counseling as a favorable activity or profession, and cannot distinguish between counseling and other professions. The task of defining counseling, for CITs at all levels, might be reflected in the following statements:

- When I talk about studying to be a counselor, my friends just give me a blank look. Even when I try to explain the work, they can't envision it.

- I am taking classes in graduate anthropology, just to add some breadth to my studies in graduate school. In that class, no one wants to talk about counseling; some of the students are scared of it. Maybe they think I am going to judge, diagnosis, or analyze them.

- Here I am about to graduate, and, I hate to admit this, but when someone asks me the difference between counseling and social work and psychology, I am still not sure how to explain the distinctions.

- I used to know the ACA definition by heart. And I kept the definition of counseling provided by the author of our Introduction to Counseling textbook written in my assignment notebook. Now that I am in internship, I define counseling much more in terms of who I am and what I do.

Let's look at your own experiences related to defining counseling.

EXPERIENTIAL ACTIVITY 8.1. DEFINITION OF COUNSELING

Have you been in a situation(s) where you were asked to how explain the nature of counseling, provide a definition of counseling, or describe your role as a counselor? What was that like for you?

Transformational Task 2: Responsibility for Professional Growth

This task represents how professional counselors understand their own professional growth, the influences on that growth, and, ultimately, the individuals who assume the responsibility for that growth. Examples of two types of responses might be represented by these two questions: "What do I need to do to meet the requirements of this assignment? What do I need to do to get better at this work?" Here are statements you might make about your own professional growth and identity, categorized by experience in the program. Note the shift in responsibility as the novice CITs rely more on external sources and the advanced CITs increase their dependence on self. External validation remains important for the advanced CITs.

Novice CITs

- I can't learn enough in my classes. My professors know so much about counseling and about working with clients.

- I wish our skills class was smaller. I feel like I need feedback from my instructor every time we practice a skill. I can't get that kind of expert response from another student.

- I am never sure if what I am doing is correct. Even when I look at my theories tapes, many times I see only a part of what I am supposed to see related to my response to the client.

Advanced CITs

- In internship, I don't always have help with clients in the moment. I am learning to think on my feet and be flexible about what I expected of a session and what happened.

- I found two seminars in a nearby city that focus on the clients I want to work with. I invited my supervisor to go along. I want to develop my expertise in working with addictions, especially teens.

- I find myself seeking supervision and help, not just from my site supervisor, but from other agency colleagues and my peers in internship.

- Oh, I had a compliment from a mother for the positive changes she sees in her daughter. The mother attributes those changes to my work with her. I felt great about those kind words. And last week was a difficult week, so I needed to hear something good.

Experiential Activity 8.2 helps you and your classmates explore the changes you are making in your responsibility for professional growth.

EXPERIENTIAL ACTIVITY 8.2. RESPONSIBILITY FOR PROFESSIONAL GROWTH

Could you describe a situation where there was a clear responsibility for your professional growth (e.g., your instructor, your site supervisor, your faculty supervisor, you)? What did you notice about who assumes the responsibility for your professional growth?

Transformational Task 3: Transformation to System Identity

The transformation to system identity describes the ways in which CITs judge their own identity relative to the professional counseling community. For novice CITs, sources of this evaluation or validation of their professional identity include validation from supervisors and clients and certification and licensure. Advanced CITs are beginning to construct their own identity and integrate it with the community in which they work. The comments of novice and advanced CITs will help you understand the transformation to systemic identity.

Novice CITs

- I remember before I began practicum, my instructors told me, "Don't worry, you are ready to begin." I trusted their judgment.

- When I think about being a counselor, I think about having my certification as a school counselor. That seems forever away!

- My clients treat me just like they treat my site supervisor. What if they are wrong?

- I am modeling myself after my site supervisor. I want to become a counselor just like her.

Advanced CITs

- When I look at who I am as a counselor, I can see many parts. I am a mixture of my professionals, one in particular, my internship supervisor, and myself. Then there is a little bit of my mom thrown in. I guess, in the end, I am my own counselor-self.

- I have been studying for the national exam. Studying has given me a different way of looking at who I am as a counselor. I am looking at myself and what I know against what the test says I should know.

- I learned an entirely different way of being a counselor at my internship site. This is my third placement. I am glad that I had three of them. Each site has required some different skills and challenged me in different ways. In this third site, working with foster care parents and providing in-home family counseling, I have built on the skills I learned in my first two placements.

Note that with the advanced CITs, their comments reflect the integration of their experiences and their personal and professional characteristics as counselors with the environment in which they work. Let's look at your own transformation of identity reflected in the Experiential Activity 8.3.

EXPERIENTIAL ACTIVITY 8.3. TRANSFORMATION TO SYSTEM IDENTITY

Who defines your professional identity: supervisors or clients, licensure or certification, your own definition, or the definition prescribed by the community in which you work? How do you communicate this identity?

CULTURAL CONSIDERATION 8.2

AND ETHICAL CONSIDERATION 8.3

The interactions that you have and the relationships you build with your supervisors and the individuals with whom you work represent a critical aspect of your professional growth and development, as does the environment in which you study and then work. Think about your own teachers, supervisors, and practicum setting in light of what you learned about acting ethically and being sensitive to multicultural and social justice issues. What have you learned from positive example? Negative example? What have you taught others? How has your academic counseling program and your practicum site influenced your commitments to ethical behavior and social justice?

Putting It All Together

The focus and contents of this chapter require a looking inward rather than an engagement in an activity or action. Counseling professional identity development is a critical component to learning to be a counselor and is a lifelong process that occurs over time. Sam, in a recent conversation with his faculty supervisor, Dr. Kim, demonstrates his counseling professional identity development (see Transcription 8.1).

TRANSCRIPTION 8.1. DR. KIM AND SAM DISCUSS SAM'S COUNSELING PROFESSIONAL IDENTITY DEVELOPMENT

Dr. Kim: Sam, thanks for joining me today for this supervision meeting. I know this is our second meeting this week, but at this time in the practicum experience, I always want to talk with my students about their counseling identity development. After reading this chapter, I always think it is a good time to have this discussion.

Sam: I think that it helped that you talked with us earlier in class about your own identity. You know we all see you as the perfect counselor. No, don't laugh. I mean it. Like, you just have so much experience.

Dr. Kim: Well I do have experience. But you know I am still developing. In fact, our class has really helped me grow. Remember two weeks ago, when we talked about the child who had been taken away twice from the family? That child was threatening to kill himself if he had to leave his family again. Janice and her site supervisor were so torn, knowing this was about to happen. I found myself tossing and turning as I thought about the options. I find myself always in development about ethical challenges.

Dr. Kim: So, Sam, could you take a moment and draw out your current thinking about professional identity development and your place in it? I brought some paper and pens, colors and magic markers, and colored pencils. I also brought some colored paper and scissors if you want to use them. We have an hour, so take about 15 minutes for your drawing if you would like. Don't go for the perfect drawing. Feel free to be as creative as you wish to express your thoughts and feelings about your own counseling professional identity.
Dr. Kim observes Sam as Sam thinks and draws and thinks and draws.
Sam begins awkwardly and haltingly and then becomes completely absorbed in his drawing.
Dr. Kim reminds Sam when there are five minutes remaining.

Sam: (looking up at Dr. Kim), I think time is up. I was really nervous about this meeting and what I was going to say. You sure caught me by surprise. Now I can't wait to hear what I have to say (laughs).
Dr. Kim and Sam laugh together.

Dr. Kim: Sam, I would like for you to just talk with me about your drawing. Take as much time as you would like. I am going to make some notes. I may stop you and ask for clarification. But this meeting is yours.

Sam: Where to begin? Maybe I will start with what I didn't draw. …
Sam talks for 20 minutes.

Dr. Kim: Sam, before we end our meeting, let's focus on three things: First, from reading this chapter and working on and talking about your drawing, what are five aspects of your professional identity development that stand out for you? Second, where do you want to go with your development? Third, what assistance do you need to support your identity development? I can pace our discussion so we will get through all three of these questions.
Dr. Kim and Sam focus on these three questions.

Dr. Kim: Sam, we are going to close this supervision session in a familiar way. As we come to the end of our time today, there are a few things that stand out to me. First, I was impressed how seriously you took this discussion today, and by how creative you were as you thought about your own development and then Gibson's process model and then your own development. I heard you talk about yourself in a different way, taking ownership for your own learning. And you seemed more confident about the differences between you and your site supervisor. Early in your practicum, you seemed to think that there was just one way to work with clients, and that was your site supervisor's way. I still hear you wishing you had more freedom to take a more Rogerian and less behavioral approach with the clinic's clients. …

Dr. Kim: Sam, let me ask you, "What will you take from this supervisory session?"

Sam: I know we only have a few minutes until close. This was so different than I thought it would be. I see now that all the work on the process model was just a way to prepare me to think about my own professional identity. I think professional identity for me was lost in the midst of everything else I was learning in classes and in practicum. I really didn't know what it meant. Even though I am still not exactly sure what it means, it still feels sort of mushy. Since I was able to draw my identity, it feels more like I understand my own development. Bet Dr. Smoot wouldn't take my drawing as an answer to his last test question (laugh).

Dr. Kim: In closing, Sam, how do you think today's supervision will influence your work in practicum?

Sam: Oh, Dr. Kim, you know I always dread that question. I just don't think fast enough to answer that. What if I come with an answer when we have supervision next week? We can begin with that.

Dr. Kim: Fair enough, Sam. And thanks for the effort and insights today. Call me if you need me.

Now it is time to focus on your own counseling professional identity development (see Reflection Question 8.2). Since professional identity development is an on-going professional task, you may want to answer this question on a regular basis. Considering identity development supports your own professional growth and development as a counselor.

REFLECTION QUESTION 8.2

APPLYING THE PROCESS VIEW OF PROFESSIONAL IDENTITY DEVELOPMENT TO YOUR OWN DEVELOPMENT

How would like for your counselor professional identity to develop during your practicum experience?

Learning about your counseling professional identity development and your own identity development is an ongoing process. It is important to recognize that each aspect of your professional development represents a unique time in your personal and professional life. Our journaling activity for this chapter will help you think about your identity development more deeply.

Summary

This chapter asks you to look inward and begin a reflective examination of your own counseling professional identity development. At this point in your growth as a counselor, the foundation for your counseling identity is the previously lived experiences you bring to your study of counseling. Your coursework and graduate experiences integrate with your earlier experiences to help build your professional self.

In order to develop a professional self, first you begin to understand what counseling is. The American Counseling Association offers the following definition: "Counseling is a professional relationship that empowers diverse individuals, families, and groups to accomplish mental health, wellness, education, and career goals" (p. 4, col.1, para 2). ACA's 20/20: A Vision for the Future of Counseling also contributes to our understanding of counseling as a profession.

Second, although understanding the nature and definition of counseling is important to your professional growth, understanding professional identity and how it develops also offers a way to explore your own growth. Looking at two aspects of this growth, personal attributes and professional training, provides insights. And, remember, these two aspects of your experience as a professional express a professional identity within a context in which the work takes place. This context might be a counseling private practice, agency, or school. Aspects of professional identity include personal-related values and beliefs and wellness and self-care, as well as professional-related competencies, lifelong learning, definitions of the profession, an ethical orientation, and a social justice orientation.

Gibson and colleagues' (2010) model of professional identity development, process view of professional counselor identity development, provides each of us a way to view our own professional identity development. Gibson and colleagues presented three transformational tasks: (a) definition of counseling, (b) responsibility for professional growth, and (c) transformation to systemic identity. Each of these three tasks represents an important part of a counselor's growth and development. Using the model to understand your professional identity development allows you intentionally shape your own identity development. The chapter closed with activities to apply the concepts introduced and anticipate and plan your professional identity development during your practicum experience.

Key Terms

20/20: A vision for the future of counseling

Continuing education and lifelong learning

Counselor professional identity

Definition of counseling

Definition of professional counseling

Identity transformation

Organizational definitions

Personal context

Process view of professional counselor identity development

Professional counselor identity development

Professional competency (knowledge and skills)

Professional ethical orientation

Professional identity

Professional or work-related context

Professional values

Prosopagnosia

Responsibility for professional growth

Social justice orientation

Transformation to systemic identity

Values and beliefs

Wellness and self-care

References

American Counseling Association (ACA). (2014). *2014 ACA Code of Ethics. Alexandria, VA: Author.*

Brott, P. E., & Myers, J. E. (1999). Development of professional school counselor identity: A grounded theory. Professional School Counseling, 2(5), 339–348.

Council for Accreditation of Counseling and Related Educational Programs (CACREP) *Section 2: Professional Counseling Identity.* Retrieved from https://www.cacrep.org/section-2-professional-counseling-identity/

Gibson, D. M., Dollarhide, C. T., & Moss, J. M. (2010). Professional identity development: A grounded theory of transformational tasks of new counselors. *Counselor Education & Supervision, 50*(1), 21–38. doi:10.1002/j.1556-6978.2010.tb00106.x

Henderson, P., Cook, K., Libby, M., & Zambrano, E. (2007). "Today I feel like a professional school counsellor." *Guidance & Counseling, 21*(3), 128–142.

Hendricks, C. B. (2008). Introduction: Who are we? The role of ethics in shaping counselor identity. *The Family Journal: Counseling and Therapy for Families and Couples, 16*(3), 258–260. doi:10.1177/1066480708317725

Luke, C. C. (2016). *Neuroscience for counselor and therapists: Integrating the science of mind and brain.* Thousand Oaks, CA: SAGE.

Luke, M., & Goodrich, K. M. (2010). Chi Sigma Iota chapter leadership and professional identity development in early career counselors. *Counselor Education and Supervision, 50*(1), 56–78.

Moss, J. M., Gibson, D. M., & Dollarhide, C. T. (2014). Professional identity development: A grounded theory of transformational tasks of counselors. *Journal of Counseling and Development, 92*(1), 3–12. doi:10.1002/j.1556-6676.2014.00124.x

Myers, J. E., Sweeney, T. J., & Witmer, J. M., The wheel of wellness counseling for wellness: A holistic model for treatment planning. *Journal of Counseling & Development, 28*(3), 251–266. doi:10.1002/j.1556-6676.2000.tb01906.x

Nugent, F. A., & Jones, K. D. (2009). *Introduction to the profession of counseling* (5th ed.). Upper Saddle River, NJ: Pearson.

Oxford English Dictionary. (2017). Transformation. Retrieved from http://www.oed.com.proxy.lib.utk.edu:90/view/Entry/204743?redirectedFrom=transformation#eid

Painter, E., & Woodside, M. (2016). Vicarious trauma: Emotional disruption and approaches to coping. *Counseling & Wellness: A Professional Counseling Journal, 5.* Retrieved from http://openknowledge.nau.edu/view/divisions/CWJ.html

Reisetter, M., Korcuska. J. S., Yexley, M., Bonds. D., Nikels, H., & McHeniy, W. (2004). Counselor educators and qualitative research: Affirming a research identity. *Counselor Education and Supervision. 44*(1), 2–16.

Ronnestad, M. H., & Skovholt, T. M. (2003). The journey of the counselor and the therapist: Research findings and perspectives on professional development. *Journal of Career Development, 30*(1), 5–44. doi:10.1023/A:1025173508081

Spurgeon, S. (2012). Counselor identity—A national imperative. *Journal of Professional Counseling, Practice, Theory, and Research, 39*(1), 3–16.

Spurgeon, S., Gibbons, M. M., & Cochran, J. L. (2012). *Creating personal dispositions for a professional counseling program. Counseling & Values, 57*(1), 96–108. doi:10.1002/j.2161-007X.2012.00011.x

Woodside, M. (2017). *The human service internship experience: Helping students find their way.* Thousand Oaks, CA: SAGE.

Woodside, M., Paulus, T., & Ziegler, M. (2009) The experience of school counseling internship through the lens of communities of practice. *Counselor Education and Supervision, 49*(1), 20–38.

Your Professional
DEVELOPMENT

INTRODUCTION

Chapter 9 focuses on an important aspect of becoming a counselor, that of professional development. This **counselor professional development** reflects the gaining and improving of the knowledge, skills, and values related to counseling and helping others. Counselor professional development requires focused effort and attention, as well as intention, and occurs over the lifespan of professional engagement. The foundations for this development include early lived experience and are enhanced both by coursework as well as related professional experiences. Counselor professional development occurs in parallel to counselor identity development.

As a counselor in training (CIT), you are patently aware of the importance of the knowledge, skills, and values you need to participate in your practicum experience. In fact, the fear and anxiety related to working with a site supervisor and with clients reflects the uncertainty you may feel about your own development of knowledge, skills, and values. By now you have experienced some success as you counseled clients in your setting. You have also encountered counseling situations where you felt your knowledge and skills lacking and/or your values challenged. You may well have observed that your confidence in your ability to help your clients tracks very closely with your increased mastery in these areas. The goals for the chapter follow.

- **Learn about aspects of professional development according to the IDM**
- **Use the IDM to determine the status of your own professional development**
- **Learn how the IDM is integrated with the supervisory experience**

ASSOCIATED CACREP STANDARDS

Section 3: PROFESSIONAL PRACTICE

Professional practice, which includes practicum and internship, provides for the application of theory and the development of counseling skills under supervision. These experiences will provide opportunities for students to counsel clients who represent the ethnic and demographic diversity of their community.

PRACTICUM

- F. Students complete supervised counseling practicum experiences that total a minimum of 100 clock hours over a full academic term that is a minimum of 10 weeks.

- G. Practicum students complete at least 40 clock hours of direct service with actual clients that contributes to the development of counseling skills (CACREP, 2016a)

Section 2: PROFESSIONAL COUNSELING IDENTITY COUNSELING CURRICULUM

- m. the role of counseling supervision in the profession (CACREP, 2016b)

The Integrated Developmental Model of Supervision (IDM)

Just as there are models that describe and illustrate counseling professional identity development, there are models that represent the ways in which counselors grow and develop throughout their careers. First, **developmental models** for counselors approach growth in terms of stages or "divisions of a journey or process" (Oxford English Dictionary, 2017). There are several assumptions made when discussing development as a series of stages, including the belief that change takes place over time. See Figure 9.1 for a graphical representation of this idea.

Recall throughout your weeks in practicum the different ways in which you have marked this record of your self-awareness, other-awareness, motivation, and autonomy. As you review your assessments, you can begin to see your development in stages of growth and development. You may discover yourself in a similar situation as Janice: "Look at my sense of autonomy; it is all over the place. The first three weeks I didn't want to let my supervisor out of my sight, but by the fourth week I wanted to strike out on my own. I thought I was ready for independent work and then I had two suicide risk assessments in one week. Don't laugh, but I went scurrying back to my site supervisor. In a hurry." (For a detailed account of Janice's experience with suicide risk assessment see Transcription 9.1.)

Second, another assumption that undergirds a stage model is its multidimensional nature. As you learned from the process view of professional counselor identity development model, development is complex. The integrated model of supervision (IDM) (Stoltenberg & McNeil, 2011; Stoltenberg, McNeil, & Delworth, 1998) is one such model that integrates three aspects of development: levels of competence, overarching structures, and specific domains of competence. Using the IDM uses several concepts to help you articulate your experience of professional growth. Sam describes his first experience using the major concepts of the IDM: "Boy is this complicated. My supervisor suggested that I take each of the concepts separately to help make sense of each. I didn't try to understand too much at once. One week I focused on my motivation and my skills the next. When trying to learn about and then implement the IDM, I would advise you to go slowly."

Third, a developmental model is based on the supposition that growth is predictable. This will help you and your supervisors anticipate many of your experiences of growth as you work with clients for the first time. One way to test this assumption is to consider your own experiences in practicum as they relate to your peers. You may recall conversations you have had with them. Sometimes, as you listened to them, you thought, "Oh my; that is exactly how I felt!" Other times, you may have felt your experiences appeared unique. Remember in Chapter 5, Kaisha encountered an ethical issue when her client Robin was using marijuana in front of her 14-year-old daughter. Jose, Janice, and Sam all had different reactions to Kaisha's situation. What was predictable was they were all struggling with the issue Kaisha confronted, unsure how to use the ethical decision-making model, and learning how to think about various perspectives on one situation.

FIGURE 9.1. Progression of counselor development

Lived experiences

Coursework and graduate experiences

Professional counselor identity

Professional knowledge, skill, values

Fourth and finally, using the IDM provides you a way to help you understand your own development as a professional counselor, to help you explain the practicum experience and your place in it, to view CACREP and program practicum goals from a different perspective, and to ask for supervision that matches your developmental needs. By the end of this chapter, you will view the IDM as a tool you can use to articulate your own development. In addition, you can use aspects of the IDM to guide your requests for and responses to supervision.

In summary, the IDM is a tool that will help you do the following:

- Organize how you reflect on your practicum experience
- Anticipate the ways in which you will grow and develop
- Integrate past experiences and classroom learning with your current practicum work
- Generate new understandings and perceptions of your professional growth
- Normalize your own work in practicum with your peers
- Discover a common language you can use to discuss practicum with your faculty supervisor, site supervisor, and peers

The IDM is complex. Before you begin to read about it, consider Janice, Jose, Kaisha, and Sam's experiences with it.

Janice: Even though the IDM uses a great deal of detail to help describe professional development, by the time I read through this chapter, I could handle the detail.

Jose: I have told you before about my site supervisor. I reviewed the overarching concepts and I got feedback about my work at the site.

Kaisha: I really had a hard time with understanding the IDM and grading myself on my work in practicum. Some of my classmates really liked it, but especially with the eight domains, these represented all the things I don't know yet. And, I am not sure I will learn them when I am in internship.

Sam: You know that I am working at the campus clinic. I think because this is such a controlled environment and because my site supervisor is directly linked to our academic program, I am able to benefit more from the study of the IDM. My placement and my work with clients is based on what I need to learn as it relates to the IDM. Now that doesn't mean that I am perfect in the eight domain areas, but it does mean that my supervisor and I can focus my work on one or two at a time.

Overview of the IDM

According to the IDM, CITs' levels of competence can be categorized as **levels of competence**, **overarching structures**, and **specific domains**. Levels of competence include **level one**, **level two**, and **level three** (Stoltenberg & McNeill, 2011). Three overarching structures, (a) **motivation**, (b) **autonomy**, and (c) **self-** and **other awareness** represent ways to measure professional growth and development for each of the three levels. Figure 9.2 presents the levels of competence (levels 1, 2, and 3) within the framework of the three overarching structures (motivation, autonomy, and self- and other awareness). Figure 9.3 illustrates the eight specific domains of counseling and therapy. These are intervention skills, assessment techniques, interpersonal assessment, client conceptualization, individual differences, theoretical orientation, treatments plans and goals, and professional ethics (Stoltenberg, McNeill, & Delworth, 1998).

You will learn about the IDM and begin to understand the three primary aspects of the IDM and how they relate to your learning experiences. These are the three overarching structures, a description of the three levels of competence and how they manifest themselves for each of the overarching structures, and a brief description of the eight specific domains.

FIGURE 9.2. IDM levels of competence

- High motivation
- Low autonomy
- Limited self-and other awareness

Level 1

Level 2

- Fluctuating motivation
- Transitioning autonomy
- Developing awareness

- Stable motivation
- Autonomous, but seeks help when needed
- Self-and other aware

Level 3

Stoltenberg & McNeil, *IDM Supervision: An Integrated Developmental Model for Supervising Counselors and Therapists.* Copyright © 2011 by Taylor & Francis.

FIGURE 9.3. IDM eight domains

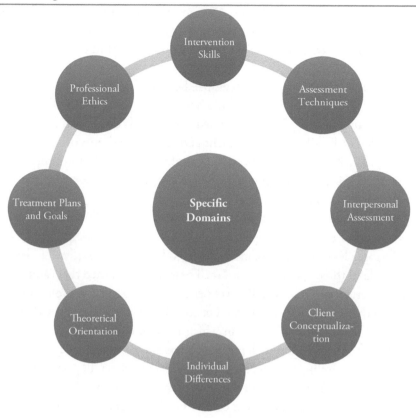

Overarching Structures

Overarching structures provide you, the practicum student, and your supervisors with a way to monitor various aspects of your performance as a counselor and your engagement in your experience of learning to be a counselor.

Let's look at the formal definition that Stoltenberg and McNeill (2011) provide for the overarching structures.

MOTIVATION. "I want to do this work." This overarching structure represents a CIT's expressed obligation or responsibility to professional development. It is an intentional commitment to gain knowledge, gain skills, and develop an understanding of the client and the client's world. Motivation means intense engagement in the learning process, a commitment to professional identity development as a counselor, and the dedication of time and energy to learning to be a counselor. Motivation can be externally directed (e.g., grades and praise) and internally directed (e.g., a sense of accomplishment and feeling positive about helping others). Motivation shifts across levels of competence.

AUTONOMY. "I am able to do this work." This overarching structure refers to a CIT's ability to act independently in the tasks and responsibilities assigned during practicum. A willingness to work independently may be related to confidence in performing tasks assigned and assuming new roles. Novices may be more dependent on supervisors and colleagues for guidance, especially during the first weeks in practicum. A sense of autonomy fluctuates depending on the skills required, novel situations, and the severity of client issues. An increasing sense of autonomy develops over time with an expanded knowledge base and skill development.

SELF- AND OTHER AWARENESS. "I recognize how my 'stuff' can interact with my client's 'stuff' in this work." This overarching structure refers to where the focus of the CIT's attentions reside. For example, often the CIT is preoccupied with a focus on the self rather than the client, especially as a novice unfamiliar with the client and few counseling skills on which to depend. The awareness can shift from self to client and insight into the self and other to be integrated into an empathetic helping relationship. This self- and other awareness contains aspects of cognitive awareness and emotional awareness.

How each of the three overarching structures manifests itself differs within each of the three levels of competence. For example, as represented in Figure 9.2, Stoltenberg and McNeill (2011) describe each of the three levels in terms of motivation: level one, **high motivation**; level two, **fluctuating motivation**; level three, **stable motivation**. These authors warned that categorizing CITs and counselors with experience at one specific level belies the complexity of professional development and growth. Using the broad category of a level of competence is too simplistic and fails to account for confidence, skill level, and the context in which the counseling occurs. For example, a CIT may develop confidence in working with pregnant teens and demonstrate a level two competence. However, even while counseling individuals in that population, as a CIT confronts a young woman threatening suicide for the first time, he or she may return to a novice or level one status. Reflection Question 9.1 will help you think about your own view of the overarching structures of the IDM.

Levels of Competence

Reviewing the general characteristics of the three levels of competence will help you understand the differences among each. And, as you think about your own development, remember that CITs may fluctuate between levels. Here is a description of this fluctuation.

Level One

Many CITs entering the counseling academic program and beginning practicum reflect level one counselor development. You can expect to exhibit many of the characteristics of level one. At this point in your practicum, you may also see an occasional shift from level one to level two. At the beginning of practicum, much of what novices know they have learned from their lived experiences and courses and experiences in the classroom (see Figure 9.1). However, by this time in practicum, you may be involved (sometimes deeply involved) performing the roles and responsibilities as a counselor. And, by now, you have adjusted to a new work environment (your practicum site), learned about expectations as a practicum student at a new site, participated in faculty and site supervision, and initiated work with real clients.

Within level one, CITs have strong emotions, such as excitement and enthusiasm for beginning their work as counselors in the world of work, and experience anxiety about their competence to do so (Stoltenberg & McNeill, 2011). As you look at the IDM's levels of competence, you will be able to assess your own level of competence according to the IDM. Understanding level one is especially important since it reflects the levels of competence of the novice.

LEVEL ONE MOTIVATION. Within the level one stage, CITs are highly motivated and enthusiastic about the practicum experience (Stoltenberg & McNeill, 2011). Here are some comments that describe CITs' experience at this level. The comments begin with CITs as they begin their practicum experience and end with those at the conclusion of their practicum experience.

- I am so excited to begin practicing my skills beyond the classroom. I am nervous, but ready, all at the same time.

- When I think about practicum, a part of me begins to think about my first job after I graduate. This is one step for me to do what I want to do: to work as a counselor.

- You know when I had to receive feedback in class, I was terrified at times. Now, I am really worried about having faculty and site supervisors tell me what I am doing wrong—and if clients can see I am just learning.

- Here, I am almost at the end of my practicum. I finally feel that I can do the work. I have clients and it seems to me I am doing real counseling. I know I am gaining skills. I don't feel so much pressure to learn, learn, learn.

- My supervisor thinks that I am ready to work with adults now. This is a new population for me. I think that I need to concentrate on my work with children rather than start all over again.

These comments from CITs reflect the dynamic nature of motivation within the same level of competence, Level One. For some, early on the motivation is high to practice skills that facilitate client growth. As comfort and confidence increases, many CITs at this level may resist new experiences; rather they want to remain with work that reinforces their competencies.

LEVEL ONE AUTONOMY. For CITs, autonomy at level one means a reliance on faculty, site supervisors, and colleagues for support and supervision (Stoltenberg & McNeill, 2011). They shy away from independent activity and prefer shadowing or working as a team with the experts.

Comments such as those that follow reflect how CITs talk about their sense of autonomy in practicum.

- A group of us were talking about practicum yesterday. We are meeting with our faculty supervisor today and we have a million questions. We want to nail down as much about the practicum experience as we can.

- In practicum class, we talked about what a good orientation to a practicum site would look like. I am going to take that list to my new site supervisor. It looks like orientation is critical to beginning well.

- My friends who are completing practicum told me stories about their first weeks in internship. Boy, each person had a really different experience. My best friend was expected to begin counseling by the end of the first week. Another friend shadowed her site supervisor for six weeks and then finally had a client all her own.

- From the very first day, when I asked my supervisor a question, he would always ask me what I thought a good answer to that question was. Early on, that response drove me crazy. I just needed him to tell me what to do; I mean first, second, and then third. A list. Now that I am into the work, I look forward to answering the questions together. I still do need answers. And sometimes, for agency policies, "it depends" just doesn't seem to me to be a really good answer.

- My faculty supervisor is fond of saying, "Well I can think of about four ways to approach this situation." I want to feel confident in my work, so I need more specific feedback. I want to believe that I have a promising career as a counselor.

- Here, near the end of my practicum experience, I feel I am acting more independently. And it seems the better I perform with one client, the more confidence I have. There are some colleagues who are coming to me to consult. Wow!

As you may note while reading these comments, autonomy shifts throughout level one. For CITs involved in practicum, autonomy is manifested in various ways. And, for the most part, CITs move from very **dependent** to more **autonomous** during the practicum experience.

LEVEL ONE SELF- AND OTHER AWARENESS. For the level one CIT, the focus begins with a strong awareness of self. These comments reflect how this focus on self is made manifest:

- I have a list in my head of the ways that I will move a client through a first session. I laid this out on a note card. And I just keep going over and over it.

- I am thinking that I am going to use a counseling approach that is very linear. Some people call this a "cookbook" approach. That is about all that I can handle.

- Yesterday I had my fifth counseling session. And I have four clients. I am still terrified that I can't do this work, but in the last session, I finally relaxed enough to actually listen to the client, and we sat together in silence a couple of times.

- My faculty supervisor and I reviewed my second tape in supervision. I could see several places where I could have responded to the client. I was still responding in terms of my goals rather than the clients. Yet, there was this one time when I said,

"Life seems particularly difficult for you." My client nodded and then talked about some of the feelings associated with the difficulty. That was the only time I focused on the client, but I can see what happens when this occurs!

- Sometimes I come into session so enthusiastic to see my client that I think I overwhelm my client. My site supervisor tells me that I must leave room for the client's emotions, too.

Within the levels of competence framework, in level one, self- and other awareness primarily represents a **focus on self**. During the practicum experience, as a CIT's comfort level with clients increases, it becomes easier for the CIT to **focus on the client** and less on the self.

Level Two

As you might expect, level two represents CITs' professional growth in terms of motivation, autonomy, and self- and other awareness (Stoltenberg & McNeil, 2011). Level two means the CITs no longer are considered novices, although they will still encounter situations in which the term novice applies. At this level, there are specific characteristics linked to seeing counseling as a more complex and complicated process. CITs are able to concentrate on clients rather than themselves; they see both clients and their work with clients more realistically. This means they wonder about the help they provide and its effectiveness. CITs functioning as level two counselors see the need to vary techniques and approaches in response to client reactions and client needs. They experience varying emotions in their work, excitement about their work, and confirmation they are making a difference, as well as frustration with their lack of success or progress with some clients. According to Stoltenberg and McNeil (2011), level two is tumultuous and changeable. Here are student comments that reflect their experiences of working at a level two.

LEVEL TWO MOTIVATION. There is a great deal of motivation during level two, including excitement with the successes of the work and discouragement from lack of success. Many times, the response links to a feeling of suitability or unsuitability for the work.

- I have had such a wonderful week working my clients. I have never been clearer that I am meant to be a counselor.

- I have several really difficult clients right now, but I know if I work hard and they work hard, then we can make progress together.

- I have this one client; he is a young boy. Just thinking about him makes me so sad. His situation is so difficult. After two months of work with him and his family, all I can see are more problems. And I will complete my work in a month. Then what will happen to him?

- My faculty supervisor says that midterm is a difficult time for practicum students. I feel like I will never know enough to help my clients. I have discovered several parts of my personality that really don't help me as a counselor.

LEVEL TWO AUTONOMY. During level two, a CIT's sense of autonomy fluctuates widely (Stoltenberg & McNeil, 2011). Much of the time, CITs are becoming more and more independent. It is often times ironic: The more independent a CIT is, the more complex and complicated client work appears and the more the CIT depends on supervision, both information based and relationship and support based. Comments from CITs include the following:

- The more success I have working with clients using narrative techniques, the more I believe I can work independently. I can really see my skill development from the beginning of the semester.

- I thought reflecting feelings was challenging when I started with my first client, but I did think that I knew the client issues. The more I know about this client, the more confused and sometimes overwhelmed I am about the issues presented. I will give you one example. My first goal was to make sure that one of my persistently mentally ill clients talked to her physician. My most recent goal was just to get her to get dressed and walk downstairs to eat breakfast and take her meds.

- Here at the end of practicum, I don't see my supervisor much, expect for our check in the mornings and our weekly meetings. Except when I need him, I need him immediately!

- I think that I summarize my status as a need to work on my own, but with support. My supervisor has been working for 10 years. She says that it is current status, too.

LEVEL TWO SELF- AND OTHER AWARENESS. This overarching structure also fluctuates widely during level two of competence. The movement seen here is from an increased awareness of other (the client) and then taking on the client's issues and problems. The following comments reflect level two self- and other awareness.

- I am feeling easy with most of my clients.

- There are times when I feel at one with my clients and I am able to focus on them. That is where my attention is.

- In one of our assignments for practicum class, we had to go back and listen to our first tape working with our first client. Then we read our notes from supervision about the tape. I am not really giving myself a hard time, but I only noticed a small part of what my client was trying to tell me. Summarizing the session was not difficult at all. Today, I also wrote a summary of that session. I turned a paragraph into three pages. Things look so complex now.

- Sometimes I feel I have insufficient skills and understanding to help my clients.

- Yesterday I left a session and I felt so badly for the client. Honestly, I had so much empathy, I felt I was the client. Then I started thinking about myself and not the client.

Level Three

Level three reflects an advanced level or a mature level of professional work. At this level, the CIT, practicum student, or intern, can be described as a professional. CITs may show evidence of this professional behavior, level three of competence during their field-based experiences. During this level, counselors may still have highs and lows in their work, require supervision and support, and encounter very difficult and challenging clients and situations. At the same time, over time, these professionals have a solid grasp of the work, an understanding of themselves as helpers, and an ability to match their skills to meet client needs. Here are some comments you might expect from counselors functioning at level three of competence.

LEVEL THREE MOTIVATION. Stability is the hallmark of motivation in level three of competence. Counselors may look inward for support, consideration, and work.

- Working with clients seems more stable and the work seems more even for me. There are fewer crises. I can remember when I wasn't sure that this was the work for me.

- I meet with five other professionals every Friday afternoon. We always bring in our evaluations of our performances and then share our critiques with each other. I don't want to think I am currently the best that I can be.

- I can remember when every month I would think about changing jobs or changing professions. I don't have those thoughts very often.

LEVEL THREE AUTONOMY. At level three of competency, autonomy continues to be consistent. Perhaps counterintuitively, understanding the ongoing need for professional development, supervision, and support actually provides the foundation for working autonomously.

- I love my work and I welcome the responsibility.

- I can remember when I was fearful that I would be without supervision when I graduated. Now I know that I can seek out supervision and consultation, and I do so regularly. I am fortunate that I work in a site where professionals support each other.

- Oh, my job has crises all of the time. I work with foster families. With every crisis, I handle it as well as I can, but always, I am seeking opinions. Suicide risk and abuse are two areas that I always seek help from others.

LEVEL THREE SELF- AND OTHER AWARENESS. Level three self- and other awareness for the counselor becomes more sophisticated. Early focus on self means trying to "get it right" during the counseling session, and the focus shifts between the counselor and the client. At this level, counseling becomes more of a dance where both counselor and client are involved. In the moment, the counselor is aware of both parties, and, in addition, the interaction as a whole. For instance, the professionals view the agreements and contradictions between what the client says and what the client does, considers several reasons for client behavior, and chooses responses from several possible ones.

- One of the things my faculty supervisor taught me was to look for what the client says and then what the client does. I feel like the communication improves if I can openly say to the client, "This is what I am seeing.... What do you think?"

- Sometimes I surprise myself because my thoughts about clients just come to me unbidden. I am always asking myself in counseling and in real life, "What could be the motive for this specific behavior?" As an aside, even if I think I have listed all realistic motivations, lots of times I am surprised by the client's response.

- In my agency, we value being able to think on our feet. We all try to be in a session and be thinking about the session, all in the same moment.

Discussion Together 9.1 provides you with the opportunity to gain a broader view of levels of competence across a range of professionals. It will also help you develop ways of talking about levels of competence and the overarching structures that describe aspects of your professional growth. Finally, participating in this exercise will develop your skills of critical reflection and provide ways of integrating this reflection into the supervisory process.

DISCUSSION TOGETHER 9.1
Levels of Competence

Describe your motivation as a counselor. Describe your motivation of learning to be a better counselor. Have you experienced times where you wished for more or less autonomy? In what ways during the counseling process have you been made aware of something about yourself you were previously unaware of? How about awareness of your client?

The IDM overarching structures and levels of competence provide you with a way to talk about your own development as a counselor. And, using the language and the concepts of the integrated developmental model can bring new insights into your experiences of supervision. In Transcription 9.1, Dr. Kim and Janice demonstrate how to use the IDM to address the way in which Janice is approaching her work with a client.

TRANSCRIPTION 9.1. IDM-FOCUSED SUPERVISION WITH JANICE

Janice has brought another video from a session earlier in the morning where she believed there was a need to conduct a suicide assessment. She was anxious to talk about this during supervision.

Janice: I had such a difficult morning at my school and I need to talk about my experience with a student who threatened suicide. I was scared to death that I would mishandle this.

Dr. Kim: Janice, can you walk us through what happened during the session?

Janice: My student Chloe I have seen four times, and I see her twice a week. She is often upset during our individual sessions. This morning she came in and dropped into the chair beside my desk. She started crying, and she began crying so hard that she couldn't breathe.

Dr. Kim: Before you tell us more about this morning, let's stop for a moment. When you think about how this counseling session began, tell me what it was like for you.

Janice: (Looking down and breathing heavily). Oh, I was in a panic.

Dr. Kim: What did this panic look like for you?

Janice: My mind was a whirl. I couldn't focus on what to do. I couldn't breathe. I wanted to cry with Chloe but I knew I couldn't do that. I was afraid that I couldn't help her. I was scared.

Dr. Kim: Janice, let's take one more deep breath before we return to this morning's counseling session with Chloe.

Janice: I told Chloe, "I really want to help you through this. I am going to get Ms. Kowalski. I think the two of us as a team could give you the best support. Is that okay with you?" and then Chloe nodded yes and I went next door and asked Ms. Kowalski to come in to join us. Together, we talked with Chloe and Ms. Kowalski and I together conducted a suicide risk assessment. And then Chloe called her mom and asked her to come pick her up from school. Chloe was calm by the time her mom came. The four of us talked about this morning and created a safety plan for home and school.

Dr. Kim: How did you assess Chloe's state when she left with her mom?

Janice: Ms. Kowalski and I talked about this. The result of the suicide risk assessment we conducted was that Chloe had no desire to hurt herself and no plan. She was shaken but had stopped crying and was breathing normally by the time her mother picked her up, and we planned for her to come to our office to see either me or Ms. Kowalski every morning the rest of the week.

Dr. Kim: Janice, let's focus on you now. We only have 15 minutes of supervision remaining. I would like for us to use the IDM overarching structures as a tool to reflect on what the morning was like for you.

Dr. Kim: Look at this form; remind yourself of the structures of motivation, autonomy, self- and other awareness. Which of these appear relevant to you?

Janice: Oh Dr. Kim, I think self- and other awareness is swirling around for me. Imagine at my age, having to go to get help to counsel Chloe. I was so frightened. I was too aware of myself. It froze me.

Dr. Kim: As you remember when we talked about what you can expect as a novice counselor, there is a continual attention to first self and then other and then back to self. And sometimes you will be able to see what you have in common with the client.

[This session continues for an addition five minutes.]

Dr. Kim: I know we are out of time for this session. Janice, even though we have not yet talked about the session from the autonomy/dependence perspective, I want to applaud you for asking your supervisor for help. You also helped Chloe see the need for your supervisor to join you. From an ethical perspective, it was important to pay attention to the risk of suicide and also to consult when needed.

Dr. Kim: Janice, I also want to affirm how challenging it is to learn to be a counselor. Suicide risk assessment is one of the most difficult issues that you will learn to tackle. I am glad we could face this together.

Janice: My feelings are just settling. But I have learned that I still have a lot to learn. I would hate to work with clients without support.

Transcription 9.1 provides just one illustration of the way in which your knowledge of the IDM and its levels and overarching structure can facilitate your professional growth. Note that Dr. Kim and Janice chose to focus on self- and other awareness. Janice's responses to Chloe represent her novice status and illustrate level one thoughts and behaviors. She affirms that Chloe's focus on self is normal. She also introduces the idea that Janice's responses may have, in part, paralleled Chloe's responses. Dr. Kim also notes that Janice's sense of shame during her work with Chloe and wants to return to that emotion during another supervisory session. Dealing with the risk of suicide is challenging for the most seasoned of counselors. As a practicum student, asking for help considering this issue and understanding the nuances of each situation may lessen your fear of this aspect of counseling. Respect for its seriousness should remain as you develop professionally.

> **ETHICAL CONSIDERATION 9.2**
>
> What ethical situations are apparent in the following transcription?

Specific Domains

Within the IDM, there are specific domains that define areas of skill development and counseling practice that are required to be an effective counselor. Let's look at a brief description of each of these eight specific domains, adapted from Stoltenberg and McNeill (2011). Figure 9.3 illustrates the eight specific domains of counseling and therapy.

INTERVENTION SKILL COMPETENCE. This domain concentrates on the professional counselor's capacity to deliver a client intervention. This is the confidence in and the ability to work within a specific context (e.g., individual, group) and deliver counseling services via a specific theoretical approach.

Development during practicum. The practicum student begins to "try on" various intervention skills for individual and group counseling work.

ASSESSMENT TECHNIQUES. Assessment techniques includes the professional counselor's trust in and skill level to choose appropriate testing materials that match counseling goals and client abilities. It also encompasses understanding assessment procedures and experience in a wide range of assessment tools, tests, and techniques.

Development during practicum. In most practicum contexts, the understanding and development of assessment techniques is not an area of focus. It is, however, vital to begin to understand ethical use and cultural considerations for interpreting results, as well as viewing assessments as one piece of the clinical picture, not the whole.

INTERPERSONAL ASSESSMENT. The focus of the interpersonal assessment relates to the counselor's ability to use the self to conceptualize the client's interpersonal dynamics. How this occurs and the subsequent interpersonal assessment is guided by the theoretical orientation and the goals of the counseling and service delivery.

Development during practicum. The practicum student is beginning to understand how to use the self to conceptualize the client's interpersonal dynamics. Limitations for this development include the fluctuation between self- and other awareness, rather than the integration of the two, and the focus on basic skills rather than more sophisticated use of theory in practice.

CLIENT CONCEPTUALIZATION. Broadly defined, client conceptualization includes an integration of a mental health status assessment, a diagnosis of mental health disorders, and the client's personal attributes, life experiences, environmental influences, and cultural dimensions. The counselor presents a client conceptualization that is the foundation for goal setting and treatment planning.

Development during practicum. By the conclusion of practicum, most students develop an in-depth case study, complete with client conceptualization. This assists students in understanding the client-in-context nature of counseling.

INDIVIDUAL DIFFERENCES. Within this domain, the counselor is able to identify characteristics and influences that define the client as a unique individual. Characteristics and influences include but are not limited to aspects of personality and influencers of gender, age, socioeconomic status, culture, and education. The importance of each of these varies according to the dynamic of the counseling process.

Development during practicum. A focus on a client's uniqueness or individual differences helps move practicum students from making generalizations about clients and using a "cookbook" approach to their counseling interactions and plans. This increases awareness on the ethical implications of cultural differences as well as the differences that exist within cultures and ethnicities.

THEORETICAL ORIENTATION. Within the framework of theoretical orientation, counselors are able to identify and use specific theory-based therapeutic approaches and understand how the self may influence the counseling approach and process. Counselors view the use of theory and approaches as complex and nuanced and begin to wrestle with the reality that theory is not a one-size-fits-all proposition.

Development during practicum. As students gain confidence in their basic helping skills, they may want to try to implement a theoretical orientation in their counseling work. Supervisors help students rein in these impulses and instead focus on the ways a particular theory of interest approaches basic relational and helping skills. Furthermore, they assist CITs to choose an orientation based on student skills and values and client needs or setting requirements.

TREATMENT PLANS AND GOALS. This specific domain refers to the counselor's ability to establish goals, plan treatment, and carry it out in an organized fashion. The way in which this activity is delivered is dependent on counselor skills, client participation, and agency resources and client environment supports and barriers.

Development during practicum. Treatment planning and establishing counseling goals begins early in practicum as students prepare to see their first clients. It goes in tandem with relationship building and becomes the vehicle to demonstrate respect, acceptance, tolerance, and self-determination. Treatment planning and goal setting helps counselor and client form a cooperative relationship. By submitting weekly treatment plans and goals to site and faculty supervisors, the practicum student can receive critical feedback and learn how to view the whole of the counseling process and the details of a structured setting.

PROFESSIONAL ETHICS. The domain of professional ethics reflects the counselor's ability and practice of ethical behavior as defined by the profession, various standards of care, and integration with personal values and beliefs.

Development during practicum. Professional ethics is a key aspect of professional identity development and professional development. Ethics, including a focus on diversity and social justice, becomes a component of each counseling consideration. Ethical dimensions of performing the counseling role and assuming its concomitant responsibilities is integrated throughout the practicum experience.

This cursory introduction to the eight specific domains ends our discussion of the three aspects of the IDM.

Experiential Activity 9.1 provides you a way to think about your performance related the eight specific domains.

EXPERIENTIAL ACTIVITY 9.1. CONSIDERING YOUR DEVELOPMENT AS A COUNSELOR: EIGHT SPECIFIC DOMAINS

As you consider the areas of the IDM, (a) intervention skills, (b) assessment techniques, (c) interpersonal assessment, (d) client conceptualization, (e) individual differences, (f) theoretical orientation, (g) treatment plans and goals, and (h) professional ethics, what areas of growth have you noted?

In your practicum experience, your time and skill level will prevent you from deeply focusing on all eight specific domains. To support your growth and development, you might choose two or three of the domains, in concert with your site and faculty supervisors in which to focus. From our experience, domains such as intervention skills, beginning client conceptualization, treatment plans and goals, and professional ethics may

> ### MULTICULTURAL CONSIDERATION 9.2
>
> How would you integrate multicultural considerations and social justice into the eight specific domains? Suggest five approaches and provide a concrete example for each.

be good choices. The domains you choose may be determined by your academic program's goals for practicum, your placement site, the clients with whom you work, and your course assignments. Our advice is to be aware of all eight and focus on only a few.

Summary

In this chapter, you learned about the integrated developmental model (IDM), developed by Stoltenberg and McNeill (2011), a model that describes the stages of a counselor's professional development from novice to experienced counselor. This model addresses ways you can anticipate and then track the knowledge, skills, and values that you will develop in practicum and beyond. Considering professional development, you learned about the three aspects of the IDM, overarching structures, levels of competence, and specific domains of competence.

Overarching structures provide you, the practicum student, and your supervisors with a way to monitor various aspects of your performance of a counselor and your engagement in your experience of learning to be a counselor. These structures represent motivation ("I want to do this work"), autonomy ("I am able to do this work"), and self- and other awareness "I recognize how my 'stuff' can interact with my client's 'stuff' in this work").

The levels of competence represent the stages of professional counselor development, ranging from levels one through levels three. (Levels one through three are describe in this chapter.) How each of the three overarching structures manifests itself differs within each of the three levels of competence and reflects different levels of competence. For example, regarding autonomy, many novice CITs at level one are dependent on their supervisors, while in level two, as CITs grow and develop, they can gain confidence and become more autonomous, only to return to dependency as they are placed in novel situations. Counselors in level three balance autonomy with consulting with others and serving as a consultant for others. You read about Janice's change from a feeling of autonomy to a need for her supervisor's intervention in transcription 9.1.

Specific domains of counseling and therapy skill development and counseling practice are required to be an effective counselor. These are intervention skills, assessment techniques, interpersonal assessment, client conceptualization, individual differences, theoretical orientation, treatments plans and goals, and professional ethics (Stoltenberg, McNeill, & Delworth, 1998). Each of these represent important knowledge, skills, and values that you need to become an effective counselor. However, as a practicum student, some are more relevant than others. Those include intervention skills, beginning client conceptualization, treatment plans and goals, and professional ethics.

Key Terms

Assessment techniques

Autonomous

Autonomy

Client conceptualization

Counselor professional development

Dependent

Developmental models

Fluctuating motivation

Focus on self

Focus on the client

High motivation

Individual differences

Integrated developmental model of supervision (idm)

Interpersonal assessment

Intervention skills

Level one

Level three

Level two

Levels of competence

Motivation

Overarching structures

Professional ethics

Self-and other awareness

Specific domains

Stable motivation

Theoretical orientation

Treatment plans and goals

References

Council for Accreditation of Counseling and Related Programs. (2016). *Section 3: Professional Practice.* Retrieved from https://www.cacrep.org/section-3-professional-practice/

Council for Accreditation of Counseling and Related Programs. (2016). *Section 2: Professional Counseling Identity.* Retrieved from https://www.cacrep.org/section-2-professional-counseling-identity/

Oxford English Dictionary. (2017). Stage Retrieved from http://www.oed.com.proxy.lib.utk.edu:90/view/Entry/188653?rskey=f7stqp&result=1&iAdvanced=false#eid

Stoltenberg, C. D., & McNeill, B. W. (2011). *IDM supervision: An integrated developmental model for supervising counselors and therapists* (3rd ed.). New York, NY: Routledge.

Stoltenberg, C. D., McNeill, B. W., & Delworth, U. (1998). *IDM supervision: An integrated developmental model of supervision counselors and therapists* (1st ed.). San Francisco, CA: Jossey Bass.

CHAPTER 10

Getting What You Need
FROM SUPERVISION

INTRODUCTION

As you learn about and experience practicum, you may notice something distinctly different about it as a learning environment. In fact, your educational experiences up to this point may have been very different. To understand this difference, it is important to look at past educational experiences. For most of our primary and secondary education and, to great extent our undergraduate educational experience, the focus may likely have been on faculty and instructors passing along information to willing or less engaged students. Students viewed this teacher as an authority figure who knows the most important information on a specific subject. Therefore, a learner's job was to tap into that all-knowing source by taking notes and reading and reviewing those notes for tests.

In most cases, by the time you are reading this chapter, you have (a) completed prerequisite counseling courses, (b) registered and enrolled in the practicum course, (c) identified a site and completed all the contracts and required paperwork, (d) met the site staff and even begun meeting with clients, and (e) become actively engaged in site and campus supervision. Based on the typical model of teaching and learning as described, you'd naturally assume that it is now the time for your supervisor and faculty supervisor to assume their responsibilities; all you need to do is listen and learn from them.

Your practicum in counseling, though, demands a very different learning experience. There is no studying for a session in the traditional sense; there is no exam to be graded, and many of the grades reflect what you do as well as what you know. For some practicum students, it can be incredibly unsettling. For others, they are relieved to leave classroom learning behind, yet are disappointed there is still classroom attendance, assignments, and other paperwork to attend to.

You will learn new ways to think about this new learning environment as a field-based experience when you have the opportunity to apply theory to practice! One unique feature of field-based learning, and specifically the practicum experience, is supervision. Supervision represents a special pedagogy with two central actors, the supervisor and the supervisee. Each have specific roles and responsibilities. And, as a supervisee, you have rights as well as responsibilities.

Field-based learning and working under supervision depart from the traditional teaching environments and the learning styles that have brought you academic success thus far, so you will need to shift your thinking from education and learning from the teacher as an authority model to a belief in and a stance of self-advocacy. Through self-advocacy, you can both promote your own learning and take full advantage of site and faculty supervision. Self-advocacy, as a belief in oneself and a strategy of learning, will support your development as a professional counselor. The goals of the chapter follow.

GOALS OF THE CHAPTER

- Identify the points of convergence and divergence between the classroom and the community
- Learn self-advocacy approaches for communicating with faculty and site supervisors
- Take ownership for your learning experiences and for growing as a counselor
- Learn what you can expect from a responsible supervisor
- Identify times when you need help with unfair, poor, or harmful supervision

RELATED CACREP GOALS

Section 2: PROFESSIONAL COUNSELING IDENTITY
1. PROFESSIONAL COUNSELING ORIENTATION AND ETHICAL PRACTICE

- k. strategies for personal and professional self-evaluation and implications for practice
- l. self-care strategies appropriate to the counselor role
- m. the role of counseling supervision in the profession (CACREP, 2016)

Defining Supervision

At this point in practicum, you work with two supervisors, a faculty supervisor and a practicum or site supervisor. You may also have a doctoral student supervisor. In Chapter 2, supervision is described as an activity that occurs when an experienced professional counselor services as a mentor to a novice professional. Within this context, the practicum student, as a novice, begins to move from the boundary of the profession into the full participation in the profession (Woodside, Paulus, & Ziegler, 2009). This movement toward participation in the profession happens with the help and support of a supervisor. The Oxford English Dictionary (2018) articulates specific action of a supervision as "overseeing, directing, or taking charge of a person, organization, activity, etc."

Within the counseling profession, the term "supervision" includes two types of supervision, **administrative supervision** and **clinical supervision** (Professional Counselor's Desk Reference, 2018). Both relate to professional development and meeting professional standards. Administrative supervision refers primarily to working with clients in an effective way and documenting that work, especially recording the steps that the supervisee takes to help clients and the clinical outcomes that resulted. In contrast, clinical supervision focuses on the counselor-client relationship and the counselor-supervisor relationship (Bernard & Goodyear, 2014) and protection of the client. Client welfare and other ethical standards are focal points of clinical supervision. The relationship between the supervisor and the supervisee is commonly referred to as the **supervisory relationship**. One fundamental difference between the supervisory relationship and the counseling relationship is a power dimension since supervisors perform an evaluative function. This function represents the basis of this power (Falender, 2014).

While you are in practicum, both faculty and site supervisors will pay careful attention to your work, especially your work with clients. Supervisors will also set aside time each week to provide honest feedback and suggest ways to improve your performance as a counselor. They will, within the context of the supervisory relationship, offer support through conversation and modeling.

Counseling in Training Self-Advocacy

Getting what you need—in supervision or anywhere else in the counseling profession—requires you to (a) know your needs and (b) know how best to meet those needs yourself. You will see this later in your career as well, but it is true enough now: No one else is likely to be as concerned about your needs and well-being as you are, nor should they be. This concern for self is **self-advocacy**. Let's look in on our cast of practicum students to see how issues of self-advocacy might arise in the context of practicum. Transcription 10.1 represents the dialogue in a practicum class several weeks into the term.

TRANSCRIPTION 10.1. THE NEED FOR SELF-ADVOCACY

Kaisha: Dr. Kim enters the classroom just as Kaisha finishes talking with her classmates. Dr. Kim can sense that she has walked into the middle of an important conversation but waits to see what emerges. As soon as she opens class, Kaisha relates the following experience: "My site has been really open and flexible with me. They have even suggested that I co-facilitate a group with another practicum student who is placed there. It feels great for them to show this kind of confidence in me. I mean, it's only week five of the semester. The problem is, our program is clear that we have to be supervised in our work at all times and that we are not supposed to have our own clients yet. This was all fine until I recorded my first video session. The supervisor was supposed to sit in on the session with me—you know, the whole constant supervision thing.

When it came time to begin the video, she helped me set up the video, then walked out and sat in a chair outside the room. She said she trusted me and she did not want to distract me or the client. I felt pressure to be okay with that because I was already nervous enough about videotaping the session. After the session, I opened the door and she (supervisor) was gone.

Dr. Kim, I wasn't sure if I should tell you this. I was anxious to tell you, but I don't want to get kicked out from my site and I don't want to the site supervisor to get into trouble. And … if I'm honest … I'm afraid you will tell me I have to redo the video because it did not conform to the assignment."

Jose: Upon hearing the discussion of Kaisha's situation at her site, Jose feels compelled to relate his experience at his site to Dr. Kim and his classmates. "Okay, since it looks like this is the group supervision session where we are going to 'go there,' I need to bring something up. We all had the group counseling course with Dr. _____ last semester, right? (lots of head nods, sighs, and groans). That class challenged me so much to look at my own life, but also presented group counseling as this engaging, transformative experience that could really change clients' lives. It may have also been one of the most personally challenging courses I've had thus far, but I left believing that I can lead group effectively. Here's the thing: I walked into the residential facility, where their primary treatment modality is group, expecting to see some amazing group work (takes a deep breath).

So far, here's what I've seen: Groups that seem to be treated more like a class, where the counselor goes over step work (12-step recovery packets), gives lots of time for the clients to complete their packets (sometimes an hour), then has them complete worksheets. There is some discussion of the social skills, triggers and coping skills, and family support worksheets, but the clients seem so bored and distracted. The co-facilitator is more like the behavior monitor and redirects client behaviors almost the whole time. The thing is, I have trouble staying attentive, and at times awake! It has gotten so bad at times that I wonder if I can even count the time as direct hours because it feels so much like a class—that clients even call it a class!! And, I was dreading bringing it up because I was afraid that I would not be able to count those hours and would have to make them up."

Janice: "Well, I guess it is my turn. The principal at the school where I'm placed is really happy to have a practicum student. She's so happy, in fact, that she wants me to see a lot of students when I'm there. The problem I'm having is that I'm being referred to the students who have been identified as having behavioral problems. The school counselor does not have time to meet with them all, given all the administrative work assigned to her. The principal is hoping that counseling will help these students modify their behavior. My concern is that these students are now in counseling, with a practicum student, and their parents may not even know this is happening. When I asked about obtaining informed consent for counseling, I was told that this falls under the purview of the school and can be framed as educational counseling. Therefore, parental informed consent is implied by virtue of the students being enrolled in the school. This did not sit well with me, so I discussed it with the school counselor, who said this is the way it works in a school setting. She added that some parents would be suspicious of counseling and would block their child from receiving this service, which would ultimately negatively affect the success potential of the child. I can't argue that these students are not higher risk, but shouldn't I still try to get consent? I've been told, off the record, that principals are the "chief executives" of their schools, so what they say goes. I'm a little afraid that if I push this issue, I'll get kicked from the site. And after all, it is beneficial for the students, right?

Sam: "My concerns at my site are a little different from the others, but since we seem to be on a roll, I'd like to get some advice or feedback. My supervisor has been really supportive and has given me multiple opportunities to get involved at the site. In fact, I could really see myself staying on for internship and taking my experience to the next level in terms of professional growth and client care. The thing is, when it comes to supervision at the site, there are a couple of challenges I'm facing.

So, Dr. Kim, you seem to model for us how to listen, hear, and provide space for us to work. When I got to my site, I apparently was expecting that my site supervisor would engage in much the same thing. It turns out, your [Dr. Kim] style is very different and I miss it when I'm in supervision at the site. When I sit down for supervision, my supervisor asks how I'm doing. Then, almost regardless of what I say, he responds by talking to (at?) me for the rest of the session—kind of dominating the flow. I feel like I get one shot to say what I think before he takes over. I feel bad because he has lots of experience and what he says makes sense, but I don't feel like there is a lot of time or room for me to express my own thoughts and concerns. Like the others have said, I'm concerned about how to approach this. I didn't want to bring it up here because I figured you [Dr. Kim] would push me to advocate for myself at the site (class chuckles in recognition of this), and I definitely don't want to offend my supervisor—I mean, how are you supposed to tell your supervisor, who's been a counselor for 20 years, that you need him to stop talking so much because you don't feel heard?!

There is limited literature in the counseling research on how to support counseling students' or counselors' in training development of self-advocacy. But, if Janice, Jose, Kaisha, and Sam's experiences represent routine difficulties that practicum students encounter, then self-advocacy is an important concept to understand and a skill to learn. Let's explore one perspective in approaching counselor in training self-advocacy. Imagine a diagram where self-advocacy is the center and is surrounded by four interconnected, dynamic components. Those components include counselor well-being, self-awareness, self-care and mutual care, and a sense of agency (see Figure 10.1)

FIGURE 10.1. Counselor in training self-advocacy model

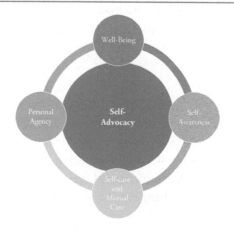

Self-Awareness

Self-awareness is a crucial factor in counselor development and counselor professional identity. This self-awareness extends also to self-advocacy. Pompeo and Levitt (2014) describe self-reflection this way: "Conscious awareness of one's action, intentions, motives, emotions, thoughts, and feelings" (p. 59). They also note that there is scant literature on self-awareness in counselor training, but that self-reflection leads to the components of self-advocacy: well-being, self-care and mutual care, and personal agency.

As you are reading this, pause to attend to your body, mind, and emotions. Do you experience any sensations related to hunger, anger, loneliness, or tiredness? If so—and these are not far-fetched experiences for graduate counseling students, especially in practicum—and if you have these sensations, then your perceptions of your environment, clients, supervisors, and even the information in this text may be obscured. Alcoholics Anonymous uses the acronym HALT (hungry, angry, lonely, tired) as a guide for halting our perception and behaviors when our physiological and/or psychological needs are unmet, leaving us vulnerable to misperception.

Well-Being

Well-being, as it relates to the practicum experience, is an important concept because it focuses on perceptions individuals have about their lives: "[w]hat people think and feel about their lives, such as the quality of their relationships, their positive emotions and resilience, the realization of their potential, or their overall satisfaction with life" (Center for Disease Control, 2018). According to Diener & Biswas-Diener (2008), "[S]ubjective well-being encompasses people's life satisfaction and their evaluation of important domains of life such as work, health, and relationships. It also includes their emotions such as joy and engagement, and the relatively rare experience of unpleasant emotions such as anger, sadness, and fear" (p. 4). Some common issues college students experience and are particularly vulnerable to include maintaining positive nutrition (eating well), physical health (exercising), and rest (improving sleep habits) (Baldwin, Towler, Oliver, & Datta, 2017). Of course, as the definitions of the term suggests, well-being can include other aspects of life beyond the physical, such as mental, spiritual, social, and others.

Well-being and self-advocacy are inextricably linked in two important ways. First, they both depend on the beliefs in the self that individuals hold. Akin to well-being, self-advocacy is "a developmental process in which the individual gradually gains confidence in expressing ambitions and emotions, taking responsibility over his or her life" (Rinat, & Haya, 2018). Second, both **self-efficacy** or the belief in one's ability to promote change and a positive approach to life are predictors of positive well-being (Karademas, 2007). Reciprocally, achieving or maintaining positive well-being facilitates positive change and growth (Biswas-Diener, 2013).

Promoting Change

The professional growth and development that occurs during practicum, in part, results in a practicum student's need for change. These changes can influence life in school, work, health, and relationship settings. Many of these changes are directly related to learning to be a counselor. These might include developing skills of responding and reflecting or case conceptualization, identifying ethical challenges or multicultural biases, or learning how to manage time and organize paperwork. The process of change could also reflect issues of a more personal nature such as examining dual relationships, establishing boundaries, and maintaining work-related and family- and friend-related social lives. Change might include establishing health goals such as positive nutrition, regular exercise, and better sleep.

In the midst of practicum, thinking about change or making self-promises to change may seem overwhelming. Prochaska & Norcross (2014) developed a process of change using a stage model. The model of change can support your efforts, regardless of the changes that you would like to make. So, you can see how the change model works. Chad offers a lighthearted take on the model (see Figure 10.2). To track your progress through the model, take some time to identify your self-talk. This will help you understand and account for your progress. Self-talk will help you identify any barriers. Third, look to identify an area of change that you would like to undertake. Use Prochaska and Norcross's (2014) **stages of change** to plan to increase your well-being.

FIGURE 10.2. Well-being and Prochaska and Norcross's stages of change: Chad's donut love story

Stage of Change Description	Chad's Self-Talk at each Stage
Precontemplation—The client/CIT is both unaware of the problem, and especially unaware of their role in it.	"What's wrong with donuts? I can eat them if I want; I'm not hurting anyone!"
Contemplation—The client/CIT has moved into some awareness that there is a problem, but is, at best ambivalent about taking responsibility for the problem or the change that is needed.	"So maybe the donut is beginning to settle around my waist, but it's not really a problem, and besides, I did not make the donuts and they're so darn good!"
Preparation—The client has moved into greater ownership of both the problem and their role in it. They are beginning to explore options for change.	"Okay, so maybe I have had to buy 'donut' pants and I can't move like I used to; but how can I say no to such a good friend?"
Action—As the name implies, the client is actively taking steps for change that reflect personal responsibility for choices.	"I have to break up with the donut; it's terrific in the moment but it's causing damage in multiple areas; time to toss the donuts and take a walk."
Maintenance—Making a change at a specific point in time (saying no to that donut that's calling your—my—name) is one thing; committing to making a change over time is a completely different one (when the donut follows you around, and having to repeatedly say no).	"Now I have to take a walk daily and reject the donut's pleas for us to be together? This is hard work!"
Relapse—Specific to the substance and process addiction groups, this stage acknowledges that re-engaging an old behavior is a part of the process of growth.	"The donut found me! We danced, and I imbibed. Darn you donut! Darn you, me. I have to figure out what was happening that let me vulnerable to that old relationship!"

Self-Care and Mutual Care

Self-care is a tricky component of self-advocacy and one that usually draws sighs and groans from students and seasoned counselors as well. In discussing self-care, we talk about **wellness**. The literature on wellness provides wonderful models to draw from, encouraging us to take care of ourselves physically, spiritually, emotionally, socially, relationally, and vocationally (Myers & Sweeney, 2004; SAMSHA, 2018). Promoting self-care is embedded in the 2014 ACA Code of Ethics (ACA, 2014) and is commonly one of the recommendations for professionals to avoid or lessen burnout, compassion fatigue, and vicarious trauma (Painter & Woodside, 2017). Self-care also, at times, evokes feelings of guilt, shame, and embarrassment for not taking care of oneself as fully as one should.

Neuroscience research provides us with some explanations of the negative effects of stress on our physiology, cognitive, and emotional functioning. A description of one study confirms the importance of self-care, and at times, the difficulties we have achieving it.

Neuroscience Research and Stress

Counseling is difficult work. Despite the efforts of faculty, supervisors, and training programs, counselors face an array of challenges on a daily, even hourly basis. Most of these challenges can result in growth for both the counselor and the client, and can feel very rewarding. However, these constant, often unpredictable challenges can take a toll. There is a body of research that focuses on the challenges for individuals who face what is called **chronic variable stress** (CVS) (Taylor et al., 2014).

What does CVS look like and how does it evolve? Recent neuroscience research with rats as the subjects look for an answer. According to an experiment with rats, when you expose them to stressors over time and you vary the intensity of the exposure in unpredictable ways, their ability to make goal-directed decisions decreases while their compulsive, habitual behaviors increases (Taylor et al., 2014). What this means is that the rats were less intentional, flexible, and adaptable. Instead, they developed propensities for addiction at the cellular level.

The explanation for these findings is reasonably straightforward. Stress signals the release of cortisol, a hormone designed to respond to stress. While these responses are adaptive in the short term, when cortisol is present in the brain too long, it begins to erode systems needed for well-being. For example, chronic stress can reduce the volume of the hippocampus, the structure most strongly associated with executive function of memory (Koolhaas et al., 2011). In a word, stress can result in short-term memory deficits.

This information is not intended to frighten you; instead, it should stimulate us all to be aware of these chronic, unpredictable stressors and their cumulative effects on our well-being. Practicum, perhaps more than any other course, due to its position as first client and agency contact for most students, can be very stressful. And, practicum exists in the context of graduate school, wherein students are trying to balance more intensive applied course material with family, work, and other roles and relationships.

Professional Support for Self-Care

These multiple stressors tax an individual's ability to cope, which is a big part of why self-care is such a vital component of training programs, both from Council for Accreditation for Counseling and Related Programs (CACREP, 2016) and American Counseling Association's (ACA, 2014) perspectives.

Both the Council for Accreditation for Counseling and Related Programs (CACREP, 2016) and the American Counseling Association (ACA, 2014) indicate the critical importance of self-care related to the development of the professional counselor. The 2016 CACREP standards state coursework and subsequent skills should include the teaching of "self-care strategies appropriate to the counselor role" (CACREP Standards, 2016, Section 2).

In relation to self-care, the 2014 ACA Code of Ethics states, "In addition, counselors engage in self-care activities to maintain and promote their own emotional, physical, mental, and spiritual well-being to best meet their professional responsibilities" (p. 7).

Self-care is something of a unicorn in the counseling field: a mythical, beautiful beast that is highly desirable but nearly impossible to find. Self-care is often discussed at length as the epitome of counselor wellness, yet seems to defy meaningful description. For example, arguably the leaders in counselor wellness, Myers and Sweeney (2004), in writing about counselor wellness, describe self-care as "taking responsibility for one's wellness through self-care and safety habits that are preventive in nature; minimizing the harmful effects of pollution in one's environment" (p. 485).

Anytime you see the term you are trying to define used in the definition, you know you have a concept that is difficult to grasp. This does not mean that self-care is nonexistent or unimportant; it means that it is often elusive. Therefore, we owe it to ourselves as individuals and as professionals to explore this concept while carefully reflecting on its implications. Self-care typically includes strategies for maintaining healthy behaviors in a number of domains: psychical, emotional, social, familial, mental, and spiritual (and there are certainly others that could be added to this list as well). As such, there are many models to choose from to illustrate wellness and self-care. Dang and Sangganjanavanich's (2015) model allows immediate application. This approach is valuable because it approaches self-care through the lens of self-advocacy and does so at three separate but interrelated domains of functioning: individual, organizational, and professional. Table 10.1 provides a summary of the information presented in the model (Dang & Sangganjanavanich, 2015, p. 13). Please note that in **Dang and Sangganjanavanich's approach to wellness**, the model integrates the notion of advocacy, wellness, and well-being.

TABLE 10.1. Descriptive Advocacy Strategies to Promote Counselor Well-Being (Dang & Sangganjanavanich, 2015)

Levels	Importance of Advocacy	Strategies
Micro level (Individual)	To examine professional counselors' personal awareness of wellness, including roles that wellness plays in their day-to-day living, as well as their bio-psychosocial wellness goals and practices To address professional counselors' needs and to enhance functioning in specific areas concerning wellness To empower professional counselors to self-advocate for their well-being	Adopting a scientific model in conceptualizing, assessing, and (re) evaluating counselors' wellness Initiating plan of actions to promote counselors' wellness Taking actions to self-advocate for counselors' personal and professional well-being
Meso level (Organization and local community)	To comprehensively understand both benefits and challenges that professional counselors encounter within their surroundings To create a web of professional support that members are accountable to ensure each other's well-being To produce positive changes within the organization and local community concerning counselors' wellness	Conducting an environmental scan Enhancing intraprofessional collaboration among professional counselors Examining the existence of relevant policies concerning counselors' wellness within the organization and community
Macro level (Profession and the general public)	To further assist counselors' professional functions To maximize the collective advocacy efforts through collaboration with professionals and professional organizations from multiple disciplines To stay alert with professional standards, social policies, and legislation concerning counselors' well-being To assure public access to quality counseling services	Active involvement of professional associations Increasing interprofessional collaboration Utilizing various advocacy efforts (e.g., presentations to government officials, testifying at hearings, litigation, constituent contact, the use of social media, lobbying) Educating the general public to seek counseling services from counselors who demonstrate their well-being

Colman and Colleagues' (2016) Meta-Analytic Study of Self-Care Among Graduate Psychology Students

Colman and colleagues' (2016) meta-analytic study of self-care among graduate psychology students provides the following summative guidance that is similar for graduate counseling students in practicum:

- [S]elf-care involves a variety of things, from exercise to mindfulness to social support
- [S]elf-care absolutely helps the majority of graduate students who engage in it, but not because it takes away stress, because it mitigates the negative effects of stress
- [I]t does not matter the form of self-care one engages in, as long as it works for the individual
- [S]elf-care effectiveness cuts across a wide variety of demographic factors

In summary, do something that is healthful for yourself, not because someone in authority told you to "get your sleep," but because daily or bi-weekly catnaps work for you. And take those naps (whatever strategy works for you), not to feel less stress so much as to help you cope with the tasks of your life.

SELF-CARE FOR CHAD: I am, like the previous example, a napper, as well as a video game player. Both help me turn down the noise in my mind to better tune in to those around me. For years I struggled with not being a runner and salad-eater. Running is great and salads are fine, but they don't enliven me. Working out is great, but it occurs intermittently. Taking a nap or building in a video game world refreshes me. I have a few very close relationships that support me in reflecting on my choices and work, and those keep me grounded and centered. Oh, and I chase my young daughter around the rest of the time, as she is a non-stop bundle of energy! For most of my career up to this point, I not only viewed my choices as self-care, I did the opposite and denigrated my efforts because I was not following a prescribed path to self-care: sleep more, eat better, exercise more, and meditate. Now, I incorporate yoga-like stretching and mild strength-training into my evening routine. I should also note, for the sake of authenticity, donuts and other high-fat, high-sugar treats continue to be the bane for me. Day by day, right?

SELF-CARE FOR MARIANNE: Much of my life I might look like I am the epitome of anti-self-care. Okay, so here is how it goes. Work, family, relationships, self. Yes, they are all important. So, reminiscent of the adage, "a woman can have it all," I have tried to have it all. During my 44 work years as a college professor, I started the day by 5:00 a.m., ran or exercised, then came home and got ready for work and helped my family get ready for their daily activities. Most days I was at work by 7:30 a.m. and managed to spend my day "without a minute wasted," heading home to pick up the kids, take them to their activities, fix nutritious meals, and make sure they and my loving husband had my attention and love and support at home. When the kids went to bed, I would return to the kitchen table to grade papers and work to get ready for the next work day! After the kids left home, I decided to learn the guitar; certainly, I could find 30 minutes to practice. And then, I assumed administrative and evening class responsibilities. Evening classes were perfect—this way I could ensure a 15-hour work day!

So, what did my concept and practice of wellness and self-care look like? I could check off the boxes of care—time for family (check); time for exercise (check); time for work (check); time for a hobby (check)! I strove for balance during those years, but, in my heart, I knew that extending the day and cramming in everything that I thought was important was not the way to gain it. Achievement was too important to me.

Today, I am able to be more at peace with self-care. I pace myself through the day. I read for pleasure in the afternoon. And, at 7:00 p.m., everything comes to a halt and I spend the evenings with my husband. That is our time and the items on my list and the commitments to achieve and "have it all" are put aside. We have started meditating together and we read aloud to one another. When I look back over my life, I am content with the past and happy about the present. I think earlier self-care was something that I did; I hope that now self-care is more of who I am.

> ### ETHICAL CONSIDERATION 10.1
>
> Take a moment and note the ways in which self-care and mutual care relate to the 2014 ACA Code of Ethics. How do they relate to the values stated in the Code of Ethics? How do they relate to specific standards?

You will want to look at your own self-care. An honest discussion with peers and supervisors may help you see self-care, not as a gold standard to reach or a mountain to climb, where there is either success or failure, but as a daily engagement termed the **4 p's of self-care**: priorities, practice, pressures, and peace. Let's engage now in Discussion Together 10.1.

DISCUSSION TOGETHER 10.1
Self-Care: Priorities, Practice, Pressures, and Peace

As you think about your own experience in practicum, brainstorm what comes to mind when you think about priorities, practice of self-care, pressures, and peace.

Mutual Care

The discussion of self-care and its focus on wellness extends to the concept of **mutual care**, a concept that is related to Barragan & Dweck's (2014) description of altruism in self-care amongst counselors. Mutual care focuses on a counselor's in training natural or innate bend toward altruism. Mutual care can also be expressed as mutual self-care, or mutuality, or reciprocal self-care. This unique dimension of self-care represents the behavior of helping professionals reach out to others in professional and personal ways. For example, one strategy that is helpful for practicum students is to communicate with others as a daily practice when they feel isolated or emotionally exhausted or otherwise vulnerable. We see this as a viable alternative to engaging in 30 minutes of exercise or eating a piece of fruit to care for themselves. Students are invited to send a text message, make a phone call, or send another form of communication to one of their friends or colleagues who may or may not be feeling something similar.

The mutuality of the act of reaching out occurs as the communication both provides care for the individual in need and enhances and embraces the need of the receiver. For instance, Kaisha sent several text messages to Sam last week. What is notable is that Kaisha began the exchange, but during the communication, Sam shares a feeling of isolation and is comforted by Kaisha. Sam wasn't depending on Kaisha for his well-being, but she was available for him during the exchange. Kaisha could describe her own needs and still help Sam with his.

TRANSCRIPTION 10.2. REACHING OUT

Text Exchange # 1, Monday

Kaisha: Hi! Tough Monday, here. New clients. Two clients not happy to be here.

Sam: Great to hear from you. My supervisor is out today. Trying to find my way.

Kaisha: Good luck. Let me know if I can help.

Sam: Thanks. You too!

Both Kaisha and Sam were able to manage their own personal needs by leveraging a natural inclination to reach out to others. A trend in the mental health field is actually the opposite of mutual care. Rather than approaching colleagues with the same nonjudgmental, nurturing disposition as with clients, counselors are vulnerable to displacing their stress onto their co-workers and even clients (Moore, 2017). You will recall that displacement is Freud's term for the defense mechanism wherein the person gets yelled out by their boss, and, since they can't do this back to the boss, they go home and kick the dog. As a field, we must find alternatives to "kicking" those closest to us in the work environment. Mutual care is an intentional behavior that allows us to ask for help and can provide to a colleague help in return. In our informal experiments with mutual care with our supervisees, CITs report success and positive results from this approach.

Personal Agency

In 1977, Albert Bandura presented his work on the concept of self-efficacy as it relates to changing behaviors. You may recall that self-efficacy is the belief in one's ability to accomplish a task. It is not confidence—a feeling about ability—rather, it is a cognitive appraisal of ability. Self-efficacy is a major component of social cognitive theory (Bandura, 1986), which describes how the social environment influences how one thinks and acts, and vice versa. Bandura's social cognitive theory, and the self-efficacy component in particular, has generated a significant amount of research. A lesser known, but still highly significant component of social cognitive theory, is **personal agency** (Bandura, 1989). Bandura (1989) defines personal agency by stating, "The capacity to exercise control over one's own thought processes, motivation, and action is a distinctly human characteristic. Because judgments and actions are partly self-determined, people can effect change in themselves and their situations through their own efforts" (p. 1175). Bandura also cautions that agency is neither a denial of the power of environment to shape behavior, nor is it that humans are completely autonomous. This middle-ground concept of agency is called emergent, interactive agency (Bandura, 1986, 1989).

So, why mention this here, in a section on self-advocacy, especially as it relates to well-being and self- and mutual care? As you have read in Chapter 9—and have

MULTICULTURAL CONSIDERATION 10.1

Not all cultures promote personal agency in the same ways. Review the material you have learned about various cultures prior to your practicum experience. What differences do you find in terms of personal agency among cultures? What differences do you find in terms of personal agency related to individual characteristics such as age, gender, sex, religious affiliation, ethnicity, and others?

likely experienced by now in practicum—CITs experience many circumstances in which they feel powerless. They don't feel that they have autonomy. While this is a natural occurrence in the context of counselor development, it can also represent a slippery slope toward externalizing responsibility to your own well-being, and even ethical behavior. Practicum is set up for growth, yet it can lead to students feeling somewhat lacking in agency for their development. Let's consider some common missed opportunities for self-advocacy and an increased sense of personal agency that might occur during the practicum experience.

Common Missed Opportunities for Self-Advocacy

In order to help you become more aware of the ways you might have experienced a lack of self-advocacy in your practicum environment, compiled are a number of student encounters. These include site-based events as well as student self-talk:

- My site supervisor is so busy, I don't want to bother him.

- My supervisor provides supervision on the fly (two- to five-minute conversations in passing), but rarely sits down with me to discuss my work.

- My site provides plenty of opportunities for indirect hours, but I'm struggling to get enough direct hours. I ask, but they tell me not to worry, because "the number of direct hours will increase soon." It's three-fourths of the way through the semester and I have less than half of my direct hours.

- At times, I feel like an unpaid staff member (e. g., doing everything that a full-time employee would; but, at other times, I feel abruptly reminded that I'm not a part of the team (e.g., "This meeting is for staff only"). I'm unclear what my role is exactly.

- I don't want to share my struggles with my faculty supervisor because they might

  o think poorly about me and my potential for success in the field;

  o feel let down that I'm still struggling in this area; or

  o might not be able to help.

- I hate to bother my faculty member because she seems so busy/unavailable; I figure that I can work it out on my own.

- My practicum instructor is "a," while my academic advisor is "b," but then there's professor "c" who oversees practicum and internship for the program. Whom can/should I talk with about my practicum experience?

The commonplace nature of these self-statements and site perceptions does not diminish their effect on students' ability to navigate them during the practicum experience. Reflection Question 10.1 will help you bolster your strengths and challenges regarding personal agency.

REFLECTION QUESTION 10.1

CHALLENGING THOUGHTS ABOUT SELF-ADVOCACY AND PERSONAL AGENCY

As you reflect on the statements in the previous section, which seem most likely to represent your thinking and experience?

Next, we offer the opportunity for you to follow up on your reflection by challenging your thoughts regarding missed opportunities in Table 10.2.

TABLE 10.2. Challenging Thoughts About Missed Opportunities for Self-Advocacy

Self-statement	Challenge Statement or Action
My site supervisor is so busy, I don't want to bother him.	
My supervisor provides supervision on the fly (two- to five-minute conversations in passing), but rarely sits down with me to discuss my work.	
My site provides plenty of opportunities for indirect hours, but I'm struggling to get enough direct hours. I ask, but they tell me not to worry, because "the number of direct hours will increase soon." It's three-fourths of the way through the semester and I have less than half of my direct hours.	
At times, I feel like an unpaid staff member (e. g., doing everything that a full-time employee would; but, at other times, I feel abruptly reminded that I'm not a part of the team (e.g., "This meeting is for staff only"). I'm unclear what my role is exactly.	
I don't want to share my struggles with my faculty supervisors because they might	
think poorly about me and my potential for success in the field;	
feel let down that I'm still struggling in this area; or	
might not be able to help.	
I hate to bother my faculty member because she seems so busy/unavailable; I figure that I can work it out on my own.	
My practicum instructor is "a," while my academic advisor is "b," but then there's professor "c" who oversees practicum and internship for the program. Whom can/should I talk with about my practicum experience?	

Balancing Gratitude, Deference, and Advocacy at the Site

One approach to self-advocacy experienced regularly by students in both practicum and internship involves the tension between gratitude and professional boundaries. On the one hand, students need to have a disposition of gratitude toward the site and site supervisor for the opportunity to experience growth and development in that particular context. This means being gracious when asked to perform tasks that are not glamorous or even clinical. For example, many students will file, update client charts, help tidy up the group counseling room, supervise clients or family members of clients, answer phones or monitor agency e-mail, and perform other tasks that can, when under stress to gain clinical experience, feel demeaning or undignified. In many, if not most cases, these are not meant to make the student feel this way; they are simply the indirect hours that provide a meaningful service to the site. One the other hand, there are times when circumstances at a site push a practicum student beyond what can be reasonably expected of them. Practicum students are not unpaid staff members, placed at the site to do work that an agency or practice is unwilling to pay a staff member to do. These situations arise as **boundary violations** that may require faculty intervention, but certainly necessitate **boundary assertions** by the practicum students. Examples include asking students to stay after their scheduled hours to perform agency tasks (occasionally volunteering to offer support in crunch times are exceptions), asking practicum students to conduct sessions when a counselor is absent so that the agency can bill for the session instead of rescheduling it, treating the student as a facilities custodian or front office administrative assistant, and the like. This is where gratitude for being able to learn at the site meets the needs to set professional boundaries.

The Quality of Supervision

Within in the context of supervision, you, as a student, have rights and responsibilities related to practicum. Munson (2002) described these in a **Supervisee Bill of Rights**. The intention was to present clear expectations for both practicum student and supervisor. Table 10.3 provides you with a list of student rights and responsibilities and supervisor desirable behaviors adapted from Munson's work (Woodside, 2017).

TABLE 10.3. Practicum Student Rights and Responsibilities and Supervisor Desirable Behaviors

Practicum Student Rights	Desirable Supervisor Behaviors	Practicum Student Responsibilities
Receives dependable supervision at regularly scheduled times	Schedules regular supervision times Is available for questions Is available for crises Makes plans for alternative site supervision when unavailable Is clear about how student prepares for and delivers services Provides appropriate developmental supervision (observation, direct supervision, indirect supervision) Provides opportunities to practice interventions.	Attends supervisory sessions Arrives on time to supervisory sessions Asks supervisor for instructions prior to providing services or assuming agency tasks or projects Asks supervisor for feedback after client work Reviews case notes and other assignments with supervisor and asks for feedback Attends relevant professional development meetings to learn about innovative interventions

Practicum Student Rights	Desirable Supervisor Behaviors	Practicum Student Responsibilities
Receives supervision that helps develop knowledge, skills, and values	Develops a supervision plan reflecting what student should learn and what student should do Plans supervision sessions based on student development and overall plan Merges supervision plan with student's expressed goals	Asks questions that facilitate learning Probes for clarity related to supervisor instructions or suggestions Make notes about work and follows up with questions
Receives supervision that demonstrates respect for student	Listens to student's description of experiences Seeks student's opinions and thoughts Respects confidential information shared by student Discusses, promptly, difficulties and challenges related to supervisory relationship Encourages student to try new skills	Shares practicum-related experiences with supervisor Remains open about strengths and limitations Shares thoughts and opinions about practicum work Uses personal disclosure to gain insight about professional growth and skill development Discusses challenges with the supervisory relationship.
Receives evaluation based on clear expectations and standards and based on data	Matches practicum goals with evaluation measures Reviews goals and evaluations Conducts informal evaluations regularly Provides clear positive and constructive feedback Conducts evaluations in a timely manner Reviews formal evaluations with student Seeks student's input in evaluations Creates a plan for growth based on evaluation	Shares professional and personal goals for practicum Seeks experiences that meet goals Prepares questions for supervisor and asks for specific feedback Provides examples of ways student believes he or she is meeting goals Keeps a list of goals to add or subtract from practicum contract Reviews the academic program evaluation forms prior to formal evaluation Identifies any areas where student needs additional work
Receives supervision from supervisor who has expertise in helping and demonstrates effective helping skills	Related to clients served: Demonstrates good attending skills Establishes rapport with clients Uses a variety of assessment techniques Formulates clear client conceptualizations Understands theories and approaches to helping Formulates treatment goals and plans Uses a variety of interventions effectively Assesses client cognitive and affective communication Responds with respect and equity to clients' individual differences Behaves in a professional and ethical manner	Prepares for supervision sessions asking questions related to the following: Intervention skills Assessment skills Conceptualizing clients Clients' individual needs and differences Treatment goals and plans Ethical issues and decision making
Receives supervision from individual who is a trained supervisor	Understands the roles and responsibilities of supervision Assesses what type of supervision the student needs Attends training related to supervision Asks for feedback from student on performance as a supervisor	Asks for help that facilitates professional growth and development Uses academic program's list of responsibilities to assess supervisor performance Provides faculty supervisor information related to supervisor performance and supervisory process When supervisor cannot provide support needed, seeks supervision from others Consults faculty, supervisor, and peers

Original work from Munson (2002); adapted from Woodside (2017)

In spite of program standards for supervision and knowledge of supervisor desirable behaviors, it is sometimes difficult to judge the quality of supervision. Naturally, supervisor behaviors are often uneven, ranging from exemplary to merely adequate or poor. You should not expect supervision to be perfect, and there are many ways to conduct supervision and develop a supervisory relationship. If you believe you are not receiving the supervision you need, based on your rights and the supervisor desirable behaviors delineated in Table 10.3, talk with your faculty supervisor and ask for suggestions about how to proceed.

Considering Poor or Harmful Supervision

More serious considerations arise when supervisors provide poor supervision or **harmful supervision**. Both these limit a student's professional growth and development (Ellis, 2001; Ellis et al., 2014). Let's examine what defines poor supervision and harmful supervision. Behaviors linked to supervisee rights and that are associated with poor supervision are listed in Table 10.4.

TABLE 10.4. Supervisee Rights and Poor Supervision

Supervisee Rights	Poor Supervision
Receive dependable supervision at regularly scheduled times	Maintains an irregular supervision schedule Consistently arrives late to supervision meeting Consistently comes to supervision ill-prepared Communicates using an aggressive tone
Receive supervision that helps develop knowledge, skills, and values	Assigns most tasks and activities on an ad hoc basis Relates all assignments to supervisor needs rather than practicum contract and goals Disregards student's interests Refuses to share ethical decision-making process
Receive supervision that demonstrates respect for student	Maintains communication at a "surface" and business level Criticizes student in front of others Demands that student's work mirror supervisor behaviors Disregards student's concerns about discrimination and oppression related to client work Ignores any ruptures in the supervisory relationship
Receive evaluation based on clear expectations and standards and based on data	Evaluates student without observation Evaluates student without reference to established goals Evaluates student without reviewing criteria for evaluation Only discusses student's limitations Surprises the student with strong criticism at the final evaluation
Receive supervision from supervisor who has expertise in helping and demonstrates effective helping skills	Only sees his or her strengths and does not see his or her limitations Only discusses his or her own strengths with student Practices outside his or her areas of competence Rarely asks other colleagues to work with student
Receive supervision from an individual who has training in the practice of supervision	Does not talk with student about how to improve supervision Does not seek training in supervision Does not consult with faculty supervisor about how to match student experience with academic program goals.

Adapted from Woodside, M. (2017)

Doing harm within the context of supervision, while at times is difficult to distinguish from poor supervision, extends beyond ineffective work with the practicum student. Harmful supervision means hurting or traumatizing the practicum student (Ellis et al., 2014). Specific behaviors that Ellis (2001) suggests are harmful include suggesting or engaging in sexual relationships, discriminating against or oppressing the student, disrespecting boundaries, or abusing the student.

Ellis (2001) presents possible outcomes of harmful supervision: psychological, functiona, emotional, and physical (see Table 10.5).

TABLE 10.5. Outcomes of Harmful Supervision

Aspects of Harmful Supervision	Outcomes of Harmful Supervision
Psychological harm	Feelings of guilt, shame, fear, and mistrust
Functional impairment in professional or personal life	Inability to maintain relationships, organize daily tasks, or follow a schedule
Emotional harm	Development and aggravation of expressions of anxiety, depression, or post-traumatic stress syndrome
Physical debilitation	Issues such as chronic illness, sleep disorders, or increased use of alcohol or substance abuse

Adapted from Woodside, M. (2017)

Whether you believe that you are involved in poor or harmful supervision, it is important for you to share the details of your experience with your faculty supervisor. If you believe that your faculty supervisor is delivering supervision in a poor or harmful way, then ask the head of your academic program or the department head for assistance. Be clear about the behaviors you have observed or experienced. And plan your next steps.

Summary

When it comes to counselors advocating for their individual personal and professional needs, the challenges are great. Addressing one's own needs can feel selfish, especially when working in a field that seems to value self-sacrifice and that asks so much of the counselor. We can tend toward martyrdom as a means of avoiding the discomfort of (a) identifying our needs, (b) asking for what we need, (c) expecting those needs to be taking seriously, and (d) taking the steps necessary to meet those needs. Self-advocacy is a process that involves self-awareness, personal well-being, personal agency, and self-care and mutual care. These constructs are dynamic and interrelated, and they shape the kind of counselor you will become. We encourage you to seek support as needed, and to challenge yourself in your interpretation of when that is.

Key Terms

4 Ps of self-care

Action

Administrative supervision

Boundary assertions

Boundary violations

Chronic variable stress

Clinical supervision

Contemplation

Dang and sangganjanavanich's approach to wellness

Harmful supervision

Maintenance

Mutual care

Personal agency

Poor supervision

Precontemplation

Preparation

Relapse

Self-advocacy

Self-awareness

Self-care

Self-efficacy

Stages of change

Supervisee bill of rights

Supervision

Supervisory relationship

Well-being

Wellness

References

American Counseling Association (ACA). (2014). *2014 ACA Code of Ethics*. Alexandria, VA: Author.

Baldwin, D. R., Towler, K., Oliver M. D. II, & Datta, S. (2017, July-December). An examination of college student wellness: A research and liberal arts perspective. *Health Psychology Open*, 1–9. doi:10.1177/2055102917719563

Bandura, A. (1989). Human agency in social cognitive theory. *American Psychologist, 44*(9), 1175–1184.

Bandura, A. (1986). *Social foundations of thought and action: A social cognitive theory*. Englewood Cliffs, NJ: Prentice-Hall.

Barragan, R. C., & Dweck, C. S. (2014). Rethinking natural altruism: Simple reciprocal interactions trigger children's benevolence. *Proceedings of the National Academy of Sciences of the United States of America, 111*(48), 17071–17074.

Bernard, J. M., & Goodyear, R. K. (2014). *Fundamentals of clinical supervision* (5th ed.). Boston, MA: Allyn & Bacon.

Biswas-Diener, R. (2013). *Invitation to positive psychology: Research and tools for the professional (The positive psychology workbook series)*. Milwaukie, OR: Positive Acorn.

Center for Disease Control. (2018). *Health-related quality of life: Well-being concepts*. Retrieved from https://www.cdc.gov/hrqol/wellbeing.htm

Council for Accreditation for Counseling and Related Programs. (2016). *2016 CACREP Standards*. Retrieved from http://www.cacrep.org/for-programs/2016-cacrep-standards/

Dang, Y., & Sangganjanavanich, V. F. (2015). Promoting counselor professional and personal well-being through advocacy. *Journal of Counselor Leadership and Advocacy, 2*(1), 1–13. doi.org/10.1080/2326716X.2015.1007179

Diener, E. (2009). *Assessing well-being: The collected works of Ed Diener*. New York, NY: Springer.

Diener, E., & Biawas-Diener, R. (2008). *Happiness: Unlocking the mysteries of psychological wealth*. Malden, MA: Blackwell.

Ellis, M. V. (2001). Harmful supervision, a cause for alarm: Comment on Gray et al. (2001) and Nelson and Friedlander (2001). *Journal of Counseling Psychology, 48*(4), 401–406.

Ellis, M. V., Berger, L., Hanus, A. E., Ayala, E. E., Swords, B. A., & Siembor, M. (2014). Inadequate and harmful supervision: Testing a revised framework and assessing occurrence. *The Counseling Psychologist, 42*(4), 434–472. doi:10.1177/0011000013508656

Falender, C. A. (2014). Clinical supervision in a competency-based era. *South African Journal of Psychology, 44*(1), 6–17. doi:10.1177/0081246313516260

Karademas, E. C. (2007). Positive and negative aspects of well-being: Common and specific predictors. *Personality and Individual Differences, 43*(2), 277–287. doi:10.1016/j.paid.2006.11.031

Koolhaas, J. M., Bartolomucci, A., Buwalda, B. D., De Boer, S. F., Flügge, G., Korte, S. M., … & Richter-Levin, G. (2011). Stress revisited: A critical evaluation of the stress concept. *Neuroscience & Biobehavioral Reviews, 35*(5), 1291–1301. doi:10.1016/j.neubiorev.2011.02.003

Moore, G. P. (2017). Critical incidents in mental health units may be better understood and managed with a Freudian/Lacanian psychoanalytic framework. *European Journal of Psychotherapy & Counselling, 19*(1), 43–60.

Munson, C.E. (2002). *Clinical social work supervision* (3rd ed.). New York, NY: Hayworth Press.

Myers, J. E., & Sweeney, T. J. (2004). Wellness counseling: The evidence base for practice. *Journal of Counseling & Development, 86*(4), 482–493. doi:10.1002/j.1556-6678.2008.tb00536.x

Oxford English Dictionary. (2018). Supervision. Retrieved from http://www.oed.com.proxy.lib.utk.edu:90/view/Entry/194558?redirectedFrom=supervisin#eid

Painter, E., & Woodside, M. (2016). Vicarious trauma: Emotional disruption and approaches to coping. *Counseling & Wellness: A Professional Counseling Journal, 5*. Retrieved from http://openknowledge.nau.edu/view/divisions/CWJ.html

Pompeo, A. M., & Levitt, D. H. (2014). A path of counselor self-awareness. *Counseling and Values, 59*(1), 80–94.

Prochaska, J. O., & Norcross, J. C. (2014). *Systems of psychotherapy: A transtheoretical analysis* (8th ed.). Stamford, CT: Cengage.

Professional Counselor's Desk Reference. (2018). The identity of professional counselors: Clinical supervision within counseling practice. *Credo Online*. Retrieved from https://search-credoreferencecom.proxy.lib.utk.edu:2050/content/entry/sppcd/clinical_supervision_within_counselingpractice/0

Rinat, M., & Haya, M. Z. (2018). Differences in self-advocacy among hard of hearing and typical hearing students. *Research in Developmental Disabilities, 72*, 118–127. doi:10.1016/j.ridd.2017.11.005

Substance Abuse and Mental Health Services Administration (SAMSHA). (2018). The eight dimensions of wellness. *Wellness Initiative*. Retrieved from https://www.samhsa.gov/wellness-initiative/eight-dimensions-wellness

Taylor, S. B., Anglin, J. M., Paode, P. R., Riggert, A. G., Olive, M. F., & Conrad, C. D. (2014). Chronic stress may facilitate the recruitment of habit-and addiction-related neurocircuitries through neuronal restructuring of the striatum. *Neuroscience, 280*, 231–242. doi.org/10.1016/j.neuroscience.2014.09.029

Woodside, M., Ziegler, M., & Paulus, T. M. (2009). Understanding school counseling internships from a communities of practice framework. *Counselor Education and Supervision, 49*(1), 20–38.

CHAPTER 11

Assessment and
EVALUATION

INTRODUCTION

Most people dislike being evaluated. It can be unpredictable, unnerving, and just uncomfortable. However, it is a necessary, even vital part of our work as counselors, both our work with clients and our own personal and professional critical reflection. It is possible that our empathy for clients can help us be patient with ourselves as we face the uncertainty and angst that being evaluated evokes.

Think about the clients that you have seen thus far. Whether these clients are children, adolescents, or adults, as they assume the client role, they have doubts and fears about their part in the counseling relationship and the counseling process. Many of these are related to evaluation: "How will I appear to this counselor? How will my counselor judge me? Will I fail or be successful in this experience?" As counselors, we try to allay our clients' fears, and we work with them to understand what might be the experience of success in counseling. We want them to have a clear awareness of what progress in counseling looks like for them. And we hope that this clarity will help them feel more supported and less evaluated.

In much the same way that clients need to have an idea of what success in counseling looks like, counselors in training (CITs) need to have a sense of how success manifests itself on their journey to becoming counselors. Of course, while the doubts and fears of the CIT may be similar to clients' beginning the counseling process, the place of evaluation is very different. Therefore, it is important to understand the process of evaluation and how that process helps you define your competence and progress on the journey of learning to become a counselor. In this chapter, laying the foundation for understanding assessment and the evaluation process supports your participation in it in a positive way. The goals of the chapter follow.

GOALS OF THE CHAPTER

- Understand the role of both assessment and evaluation in practicum student development
- Reflect on the place that supervision has in the assessment and evaluation process
- Use the IDM to explore the assessment of the competencies of a professional counselor
- Examine an empirically validated approach to assessment and evaluation

RELATED CACREP GOALS

Section 3: PROFESSIONAL PRACTICE, ENTRY-LEVEL PROFESSIONAL PRACTICE

- B. Supervision of practicum and internship students includes program-appropriate audio/video recordings and/or live supervision of students' interactions with clients.
- C. Formative and summative evaluations of the student's counseling performance and ability to integrate and apply knowledge are conducted as part of the student's practicum and internship. (CACREP, 2016a)

Section 5: ENTRY-LEVEL SPECIALTY AREAS, C. CLINICAL MENTAL HEALTH COUNSELING: 3. PRACTICE

- a. intake interview, mental status evaluation, biopsychosocial history, mental health history, and psychological assessment for treatment planning and caseload management
- b. techniques and interventions for prevention and treatment of a broad range of mental health issues
- c. strategies for interfacing with the legal system regarding court-referred clients
- d. strategies for interfacing with integrated behavioral health care professionals
- e. strategies to advocate for persons with mental health issues (CACREP, 2016b)

Defining Assessment and Evaluation

Both **assessment** and **evaluation** are integral parts of an academic program focused on educating and training professional counselors. These terms, while related, represent different ways to understand the details of your profession development and its various parts or aspects. Assessment and evaluation also help you and your supervisors understand your professional development, monitor it, and establish goals for growth.

Specifically, an assessment process guides the developmental process of professional growth and highlights opportunities for growth in particular areas. Assessment in this sense can be seen as continuous or **formative**. This means that the assessment occurs over time, focusing on what is going well and progress being made and indicating where improvements are in order. The formative assessment focuses on refinement of skills and improvement. It is during formative evaluation that you and your supervisor may identify strategies for enhancing skill development, especially that which supports client growth. When, during your practicum experience, you have prepared documentations, such as a transcription of a counseling session, case notes, a case study, and/or notes from supervision, you are providing concrete ways for you and your supervisor to assess your work. Critical reflection of this document allows you to view these documents to enhance your own self-assessment.

Evaluation, on the other hand, is a **summative** process that represents a review and analysis of a counseling student's growth. It is a punctuated, threshold-based process. A common time for evaluation is at the conclusion of an experience, or, in the academic world, at the conclusion of a term. In other words, assessment is ongoing, while evaluation may be thought of as cumulative, an ending. Tools of evaluation are represented by a final evaluation that measures counselor competencies.

Let's look at your current experiences of assessment and evaluation in practicum. This reflection will establish a foundation from which you can apply the principles of evaluation you learn throughout this chapter (see Reflection Question 11.1).

REFLECTION QUESTION 11.1

PARTICIPATING IN THE EVALUATION PROCESS

Think back to the first or second time you watched or listened to your video- or audio-taped session with a client.

1. When I first heard my voice, I felt … .
2. When I listened for my response to my client … .
3. I felt embarrassed when … .
4. When I saw/heard myself make an error, I … .
5. When I thought I responded well, I … .
6. When my supervisor asked me to stop the tape, I … .
7. When my supervisor responded, "Tell me about your thoughts about your client," I … .
8. Describe any feelings of fear, guilt, shame, embarrassment while listening to the tape.
9. Describe any feelings of fear, guilt, share, embarrassment while talking with your supervisor about the tape.
10. Describe any evaluations (thoughts, emotions, behaviors) about your work.

Purposes of Evaluation

Assessment and evaluation during the experience of practicum is critical to the learning process. Their purposes reflect four areas of focus: protecting the client, protecting the counseling student, counseling student welfare and growth, and remediation and gatekeeping. At the heart of these four purposes are a strong commitment and ethical and legal values and standards that undergird supervisor adherence to considering the welfare of the client, and, at the same time, protecting the counseling student (St. John's University, n.d.). These include the following:

STANDARD OF CARE: Normative or expected professional practice

STATUTORY LIABILITY: Written standards and penalties in the law

NEGLIGENCE: Failing to observe standard of care

NEGLIGENT LIABILITY: Failing to provide a standard of care

VICARIOUS LIABILITY: Responsible for others based on authority

DIRECT LIABILITY: Being responsible for one's one actions

PRIVILEGED COMMUNICATION: Confidential communications

DUTY TO PROTECT: Obligation to protect a client in danger

DUTY TO WARN: Obligation to report abuse in a timely manner (St. John's University, n.d., slide 19).

In addition, each of these purposes are directly linked to the American Counseling Association's 2014 Code of Ethics (ACA, 2014).

Protecting the Client

By the time you reach practicum, if not before, you have the power help others in need. However, you also have access to those who may be harmed and the power to cause harm. Speaking of your position of influence or power is a difficult way to begin a section about the purposes of assessment and evaluation. But, the reality is that since we, as counselors, have access, opportunity, and means to do good for clients, *we also can do harm*. This statement is not intended to paralyze you with fear and trepidation; instead, it is intended to help you recognize the reality of your obligations and responsibility. Spurred by your own responsibility for **client welfare**, it is important to keep this idea of potential harm present in your thinking and seek out and participate willingly in the assessment and evaluation processes during practicum. Supervision is one way to participate in the assessment and evaluation processes.

When we are learning to be a counselor, it is easy to focus on our own goals. Within the context of this self-focus, seeking and accepting positive feedback regarding our work may facilitate an avoidance of fears and feelings of inadequacies. As graduate students in counseling, we tend to be high intensity, driven individuals who seek affirmation. You are here because you do well in school, and, in all likelihood, up to this point in your training and college experience in general, you may have received regular affirmations regarding your written work. Yet, on reaching practicum, the commitment to protecting client welfare requires you to make the shift from your need for high achievement and outstanding academic performance to rigorous self-examination. This is especially true as it pertains to the skills that influence and protect clients. The 2014 ACA Code of Ethics reflects this need for engaging in supervision to protect client welfare (ACA, 2014) (see Figure 11.1).

FIGURE 11.1. Counselor supervision and client welfare

F.1. Counselor Supervision and Client Welfare

F.1.a. Client Welfare

A primary obligation of counseling supervisors is to monitor the services provided by supervisees. Counseling supervisors monitor client welfare and supervisee performance and professional development. To fulfill these obligations, supervisors meet regularly with supervisees to review the supervisees' work and help them become prepared to serve a range of diverse clients. Supervisees have a responsibility to understand and follow the ACA Code of Ethics.*

Source: American Counseling Association, https://www.counseling.org/resources/aca-code-of-ethics.pdf, pp. 12. Copyright © 2014 by American Counseling Association. Reprinted with permission.

Questions for Supervisors and Practicum Students

Here are three questions that will help you reflect on the protection of the clients you serve. They may appear simplistic, but they will help you build the critical reflection you need to meet client welfare.

1. What are the client needs, issues, and challenges?

2. Do I (the practicum student) have the knowledge, skills, and values to help meet the client's needs?

3. Where might I do harm to this client?

Protecting the Counseling Student

Role ambiguity is a challenge for students and site supervisors alike, especially as practicum students share responsibility for client care, yet are in a subordinate role in an agency or school setting (Brat, O'Hara, McGhee, & Chang, 2016). Within the academic program, even during practicum, students remain in the "student role" even though they are assuming responsibilities for client care and acting as representatives of the academic institution and the academic program. This means that **protecting the counseling student** is important. Nevertheless, as a CIT, your responsibility for client welfare, even under supervision, is an important one. It is your faculty supervisor and your site supervisor's responsibility to guide you in this role as you step into your professional role and identity. This can be a challenging process and requires support and challenge from these two supervisors. A strong supervising relationship is key to maintaining these dual roles (Ladany & Friedlander, 1995). Reading Figure 11.2, F.7.i of the 2014 ACA Code of Ethics, reflects this need for engaging in supervision to protect client welfare (ACA, 2014).

FIGURE 11.2. Field placements

F.7.i. Field Placements

Counselor educators develop clear policies and provide direct assistance within their training programs regarding appropriate field placement and other clinical experiences. Counselor educators provide clearly stated roles and responsibilities for the student or supervisee, the site supervisor, and the program supervisor. They confirm that site supervisors are qualified to provide supervision in the formats in which services are provided and inform site supervisors of their professional and ethical responsibilities in this role.*

Source: American Counseling Association, https://www.counseling.org/resources/aca-code-of-ethics.pdf, pp. 14. Copyright © 2014 by American Counseling Association. Reprinted with permission.

Questions for Supervisors and Practicum Students

Following are four questions that will help you and your supervisor consider your own growth and development as a counselor:

1. What are my specific needs as a practicum student?
2. What roles and responsibilities will I assume during practicum to meet those needs?
3. In what areas of professional growth will the supervisor refer me to other staff?
4. How will I, as a practicum student, talk to my supervisor about ethical and multicultural issues?

Counseling Student Welfare and Growth

Change during your counselor training experience is not only likely, it is expected. This means that the person you are upon entry into your training program is somewhat different than the person you are as you enter and then exit the practicum experience. The difference reflects both **counseling student welfare and growth**. Practicum is a prime time for you to determine if a profession that requires such growth is a good fit for you. In our work with clients, counselors must continue to stretch and grow to monitor both their own behaviors and to model for clients an orientation toward change that is inviting and normalizing. Not everyone is comfortable with this state of flux as a professional and may find the growth process too onerous and otherwise intimidating. This crisis, if you will, is an excellent opportunity for you to seek guidance from your practicum instructor, advisor, and others to determine your fit. Reading Figure 11.3, F.8. of the 2014 ACA Code of Ethics (ACA, 2014), reflects this concern that faculty and site supervisors have for student welfare.

FIGURE 11.3. Student welfare

F.8. Student Welfare

F.8.c. Self-Growth Experiences

Self-growth is an expected component of counselor education. Counselor educators are mindful of ethical principles when they require students to engage in self-growth experiences. Counselor educators and supervisors inform students that they have a right to decide what information will be shared or withheld in class.

Source: American Counseling Association, https://www.counseling.org/resources/aca-code-of-ethics.pdf, pp. 14. Copyright © 2014 by American Counseling Association. Reprinted with permission.

Questions for Supervisors and Practicum Students

The following questions will help practicum students and supervisors sort out issues related to practicum student welfare and professional growth:

1. Where do I feel the stresses and stretches of my practicum experience?
2. How do I work through these crises of the practicum experience?
3. Do I have any thoughts or feelings of being unworthy or ill prepared for my responsibilities?
4. Have I shared these thoughts or feelings?
5. Am I supported by my supervisors? Are the issues of lack of support serious enough to ask for help from others?

Remediation

One of the values of a developmental approach to helping others is the hopefulness of a positive orientation toward a client's personal growth. Rather than viewing clients as having a disease that is incurable or that will require lifelong treatment, wellness and developmental approaches offer a view of growth as the natural state of things. For example, a client with depression can be viewed as having this illness or as being in a state of change without the resources needed to grow through it. The latter assumption is that once these resources are in place, depression will be reduced.

Assuming this positive orientation toward the professional growth of practicum students is important. This includes believing in growth and providing honest feedback, and then support, when students need support. This support occurs in terms of **remediation**.

What is remediation as it relates to the practicum experience? Evaluation leading to remediation in counselor training represents the view that students are in a state wherein their skills or dispositions are in need of support. When remediation occurs, supervisors have assessed or evaluated the counseling student and the counseling student's performance in practicum and have decided the student, if allowed to continue, unchallenged and unsupported, may cause harm to self or clients, or both. A remediation response, therefore, is to respond to the assessment or evaluation with specific supports that provide counseling students with the tools to *grow through* their counselor development struggles. Often, this remediation—a type of returning to an earlier developmental stage to be better prepared to meet the expectations of the current stage—is sufficient to course correct and continue to becoming a competent counselor. Reasons for remediation based on a lack of professional competence may include a CITs' developmental issues, discussed earlier, and/or unethical behavior or less-than-favorable dispositions. In addition, there may be limitations related to the academic program or the practicum site such as a lack of adequate professional counselor training or inadequate supervision (Johnson et al., 2008).

The 2014 ACA Code of Ethics (ACA, 2014) indicates the importance of providing honest and critical evaluation. Figure 11.4, F.9 a, b, and c of the 2014 ACA Code of Ethics (ACA, 2014) reflects this need for engaging in supervision to protect client welfare and support student professional development.

FIGURE 11.4. Field evaluation and remediation

F.9. Evaluation and Remediation

F.9.a. Evaluation of Students

Counselor educators clearly state to students, prior to and throughout the training program, the levels of competency expected, appraisal methods, and timing of evaluations for both didactic and clinical competencies. Counselor educators provide students with ongoing feedback regarding their performance throughout the training program.

F.9.b. Limitations

Counselor educators, through ongoing evaluation, are aware of and address the inability of some students to achieve counseling competencies. Counselor educators do the following:

1. assist students in securing remedial assistance when needed,
2. seek professional consultation and document their decision to dismiss or refer students for assistance, and
3. ensure that students have recourse in a timely manner to address decisions requiring them to seek assistance or to dismiss them and provide students with due process according to institutional policies and procedures.

F.9.c. Counseling for Students

If students request counseling, or if counseling services are suggested as part of a remediation process, counselor educators assist students in identifying appropriate services.*

Source: American Counseling Association, https://www.counseling.org/resources/aca-code-of-ethics.pdf, pp. 15. Copyright © 2014 by American Counseling Association. Reprinted with permission.

Questions for Supervisors and Practicum Students

Remediation can be a difficult and stressful process. The following questions can help you, as a practicum student, participate fully in this process:

1. What is the purpose of remediation?

2. Do I understand the academic program's remediation process?

3. Do I have an advocate during the process?

4. Do I understand due process? Has due process been following during my remediation process?

Gatekeeping

Gatekeeping is an important role of supervision and is related directly to the evaluation process (as is defined in Figure 11.5). Ultimately for you, a CIT, your instructors, site supervisors, and faculty supervisors will have an important role in evaluating your knowledge, skills, values, and readiness to become a professional counselor. There are numerous steps in becoming a professional counselor, including class performance, satisfactory performance in practicum and internship, demonstration of personal dispositions needed for professional work, and graduation. Once you have met the criteria for graduation, faculty in an academic program write an endorsement for you for licensure or certification. At that point, other professional organizations and state regulatory bodies become involved in certifying and licensing your professional status.

Gatekeeping, as it relates to your practicum experience, occurs during your time at your practicum site, during supervision, and in your group supervision. Gatekeeping is tied directly to work with clients, your written work in practicum class, and the results of your midterm and final evaluations. Remediation, the process discussed earlier, is one component of the gatekeeping process. Perhaps remediation does not occur as often as it should or site supervisors miss opportunities to challenge their practicum students and then support their development. There are reasons that site supervisors in particular are reluctant to evaluate students in a way that suggests a need for remediation. Site supervisors see their role as one of support, rather than one of challenge. In fact, site supervisors indicate that negative evaluations of a CIT may hamper their ability to encourage students, give them confidence in their abilities, and help them work autonomously (Freeman, Garner, Fairgrieve, & Pitts, 2016). Site supervisors do support the type of evaluation that demonstrates growth, expecting that practicum students will not necessarily perform well at the beginning of their field-based experiences. Another reason that site supervisors also show reluctance to evaluate their supervisees in a negative way reflects their fear that they will damage the supervisory relationships, especially if they indicate a CIT's lack of competence (Miller & Koerin, 2002). A final reason supervisors struggle with indicating students who need remediation represents the legal challenges they may face in doing so (Bernard & Goodyear, 2014). Our society is increasingly litigious and that trend is reflected in legal student challenges to remediation or release from a counselor education program. The professional, emotional, and financial impact of legal action is daunting (Henderson & Dufrene, 2011; McAdams & Foster, 2007).

Remediation, as a part of gatekeeping, may be difficult because the students receiving a remediation or development plan do not respond in ways that lead to growth through the process

(Figure 11.5). Students may resist participating in the development plan or they may not be able to develop the competence (knowledge, skills, and values) required for program students during the time limitations of the plan. This lack of success requires that students and faculty get together to reflect on student goals and motivations in pursuing the degree in professional counseling. In short, students may decide to leave the counseling program. And, where the process of remediation does not promote self-awareness leading to self-selecting out of training for professional counseling, program faculty may take action to remove that student.

The intent of remediation is to support the student's professional growth, helping the student develop competencies, professional and personal dispositions, and an ethical and culturally sensitive orientation to client care. However, for a few students engaged in remediation, leaving a professional counseling program may be the ultimate result of self-assessment and self-reflection. In some sense, students who leave a counseling program have found the answer to the question you considered in Chapter 1: "Is the profession of counseling right for me?" So, as dark or difficult as this may feel, it is important that, during practicum, you closely monitor your own behaviors and reactions to working with clients and in community mental health or school settings.

FIGURE 11.5. Gatekeeping and remediation

F.6. Counseling Supervision Evaluation, Remediation, and Endorsement

F.6.a. Evaluation

Supervisors document and provide supervisees with ongoing feedback regarding their performance and schedule periodic formal evaluative sessions throughout the supervisory relationship.

F.6.b. Gatekeeping and Remediation

Through initial and ongoing evaluation, supervisors are aware of supervisee limitations that might impede performance. Supervisors assist supervisees in securing remedial assistance when needed. They recommend dismissal from training programs, applied counseling settings, and state or voluntary professional credentialing processes when those supervisees are unable to demonstrate that they can provide competent professional services to a range of diverse clients. Supervisors seek consultation and document their decisions to dismiss or refer supervisees for assistance. They ensure that supervisees are aware of options available to them to address such decisions.*

Source: American Counseling Association, https://www.counseling.org/resources/aca-code-of-ethics.pdf, pp. 13. Copyright © 2014 by American Counseling Association. Reprinted with permission.

Questions for Supervisors and Practicum Students

The following questions will help you and your supervisor think more deeply about gatekeeping, remediation, and evaluation:

1. What strengths do I, as a practicum student, bring to the practicum experience?

2. How do I now answer the question, "Is the profession of counseling right for me?"

3. Do I have any serious limitations that need to be addressed during supervision?

4. How will my supervisor and I address these?

5. What type of supervisory relationship do we need to have to answer these difficult questions?

Place of Supervision in Evaluation

> ### ETHICAL CONSIDERATION 11.1
>
> Ethical guidelines permeate this section related to assessment and evaluation. Choose one of the terms and its related ethical standard and talk about why this standard is important to you and what barriers you might encounter related to living with the standard in your work as a counselor.

During the practicum experience, continuous or formative assessment occurs during supervision. In fact, you will note that throughout the earlier discussion of assessment and evaluation and their definitions and purposes, the work of the supervisor is at the forefront of these activities. This **supervision** represents a developmental conversation about the practicum student's experience related to the development of professional competencies. A similar conversation occurs with faculty supervisor, individual or triadic, and practicum group supervision. The Council for Accreditation of Counseling and Related Program (CACREP) provides guidance for standards of supervision, such that supervision and, by extension, assessment are weekly events incorporated into professional practice culture (see Figure 11.6).

FIGURE 11.6. Section 3 Professional Practice

Section 3 Professional Practice

H. Practicum students have weekly interaction with supervisors that averages one hour per week of individual and/or triadic supervision throughout the practicum by (1) a counselor education program faculty member, (2) a student supervisor who is under the supervision of a counselor education program faculty member, or (3) a site supervisor who is working in consultation on a regular schedule with a counselor education program faculty member in accordance with the supervision agreement.

I. Practicum students participate in an average of 1½ hours per week of group supervision on a regular schedule throughout the practicum. Group supervision must be provided by a counselor education program faculty member or a student supervisor who is under the supervision of a counselor education program faculty member. **

Source: Council for Accreditation of Counseling and Related Programs, http://www.cacrep.org/section-3-professional-practice/.
Copyright © 2016 by CACREP.

Engaging in assessment and evaluation of the CIT and encouraging the CIT to participate in self-assessment are two major responsibilities that supervisors assume when they accept a supervisory role. That said, many supervisors are uncomfortable in their supervisory roles and many lack the skills and competence to perform them. Let's listen to a panel discussion among site supervisors about their experiences with supervising counselors in training (see Transcription 11.1).

TRANSCRIPTION 11.1. SUPERVISORS TALK ABOUT THEIR EXPERIENCES WITH ASSESSMENT AND EVALUATION

Moderator: I want to thank the members of our panel of supervisors who are currently working with master's students in clinical mental health counseling and school counseling. My first question to you is, "What are your thoughts about assessing and evaluating your practicum students in counseling? What are the issues you face?"

Ms. Dunn: Do you want me to be honest? I don't like that part of my role. I feel really uncomfortable. When I am a counselor, I don't evaluate my clients. I don't want to evaluate my supervisees.

Mr. Tabor: Ms. Dunn, I think about this a little bit differently. I am glad to engage in evaluation. In fact, I think that everything we do with our practicum students is part of evaluation. For instance, when I choose a first client for my practicum student to see, I am assessing what I think the skills of this student are and what client she or he can work with best. I am unclear the difference between assessment and evaluation. I just think of it all as evaluation.

Ms. Loas: Well, I might be able to evaluate better, but the clinical mental health program students I work with don't have much direction. So, I am not clear what the program wants. They provide some general guidelines about knowledge, skills, and professional behavior. But it is difficult for me to tell a student, "You don't listen and reflect emotion and content of the client," when the academic program doesn't tell me what that is.

Ms. Dunn: That doesn't seem so difficult for me. I have created some work sheets that provide examples of listening and responding behaviors. I observe my students with their clients and then ask them to show me where they demonstrated specific behaviors. But I see this as teaching and not as evaluating.

Mr. Herscher: [laughs]. Oh. I think I am really good at assessment and evaluation when I have an excellent student, like this term. The work seems to take care of itself. I have a list of goals for my practicum students. And then, using a practicum contract, I asked the students to add their personal and professional goals. And then we look at the final evaluation form and add goals that match that form. We use this as a road map. It may seem complicated, but it really is easy.

Ms. Loas: But what about when is it difficult? This is my first semester as a site supervisor. I sure could use some help.

Mr. Herscher: Last semester, supervision was really difficult. I had a student who was participating in remediation. For legal reasons, I had to document in detail all my work with the student. And we had to follow a remediation plan. And to be honest, the student was not mature enough to be in practicum. She couldn't get to work on time. She didn't want to follow the school rules. And she was very defensive about my challenging her work.

Ms. Dunn: Well, I will admit that assessment and evaluation are very difficult when you can give support, but you also have to challenge. That means that I also worry about the relationship I have with my supervisee. I think that that relationship is key to my work as a supervisor. I don't want to jeopardize it.

Moderator: Thanks so much for all your responses to this question. We will move on to another question.

Many supervisors describe the assessment and evaluation responsibilities as difficult and challenging (Elman & Forest, 2007; Jacobs et al., 2011). They indicate issues similar to those site supervisors on our panel: a concern for the supervisory relationship; a limited understanding of knowledge, skills, and values that represent competence; a lack of knowledge about academic program goals, self-developed areas of focus, and CIT goals; a lack of criteria for competence; and difficulty challenging CITs and a preference for supporting them.

A summary list of **favorable conditions for evaluation** suggested by Bernard and Goodyear (2014), based on scholarly work and research presented over the years (see Table 11.1), will help you understand how a positive environment is created. These conditions, which represent both behaviors, emotions, and ethical and multicultural considerations, offer insights about CIT self-advocacy in supervision. The favorable conditions represent both supervisor and practicum student role and responsibilities. At times there is considerable overlap, while other times these vary widely.

TABLE 11.1. Favorable Conditions for Evaluation

Favorable conditions	Supervisor role and responsibilities	Practicum student role and responsibilities
Power is embedded in supervision	The supervisory relationship is not among colleagues. Be empathetic and compassionate.	The supervisor bears responsibility for your actions. Be respectful. Ask for support.
Evaluation of student reflects the site and the academic program	Advise the student with whom you will share the results of your assessment and evaluation.	Ask supervisor what information he or she will share with faculty. Ask to be kept in the loop of communication.
Recognize student defensiveness is natural	Teach students how to receive feedback. Talk openly about defensiveness.	Ask for time to digest challenging feedback. Ask for specifics about how to move forward.

Continued

TABLE 11.1. Favorable Conditions for Evaluation *Continued*

Favorable conditions	Supervisor role and responsibilities	Practicum student role and responsibilities
Individual differences exist between the supervisor and the student	Articulate the individual differences, especially as they relate to evaluation. Address gender, race, and ethnic issues early and continually.	Spend time reflecting on the part that your background, gender, race, and ethnicity influence your ability to receive corrective feedback and your reaction to your supervisor's evaluation of your performance.
There should exist a common understanding of the components of evaluation	At the beginning of practicum and regularly thereafter, review with the student the academic program goals, your goals, and the student's goals that will be included in the evaluation. Midterm evaluation is an excellent time to review goals and make a plan, based on the goal achievement, for the focus of the second half of the term.	Review at least a few of the goals of practicum with your supervisor every week or two as a regular part of supervision. During midterm evaluation, review each goal. Make a plan, based on the goal achievement, for the focus of the second half of the term.
Understand the evaluation process within which the academic program works	Ask the academic program faculty how your evaluations will be used. Understand the due process followed in the academic program.	Ask your faculty supervisor how the site supervisor faculty evaluations will be used. Be sure you understand the process to use if you believe your evaluation is inaccurate or unfair.
Avoid early judgements or inflexible perceptions of your student	Conduct a continuous assessment of your student's work. Discuss evaluations in terms of development.	
Engage in professional development related to client care and supervision	Ask for feedback from student. Act on that feedback. Engage in professional development and discuss this with student. Understand and talk about one's limitations and the process of addressing them.	Provide new information for supervisor. Work with supervisor to incorporate the new information in his or her work.
Monitor the supervisory relationship	Maintain a relationship that is respectful, open, and professional. Attend to ruptures, especially those that occur during evaluation.	Be open and practice self-disclosure about growth and development and incidents that occur during practicum. Be open to communicate through ruptures in the relationship.
Supervise only if willing to assume responsibility	Conduct a personal assessment of willingness to supervise before accepting the responsibility.	

Adapted from Bernard & Goodyear (2014)

Janice, Jose, Kaisha, and Sam share their perspectives and experiences of assessment and evaluation. They addressed the prompt, "Describe your worries and concerns about assessment and evaluation."

TRANSCRIPTION 11.2. PRACTICUM STUDENTS TALK ABOUT THEIR EXPERIENCES WITH ASSESSMENT AND EVALUATION

Janice: "I know myself pretty well. Though, while in the counseling program, I have learned that I don't know myself as well as I thought. When it comes to being evaluated, my first response is to become rigid. As a returning student, early in our program I didn't have much confidence. And when I started in practicum, I feel that I returned to that state. I didn't see my site supervisor as the enemy or punitive, but I didn't believe that I could measure up. At the same time, I wanted to be perfect in my work. My faculty supervisor, Dr. Kim, suggested that I talk with my site supervisor about my anxieties about doing well and to help me work on accepting critical feedback as a way to improve, rather than as a condemnation of who I am. This isn't easy for me to do.

Jose: "You know, I am really easy going. And I am motivated but fairly low key. I know I am going to make mistakes, but I say, 'Give it to me straight, man,' I can handle it. My supervisor doesn't say much, so I find I have to ask for feedback. In the group supervision we had with Dr. Kim, she suggested that I ask for feedback each week from my supervisor. So, I take the lead. I think that my supervisor is getting used to giving me feedback."

Kaisha: "Okay, I am going to be honest. I think that I receive negative evaluations sometimes because I am Black. And it doesn't help that I am young, too, without much experience. We talked about oppression and bias in our diversity class. From that class, I could see how this could occur. And I am working in a rural area where there are few Blacks. I think that people look at me and think, 'Can she do this job?' And I have felt this type of discrimination occurring throughout my college career. I talked about this with Dr. Kim early in my practicum, and we talked about strategies that I could use in developing a relationship with my site supervisor."

Sam: "Evaluation is something that has been worked out very carefully since I am working in the university clinic. I think that my faculty supervisors want to model excellence in assessment and evaluation process. Everything is run by the numbers. For example, we discussed due process early in practicum. And each supervisory session, at least once, we refer back to my practicum contract. And, I rate each supervisory meeting and provide my supervisor feedback. When we talk in practicum class, I find my experience is very different from my other classmates. In some ways, I have it easy. But I am not learning to advocate for myself as much."

As you can see, each of our practicum students is having a very different experience of assessment and evaluation. In part, the experience reflects individual differences of the student. Also, the type of site and the supervisory strengths and abilities contribute to a unique environment in which assessment and evaluation takes place. What is clear is that the discussion of critical feedback during group supervision has helped each of the students understand both their own role and the role of their supervisor. And Dr. Kim is actively involved in supporting the development of self-advocacy for each.

Earlier in Reflection Question 11.1, you reflected on the emotions you have had regarding the assessment and evaluation process. Now, please take a moment to think about your own practicum experience as that experience reflects the favorable and less favorable conditions for evaluation that exist (see Reflection Question 11.2) and then discuss your thoughts with your faculty supervisor (see Discussion Together 11.1).

REFLECTION QUESTION 11.2

FAVORABLE AND LESS FAVORABLE CONDITIONS FOR EVALUATION

Consider your attitudes toward assessment and evaluation and your responses to being evaluated. What similarities and differences do you notice between yourself and your supervisor regarding supervision?

Discussion Together 11.1 will guide you and your classmates in a discussion with your faculty supervisor about your role and responsibility for creating favorable conditions for your assessment and evaluation experience.

DISCUSSION TOGETHER 11.1

Asking for Help: The Assessment and Evaluation Experience

How can you and your supervisor work together to build on strengths and address limitations related to assessment and evaluation?

Using the Integrated Developmental Model for Assessing Counseling Competencies

There are a number of ways to conceptualize the primary skill domains that counselors need in order to be successful (Welfare & Borders, 2010). Therefore, for the sake of simplicity (though it is hardly simple), let's look again at the integrated developmental model (IDM) proffered by Stoltenberg & McNeil (2011) introduced in Chapter 9. Specifically, in relationship to assessment and evaluation, consider the **IDM eight domains of counselor skill development** illustrated in Figure 9.3 and described afterward. As you look at Figure 9.3, each domain has a specific location. However, each domain's location is incidental—two domains located next to one another are not necessarily more closely related than two that are on opposite sides of the figure.

As you review these eight domains, note that you may feel stronger in some domains and weaker in others. It is vital to your wellness and development that you understand that during practicum, it is not realistic to expect to feel competent in all domains at all times. Therefore, view each domain individually and assume that each domain has a developmental trajectory. Competence in these domains are not fixed points; rather, they are targets of development and focus. In fact, you may find that as you focus closely on developing one domain, you may be weaker in the other domains, since these domains will have received much less of your attention. Making each of these domains more concrete by using evidence of your practicum work (i.e., counseling session transcripts, case notes, a case study, notes from supervision) will help you evaluate your professional growth (see Reflection Question 11.3).

LINKING IDM EIGHT DOMAINS TO YOUR PRACTICUM WORK

In reflecting on the eight domains in the IDM, (a) intervention skills, (b) assessment techniques, (c) interpersonal assessment, (d) client conceptualization, (e) individual differences, (f) theoretical orientation, (g) treatment plans and goals, and (h) professional ethics, what areas of development seem most salient to you?

MULTICULTURAL
CONSIDERATION 11.1

We know that supervision is influenced by multicultural dimensions of the supervisor and the supervisee. Review step eight of Reflection Question 11.3, "Review the results of this exercise in individual or triadic supervision," and note how multicultural similarities or differences might influence a discussion of supervision, and, in particular, practicum student performance in the IDM eight domains.

Using the Counseling Competencies Scale, Revised, for Evaluating Counseling Competencies

Evaluating your counseling skills, conditions, dispositions, and behaviors to endorse your professional competence is a difficult task. In fact, thinking about counseling competence raises a number of questions, doesn't it? For example, how would you yourself know when you met a competent counselor? If a loved one was seeking counseling services but did not know where to begin and asked you for advice, how would you respond? What would you tell them to look for in a counselor, beyond credentials? How will you know when (and if) you have become a competent counselor?

It is one thing to belief yourself to be skilled, but another to be evaluated in a way that is recognized by others. In fact, there are many times you will have the necessary skills and dispositions but do not perceive yourself that way. In these times, it helps to know there is a psychologically sound—valid and reliable—measure. Measures like these not only protect your future clients, they also support you in your program.

Measuring competencies and evaluating competence is directly related to due process. **Due process** is a legal term that defines your rights as a student. Due process in counselor education has been described as the supervisees' "right to be made aware of performance requirements, receive regular evaluation and feedback including notification of underperformance, have consequences of underperformance explained to them, and have an opportunity to discuss their underperformance and resultant consequences" (Welfare, 2010, p. 338). One approach to combine due process, assessment, and evaluation is to use a standardized instrument, such as the **counselor competencies scale, revised** (CCS-R) (Lambie, Mullen, Swank, & Blount, 2018).

The counselor competencies scale, revised (Lambie, Mullen, Swank, & Blount, 2018) is an example of a practicum assessment tool that promotes due process, self-assessment, and site and faculty evaluation of counselors in training. The CCS-R is divided into two development sections: counseling skills and therapeutic conditions, which contains 11 items and "focuses on primary counseling skills (verbal and nonverbal) and conditions that facilitate a therapeutic relationship with the client" (Lambie et al., 2018, p. 11); and counseling dispositions and behaviors, which includes 11 items that "focus[] on qualities and behaviors [for] counselors-in-training that are crucial for counseling competency" (Lambie et al., 2018, p. 11). The value of the CCS-R and its role in your development as a counseling, can be seen in the CCS-R training manual, where the authors assert,

> The development of effective and ethical professional counselors necessitates that individuals demonstrate the core counseling conditions and skills, such as congruence or genuineness, compassion, empathy, and the development of a strong therapeutic relationship. A primary goal in counseling is to foster a strong therapeutic relationship between the counselor and his or her client(s) based on the client(s) presenting problem/concern and systemic influences (e.g., family, work, friends, and educational system) within a multicultural society. (Lambie & Swank, 2016, p. 4)

A summary of the two dimensions of the CCS-R is as follows: (a) the introduction, (b) a description of what the CCS-R purports to measure, and (c) the manner in which the CCS-R measures the skills, conditions, dispositions, and behaviors.

Introduction to the CCS-R

An introduction to a measurement instrument helps the user understand the purposes of the instrument. In this instance, the introduction summarizes the ways in which the CCS-R supports the evaluation efforts of counselors in training and developing professional counselors. According to the introduction of the **CCS-R,** the scale

> assesses counselors' and trainees' skills development and professional competencies. Additionally, the CCS-R provides counselors and trainees with direct feedback regarding their demonstrated ability to apply counseling skills and facilitate therapeutic conditions, and their counseling dispositions (dominant qualities) and behaviors, offering the counselors and trainees practical areas for improvement to support their development as effective and ethical professional counselors." (Lambie & Swank, 2016, p. 1).

What the CCS-R Purports to Measure

The specific skills, conditions, dispositions, and behaviors that the CCR-S purports to measure reflect the 11 items focused on skills and the 11 counseling dispositions and behaviors. In Tables 11.2 and 11.3, each item and a description of each is presented. These operational definitions for each of the items in the CCS-R are described in the training manual (Lambie & Swank, 2016, pp. 8–30). This information is helpful for you and your supervisors for it provides a basis for discussion and subsequent agreement about the skills you are learning and the dispositions you are demonstrating. For example, look at the term, "focus of counseling." Are you clear what that term means and what you are doing to use this skill? Is your supervisor considering this term in the same way? These definitions will help you and your supervisors develop together a common understanding of the term and what it means in your evaluation process.

TABLE 11.2. Counseling Skills and Therapeutic Conditions: CCS-R Descriptions

Counseling Skills and Therapeutic Conditions

1.A. Nonverbal skills. Actions taken by counselors that communicate that they are listening to the client. The nonverbal skills category may include (a) eye contact, (b) posture, (c) gestures, (d) facial expressions, (e) physical distance, (f) movements, (g) appropriate physical touch, (h) attentive silence, and (i) vocal tone, including rate of speech (attuned to the emotional state and cultural norms of the clients).

1.B. Encouragers. A verbal utterance, phrase, or brief statement that indicates acknowledgement and understanding and encourages the client to continue speaking (e.g., door openers such as "Tell me more about ...").

1.C. Questions: Open-ended and closed-ended questions. Open-ended questions—further exploration involving more than a one- or two-word answer (e.g., What brings you to counseling today?). Closed-ended questions—seeking facts that involve a one- or two-word answer or yes or no response (e.g., Who lives in your home with you currently?).

1.D. Reflection: Paraphrasing. A rephrasing of clients' stated thoughts and facts in a nonjudgmental manner, without repeating the exact word-for-word description used by the clients—a basic reflection of content. With couple and family client configurations, paraphrasing the different clients' multiple perspectives.

1.E. Reflection: Reflection of feelings. A statement or rephrasing of clients' stated or implied feelings in a nonjudgmental manner, without repeating the exact feeling word used by the client(s). With couple and family client configurations, reflection of each client's feelings.

1.F. Reflection: Summarizing. A summary of the client's expressed or implied feelings, behaviors, thoughts, deeper meaning, or future plans that the counselor may use for clarification or transition to a new topic. With couple and family client configurations, summarizing relational patterns of interaction.

1.G. Advanced reflection: Meaning. A statement that assists clients in connecting with their core beliefs and values, beyond simply reflecting thoughts and feelings stated or implied by the clients—taking counseling to a deeper level.

1.H. Confrontation. Counselor brings to clients' attention discrepancies existing within their words, behaviors, or thoughts that may present as being out of clients' awareness.

1.I. Goal setting. A process that the counselor and client engage in together to transform the identified problem/concern areas into goals to work toward accomplishing throughout the counseling process—counseling goals should be realistic, appropriate, and attainable. With couple and family client configurations, goal setting supports clients in establishing common therapeutic goals.

1.J. Focus of counseling. The counselor's ability to transition from greeting clients to focusing the counseling session on addressing the therapeutic issues and mutually defined goals in a timely manner, and then providing closure to the counseling session that includes preparing clients for future sessions and/or termination—counseling is purposeful rather than being random discussion.

1.K. Facilitate therapeutic environment: Empathy and caring. Empathy/care—actions taken by the counselor to accurately communicate understanding and meaning of clients' experience in a nonjudgmental manner that involves both immediacy and concreteness

1.L. Facilitate therapeutic environment: Respect and compassion. Respect and compassion—the counselor's demonstration of respect for clients and valuing the clients as worthy human beings; exhibited in the counselor's verbal and nonverbal messages communicated to the clients.

Source: Adapted from Lambie & Swank (2016, pp. 8–19)

TABLE 11.3. Counseling Dispositions and Behaviors: CCS-R Descriptions

2.A. Professional ethics counseling dispositions and behaviors. Using effective decision-making skills and engaging in behaviors consistent with the established codes of ethics for the helping professions such as the American Counseling Association (ACA, 2014) Codes of Ethics.

2.B. Professional behaviors. Interactions with peers, supervisors, and clients that include behaviors and attitudes that promote a positive perception of the counselor and the profession. The professional behavior category also includes maintaining a professional appearance regarding dress and grooming. The counselor is respectful and appreciative to the culture of colleagues and is able to effectively collaborate with others. Thus, the definition for professional behaviors focuses on the counselor's appropriate behaviors, attitudes, and appearance.

2.C. Professional and personal boundaries. Counselor maintains appropriate physical and emotional boundaries when interacting with clients, peers, and supervisors; includes the demonstration of appropriate verbal and nonverbal behavior.

Continued

2.D. **Knowledge and adherence to site and course policies.** Counselor adheres to all systemic policies and demonstrates knowledge and understanding of procedures related to the counseling site and course requirements.

2.E. **Record keeping and task completion.** Counselor completes all documentation (e.g., progress notes, reports, and treatment plans) in a correct, complete, and professional manner by the required deadline. In addition, the counselor completes all activities in an ethical and effective manner, including counseling sessions (individual, family, and group) and documentation as described in record keeping.

2.F. **Multicultural competencies in the counseling relationship.** The counselor demonstrates respect for culture (e.g., race, ethnicity, gender, spirituality, religion, sexual orientation, disability, social class, etc.) and awareness of and responsiveness to ways in which culture interacts with the counseling relationship.

2.G. **Emotional stability and self-control.** Counselors' ability to regulate their emotions and to exhibit self-control in a manner that allows clients to explore personal issues without the focus shifting to the counselors' emotional state; includes interactions with colleagues, such as during case consultation and clinical supervision. Specifically, the counselor demonstrates self-awareness and emotional stability (i.e., congruence between mood and affect) and self-control (i.e., impulse control) in relationships with clients.

2.H. **Motivation to learn and grow/Initiative.** The counselor's willingness to continue to grow personally and professionally; may involve a variety of personal and professional development activities such as reflection, scholarly readings, and participating in workshops and professional seminars.

2.I. **Openness to feedback.** Counselor's willingness to hear the suggestions and opinions of the supervisors and colleagues without becoming defensive and to integrate the feedback as appropriate within the performance of his or her counseling responsibilities.

2.J. **Flexibility and adaptability.** Counselor's ability to adjust to changing circumstances, unexpected events, and new situations; includes interactions with clients, colleagues, and supervisors.

2.K. **Congruence and genuineness.** Counselor's ability to be true to oneself; counselor does not present a facade when interacting with others within his or her role as a professional counselor.

Source: Adapted from Lambie & Swank (2016, pp. 20–30)

The Manner in Which the CCS-R Measures Competencies

When thinking about counseling skills, conditions, dispositions, and behaviors, one question that supervisors and CITs ask goes beyond the response, "Yes, you do demonstrate this skill (active listening)" or, "No, you don't have this disposition (flexibility)." A demonstration of competencies or dispositions occurs in degrees. In other words, thinking in terms of degrees of behavior allows you to articulate how well or how poorly a skill or disposition is demonstrated. To address the degrees of competency, the CCS-R uses a five-point scale to score those skills and dispositions being measured. The five measurements and descriptors follow in Table 11.4.

TABLE 11.4. CCS-R Evaluation Guidelines

Exceeds expectations/Demonstrates competencies (5) = The counselor or trainee demonstrates **strong** (i.e., *exceeding* the expectations of a beginning professional counselor) knowledge, skills, and dispositions in the specified counseling skill(s), ability to facilitate therapeutic conditions, and professional disposition(s) and behavior(s).

Meets expectations/Demonstrates competencies (4) = The counselor or trainee demonstrates **consistent** and **proficient** knowledge, skills, and dispositions in the specified counseling skill(s), ability to facilitate therapeutic conditions, and professional disposition(s) and behavior(s). A beginning professional counselor should be at the "Demonstrates Competencies" level at the conclusion of his or her practicum and/or internship experiences.

Near expectations/Developing toward competencies (3) = The counselor or trainee demonstrates **inconsistent** and **limited** knowledge, skills, and dispositions in the specified counseling skill(s), ability to facilitate therapeutic conditions, and professional disposition(s) and behavior(s).

Below expectations/Insufficient/Unacceptable (2) = The counselor or trainee demonstrates **limited** or **no evidence** of the knowledge, skills, and dispositions in the specified counseling skill(s), ability to facilitate therapeutic conditions, and professional disposition(s) and behavior(s).

Harmful (1) = The counselor or trainee demonstrates harmful use of knowledge, skills, and dispositions in the specified counseling skill(s), ability to facilitate therapeutic conditions, and professional disposition(s) and behavior(s).

Source: Adapted from Lambie & Swank (2016, pp. 20–30)

Using the limited information provided from the CCS-R, think about its relevance to your evaluation of your own counseling skills, conditions, dispositions, and behaviors. What dimensions of the CCS-R would you rate yourself as a "3" of less? How would you like to improve these scores as you near completion of your practicum experience?

Summary

This chapter focuses on the meaning of and the process of assessment and evaluation that you will experience during practicum. Terms such as formative and summative evaluation expand your understanding of the very different ways that you will be (have been) evaluated during your field-based experience. Both have value for your critical reflection and your professional and personal growth and development. It is important to note that the purposes of evaluation are grounded in the 2014 ACA Code of Ethics (ACA, 2014) and describe the professional responsibility of you and your supervisors. Specifically, evaluation provides a protection for clients and for practicum students alike, with responsibility for each resting with you and your supervisors and the academic program.

Supervision has a key role in the assessment and evaluation process, and it is up to the supervisor and the practicum student to establish favorable conditions for supervising. Since quality supervision includes support and challenge, assessment and evaluation may be difficult. Providing challenge to the practicum student requires a sense of trust between supervisor and practicum student, as is a student's willingness to hear critical feedback and use that feedback to facilitate improvement of knowledge, skills, and values. One way in which the practicum student can enhance the assessment process is to ask for help and to advocate for self. We provide ideas about how to do both in a professional way.

The integrated model of development (IDM) supports an assessment of the basic skills that you are learning in practicum. Using the model provides specific domains that practicum students use when working with clients. Using the IDM as an ongoing assessment tool helps facilitate communication between the supervisor and the practicum student about learning objectives, client work, and ways to target and then track growth. In addition, the Counselor Competencies Scale, Revised (CCS-R), is useful for counseling academic programs and supervisors to provide specific skills, conditions, dispositions, and behaviors that students are learning in practicum and then measure performance in a valid and reliable way.

Key Terms

Advanced reflection meaning

Assessment

Client welfare

Closed questions

Confrontation

Congruence and genuineness

Counseling student welfare and growth

Counselor competencies scale, revised

Due process

Emotional stability and self-control

Empathy

Evaluation

Favorable conditions for evaluation

Flexibility and adaptability

Focus of counseling

Formative assessment

Gatekeeping

Goal setting

Idm eight domains of counselor skill development

Knowledge and adherence to site policies

Motivation to learn and grow
Multicultural competencies
Open questions
Openness to feedback
Professional and personal
boundaries
Professional behaviors

Professional ethics
Protecting the counseling
student
Record keeping and task
completion
Reflection of feeling
Reflection paraphrasing

Reflection summarizing
Remediation
Respect and compassion
Summative
Supervision

References

American Counseling Association (ACA). (2014). *2014 ACA Code of Ethics*. Alexandria, VA: Author.

Bernard, J. M., & Goodyear, R. K. (2014). *Fundamentals of clinical supervision* (5th ed.). Boston, MA: Allyn & Bacon.

Brat, M., O'Hara, C., McGhee, C. M., & Chang, C. Y. (2016). Promoting professional counselor advocacy through professional identity development efforts in counselor education. *Journal of Counselor Leadership and Advocacy, 3*(1), 62–70. doi:10.1080/2326716X.2016.1145560

Council for Accreditation of Counseling and Related Programs. (2016a). *2016 CACREP Standards: Section 3: Professional Practice*. Retrieved from http://www.cacrep.org/section-3-professional-practice/

Council for Accreditation of Counseling and Related Programs. (2016b). *2016 CACREP Standards. (2018). Section 5: Entry-level Specialty Areas—Clinical Mental Health*. Retrieved from https://www.cacrep.org/section-5-entry-level-specialty-areas-clinical-mental-health-counseling/

Elman, N. S., & Forrest, L. (2007). From trainee impairment to professional competence problems: Seeing new terminology that facilitates effective action. *Professional Psychology: Research and Practice, 38*(5), 711–721.

Freeman, B. J., Garner, C. M., Gairgrieve, L. A., & Pitts, M. E. (2016). Gatekeeping in the field: Strategies and practices. *Journal of Professional Counseling: Practice, Theory, and Research, 43*(2), 28–41.

Henderson, K. L., & Dufrene, R. L. (2011). *Student remediation: Practical considerations for counselor educators and supervisors*. Retrieved from http://counselingoutfitters.com/vistas/vistas11/Article_45.pdf

Jacobs, S. C., Huprich, S. K., Grus, C. L., Cage, E. A., Elman, N. S., Forrest, L., ... & Kaslow, N. J. (2011). Trainees with professional competency problems: Preparing trainers for difficult but necessary conversations. *Training and Education in Professional Psychology, 5*(3), 175–184. doi:10.1037/a0024656

Johnson, W. B., Elman, N. S., Forrest, L., Rodolfa, E., Robiner, W. N., & Schaffer, J. B. (2008). Addressing professional competence problems in trainees: Some ethical considerations. *Professional Psychology Research and Practice, 39*(6), 589–599. doi:10.1037/a0014264

Ladany, N., & Friedlander, M. L. (1995). The relationship between the supervisory working alliance and trainees' experience of role conflict and role ambiguity. *Counselor Education and Supervision, 34*(3), 220–231.

Lambie, G. W., Mullen, P. R., Swank, J. M., & Blount, A. (2018). The counseling competencies scale: Validation and refinement. *Measurement and Evaluation in Counseling and Development, 51*(1), 1–15. doi:10.1080/07481756.2017.1358964

Lambie, G. W., & Swank, J. M. (2016). Counseling competencies scale–revised (CCS–R): *Training manual* (Unpublished manuscript). Department of Child, Family, and Community Sciences. Orlando, FL: University of Central Florida.

McAdams, C. R. III, & Foster, V. A. (2011). A guide to just and fair remediation of counseling students with professional performance deficiencies. *Counselor Education and Supervision, 47*(1), 2–13.

Miller, J., & Koerin, B. B. (2002). Gatekeeping in the practicum. *The Clinical Supervisor, 20*(2), 1–18. doi:10.1300/J001v20n02_01

St. John's University (n.d.). *Site supervisor training for internship and practicum supervisors*. Retrieved from https://www.stjohns.edu/sites/default/files/documents/academics/SOE/site_supervisor_training_for_internship_and_practicum_supervisors.pdf

Stoltenberg, C., McNeill, W. (2011). *IDM supervision: An integrative developmental model for supervising counselors and therapists* (3rd ed.). New York, NY: Routledge.

Welfare, L. E., & Borders, L. D. (2010). Counselor cognitions: General and domain-specific complexity. *Counselor Education and Supervision, 49*(3), 162-178.

CHAPTER 12

Taking Leave
FROM PRACTICUM

INTRODUCTION

We, as humans, do not do very well with transitions, especially leaving relationships. Take a moment as you begin this chapter, to reflect on the last relationship you took leave from. How did that go? Whose decision was it, yours or the other person? These days, a whole generation of people terminate relationships via text or instant message. Rather than being a criticism of technology or social media, use of technology in this way highlights the importance of taking leave and suggests it does not always occur in a healthy way. Transitions out of relationships, from romantic to business, formal to informal, evoke a range of responses from people, from denial to cut-and-run. It is critical to leave practicum in a positive and professional manner.

By the time you are reading this, you are feeling at home at your practicum site. In fact, you may be thinking, "I don't really know how I can leave this site (and these people). I feel that I am part of the team and really belong to this work place." You are worried about what will happen to many of your clients and asking who will carry through many of the projects that you have started. And you have dreams about contributing to the site long term! You wonder if you could work at this site full time. Perhaps many of your new colleagues have suggested that very thing.

There is anxiety associated with **taking leave**, too! When you transition to internship, sure it will be exciting, but you will have to begin again. You may be thinking, "I feel so comfortable here in practicum, and I don't want to feel like a stranger again. Right now, I am more than a practicum student. I don't want to go back to being just a student, 'just being an intern.'"

In spite of these misgivings, you are coming to the end of your practicum. You will want to conclude your work at your practicum site in a professional way and plan to take leave in a gracious, helpful, and intentional way, with an emphasis on client care. Guidelines offer ideas about how to accomplish this. In addition, you will be ending your work with your practicum class, too. How you conclude your work in practicum will help establish a positive tone to the way you enter your internship class. The goals for the chapter follow.

GOALS OF THE CHAPTER

- **Plan how you will conclude your work at your practicum site**
- **Describe guidelines for concluding your work with clients**
- **Discuss how you will conclude your work with your supervisor and with other staff**
- **Plan how you will conclude your practicum course work**
- **Plan your practicum course for taking leave**

RELATED CACREP GOALS

SECTION 3: PROFESSIONAL PRACTICE

- F. Students complete supervised counseling practicum experiences that total a minimum of 100 clock hours over a full academic term that is a minimum of 10 weeks.

- G. Practicum students complete at least 40 clock hours of direct service with actual clients that contributes to the development of counseling skills.

- H. Practicum students have weekly interaction with supervisors that averages one hour per week of individual and/or triadic supervision throughout the practicum by (1) a counselor education program faculty member, (2) a student supervisor who is under the supervision of a counselor education program faculty member, or (3) a site supervisor who is working in consultation on a regular schedule with a counselor education program faculty member in accordance with the supervision agreement.

- I. Practicum students participate in an average of 1½ hours per week of group supervision on a regular schedule throughout the practicum. Group supervision must be provided by a counselor education program faculty member or a student supervisor who is under the supervision of a counselor education program faculty member. (CACREP, 2016)

Taking Leave and Your Practicum Experience

As you approach the conclusion of the practicum experience, an interesting way to think about it is **beginning with the end in mind**. This means that taking leave from practicum occurs in several stages, and, in reality, the end is built on the foundation of its initial and following stages (see Figure 12.1). The initial stage of practicum occurs when faculty and students are engaged in the pre-practicum preparatory work; the second stage represents early days in practicum. The third stage occurs when, as a practicum student, you begin counseling your first clients. During a fourth stage, there follows a significant time of intense growth and development. You become involved in counseling clients, integrate the theory you have learned and are learning into your counseling, and continue to develop your identity as a professional counselor. Finally, in a fifth stage, and relevant to this chapter, you plan and perform a professional leave taking.

FIGURE 12.1. Stages of practicum

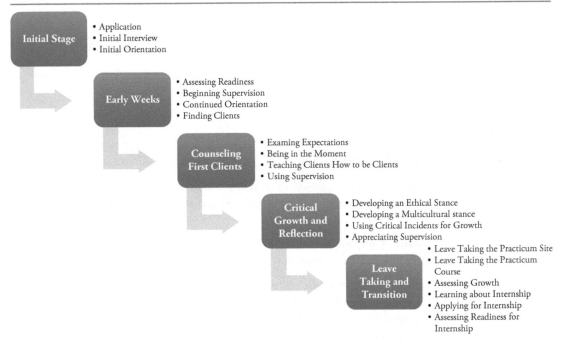

Your practicum experience is unique in many ways that reflect its temporal nature and limited scope. Most practicums are bounded by the academic calendar. Before you apply for practicum and interview for participation at a site, the approximate start and end date are set by the academic institution and the counseling program. In fact, the academic program establishes the parameters and requirements of practicum related to (a) the direct and indirect number of hours spent counseling clients, (b) the knowledge, skills, and professional behaviors you must demonstrate, and (d) the specific tasks you must complete. And, because of the start and end dates, there is a defined amount of time in which you must accomplish this work. Just as an early part of this text emphasized beginning practicum, attention now is on the way in which you end practicum.

There are three reasons to plan for a successful ending to your practicum experience. First, you have spent time at your practicum site and have, most likely, become part of the team while working there. Your supervisor, agency or school staff, and clients have begun to depend on your presence and your work. Over a period of time you have assumed many roles and taken on various responsibilities. Just as with ending volunteer commitments or gainful employment, other supervisors, staff, or volunteers will need to assume many of the roles and responsibilities when you leave. A **well-ordered transition** is essential if your work is to continue.

The primary reason developing a **transition plan** is important relates to your work with clients and client groups. Clients depend on you and count on the helping relationships you have established with them. In fact, in some instances, you are now an important part of their daily lives. Many clients are making progress and are committed to change; they view you as a part of the progress they are making and as a member of their support system. Even though in your informed consent statement and your professional disclosure statement you indicated that your work with them was time limited, the reality of your leaving may take them by surprise. Since one role of the counselor is to model effective behaviors for clients, to ensure client care, it is critical that you prepare your clients for your departure. In doing so, you will model for them an effective way of transitioning from relationships. In counseling we use the term "**termination**" to refer to the process of client leave taking.

Another reason to carefully consider how to end your practicum reflects its place in your academic program. Practicum, a field experience designed to help you develop your counseling skills and expand your identity as a professional counselor, precedes internship. You will want to make a strong and meaningful transition between these two field-based learning experiences, engaging the help of your site and faculty supervisors. In addition, because of the support you have received from your supervisors previously, you will want to both provide constructive feedback and offer appropriate thanks for their guidance and mentoring. Finally, as with most successful professional experiences, you want to develop a way to maintain these relationships. You will nurture the relationships you have with other professionals. And, for clients, a healthy departure improves the chances that they will be able to develop healthy therapeutic relationships with the next counselor they encounter, who takes your place. In Reflection Question 12.1, you will articulate your thoughts and feelings about the concluding of practicum and how you envision taking leave.

REFLECTION QUESTION 12.1

THOUGHTS AND FEELINGS RELATED TO ENDING PRACTICUM

As you anticipate the end of practicum, what thoughts and feelings stand out to you?

The Practicum Site: Guidelines for Taking Leave

Your practicum site represents one component of your practicum experience. There are three aspects of taking leave from the site: your clients, the work site, and your site supervisor. Figure 12.2 presents on overarching description of taking leave at the practicum site.

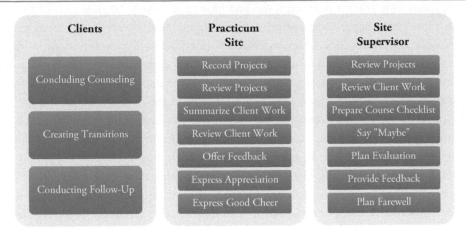

Terminating Your Work with Clients

In counseling, we often discuss the occurrence of termination as the final stage in the counseling process. In relationship to practicum, concluding your work with a client may have various meanings. This includes **concluding counseling, creating transitions, and conducting follow-up**. For instance, you and the client together may agree the client goals have been met and reach a decision together that it is time for the helping process to conclude counseling. Another way that counseling concludes relates to time boundaries. Counseling services may be time limited; this can occur because your practicum reflects the boundaries of the academic term. Or, you may offer to an individual client or a client group a limited number of sessions. Often times, these sessions have a specific focus such as assertiveness training, anger management, friendship focus, or wellness focus, to name a few. Also, if counseling with and support for a client is to continue after your practicum ends, you will be conducting transitions for your client to work with another counselor. You also may lose some clients as they drop out of the counseling process without a formal final session. Clients may end their work with you for a variety of reasons, either because they are unwilling or unable to participate. Something important to remember is that *counselors do not wait until the final session to terminate the counseling relationship.* Termination is as ongoing process that actually begins at the first session.

Concluding Counseling

Termination of the counseling process represents an important aspect in the stages or process of counseling. As difficult as termination of a counseling relationship is, making it an important part of the counseling process holds value for the counselor and the client. At the date of termination, clients often talk about new issues or discuss previously discussed issues in greater depth. For other clients, they terminate the relationship prior to the last meeting or become angry or confused at the mention of the conclusion of the counseling relationship (Howes, 2008). Taking leave, for most of us, brings up feelings of loss and grief. Positive, intentional leave taking or termination provides an opportunity for clients to learn how to conclude a relationship and normalize the feelings of loss. It is helpful to recognize that **concluding counseling** is a process.

For the counselor and the client, there are aspects of termination during the initial counseling session. Specific attention to termination with clients should begin three or four weeks prior to the end of practicum. The final meeting is a special time for a positive, supportive, and memorable end to the counseling process. Let's look at what taking leave can look like with many of your clients.

THE FIRST CLIENT CONTACT. It is within the first client contact that counselors introduce themselves and present their professional disclosure (see Figure 2.1), describe the process of counseling, and discuss counselor ethical and legal obligations and informed consent (see Figures 2.2 and 2.3). Discussing issues such as confidentiality, the purpose of practicum, and the nature of supervision all help the client understand your unique status as a practicum student. One aspect of this introduction relates to the time-limited nature of practicum and your own availability as a student to provide services. It may be helpful to think of it this way: Each individual session has a beginning and end, and the beginning comes with the end in mind; in the same way, a counseling relationship comes with a beginning and end, and the beginning holds the end in mind, with the expectation of new beginnings; likewise, practicum begins with the end in mind, pointing the way to new beginnings. In a sense, terminating counseling with a client represents a new beginning for you both.

For clients, information about concluding services may not register with them during this early stage of the counseling process. Clients are much more focused on issues such as "What is counseling? What do you expect of me? What can I expect of the counseling process? Who will know I am receiving counseling?" Clients feel anxious and fearful of the unknown, even those who are positive about their participation in the process. Hence, their attention is on the beginning of the process, rather than the end of it. Nevertheless, we help them keep a sense that the relationship, while meaningful, is temporary. Just as the ethical responsibility of informed consent is not satisfied by merely signing a document, ethical termination is not satisfied by a farewell at the end.

A MONTH PRIOR TO THE END OF PRACTICUM. As a practicum student, when you begin your work with clients, your attention is also on the beginning of the counseling process. However, around the midterm evaluation, you become more aware of the limited time remaining in practicum. You are involved with your clients as you deepen your relationships and your work with them. It is at this time that you begin to wish for more than the five or six weeks that you have remaining! Still, it is time to make your leave taking part of your work. (This is equally true if your counseling is limited by number of sessions or if you and your client can see that your goals and objectives are nearing completion.) And, taking leave will mean different things to different clients, whether those differences are rooted in race, gender, trauma history, early childhood, a recent breakup, or any number of factors that make the client in front of you an individual.

As the counselor, it is your responsibility to remind the client that counseling with you will be concluding. The tool or process of counting down represents one way to help clients remember that your work with them will end and includes presenting the client with a calendar of times together and coming to agreement about how to spend the final sessions. During this time, counselor and client can assess goals and objectives met and revise, if necessary, expectations and priorities for the final month. The process of **counting down** supports clients as they move purposefully from one session to the next. In planning for a session, counting down might be a helpful way to summarize a session, reminding clients about the number of sessions or the numbers of weeks remaining and what may happen between the current session and the final one.

Sam participates in a roleplay with Dr. Kim about how he might begin taking leave with one of his clients; Sam plays the role of his client. In this way, Dr. Kim is able to model performing a complicated task in which the practicum students have never engaged. Their interaction is excerpted in the Transcription 12.1. Afterward, Dr. Kim worked with Sam and the rest of the class to develop a basic form that they might adapt for each of their clients to plan and record their taking leave process. (see Figure 12.3).

TRANSCRIPTION 12.1. COUNTING DOWN

Dr. Kim as counselor: We have a few more moments before our session ends. Usually we end our sessions by summarizing what happened this past hour, deciding what homework might be helpful to you this next week, and confirming our next session. Today, I also want to mention that our sessions will be ending a month from now.

Sam as client: Oh, I don't think we can stop meeting. I still get angry at my kids. You help me yell less.

Dr. Kim as counselor: Our work helps you be less angry, and you feel uncomfortable with the thought of not continuing our work together.

Sam as client: Yes! Sometimes when I start yelling, I remember the homework we are doing. Don't laugh, but I put myself in time-out. I forgot that you are a student. What am I going to do?

Dr. Kim as counselor: This is an important question, because our time together has been meaningful for us both. We will want to celebrate that and also plan for the transition. You may actually find that it makes our work together even more productive. I have something that you and I can use together to plan how we will end our work together.

Sam as client: I can't think about this now.

Dr. Kim as counselor: (uses silence)

Sam as client: How many sessions did you say we have left?

Dr. Kim as counselor: What is the feeling you are experiencing right now?

Sam as client: I think I am a little angry with you (seems surprised to hear himself say this).

Dr. Kim as counselor: Anger is legitimate. You may be feeling other things as well, and I look forward to hearing more about them. This is why we begin the leaving process now and not during our last session.

Sam as client: Makes sense, I guess. I still wish we did not have to end.

Dr. Kim as counselor: That is completely understandable. It means a lot that you have let yourself get close to me and feel connected. Maybe we can use this form to plan our work next week. Let's do this together. Why don't you write. This will be our plan.

Sam as client: Okay. But I don't have to like it, right?

(both smile)

FIGURE 12.3. Planning sheet: "The End of Our Work Together: Counting Down"

Planning Sheet: "The End of Our Work Together: Counting Down"

As you may remember from our first meeting, because I am a counselor-in-training enrolled in practicum, my time here comes to an end on December 21, XXXX. I think that it is important that we plan our next month's sessions so we can focus our counseling efforts on your goals. I also want us to end our work together in a good way.

We can begin to fill out this form together and then refer to it at the end of each session.

Session	Goals	Summary of Session
11/29		
12/5		
12/12		
12/19		

Future Plans:

Many clients have not thought about the end of the counseling process. Expect that when confronted with the thoughts of concluding counseling, they may respond in a variety of ways. Clients may respond with surprise when you bring up the topic. They may also be frustrated or angry that you are leaving them. And, clients may also feel a sense of loss. These emotions underscore the reasons for this intentional leave taking and developing transition plans that represent a sense of continuity of care.

THE FINAL SESSION. During the final session, the practicum student and the client have several matters to address. You will want the client to participate fully in this session. There may be important client emotions to consider, and the client may need time to process these. The client may also have questions to ask and issues to address. Being positive and normalizing the end of the counseling process helps the client say goodbye. Perhaps as important as anything else in this section, make the ending concrete and permanent. This sounds (and feels) harsh, but departing words such as "see you later" or "here's my e-mail" or "let me know if you need anything" actually hurt clients more than they help. As you plan your final sessions, these guidelines might be helpful:

- Write or discuss a summary of your work together.

- Review what has been accomplished during the counseling process. You might want to include goals and changes in emotions, thoughts, and behaviors.

- Articulate client strengths (e.g., values, cultural influences, personal traits, and external support).

- Explore client feelings related to ending the counseling process.

- Help the client discuss thoughts about the future.

- Describe specific plans for the transition. If formal counseling is ending, help client generate a list of ways to find support.

Creating Transitions

As practicum students end their work with clients, they and their site supervisors construct a plan for each client; in other words, they are **creating transitions**. One possible option is to transfer the client to another client or agency. If the client is to be transferred, it is a good time to review the needs of the client that may have increased, decreased, or changed since you began counseling this client. You also need to note the expertise needed to adequately provide services for the client. It is also important to look at client preferences. You and your site supervisor are familiar with this type of transfer since it resembles a client referral. This includes contacting the counselor receiving the referral, sharing information with the new counselor and the client, and supporting the client through the referral process.

CONTACT THE NEW COUNSELOR. As you transition your client to another counselor, you will want to ascertain if the receiving counselor has the time and expertise to work with your client. If this transition is possible and positive for the client's continued growth, you will want to share relevant information about goals and objectives and your work with the client, respecting the limits of confidentiality. If you are going to share information about the client, you will need to inform the client and describe the information to be shared. If the client will be receiving services in another agency or school, you will need client consent.

MAKE ARRANGEMENTS/SUPPORT FOR THE CLIENT. You will also want to work with the receiving counselor about the details of this transfer (e.g., introducing the client to the new counselor; date, time, and place of first meeting; how the client can prepare for the meeting). As discussed earlier, if the client is to be referred to another agency, with the client's consent, you will send client information that supports the client's transfer. If the client has reservations about this transfer, you can plan to attend the first meeting with the client. Experiential Activity 12.1 prepares you for concluding services and the challenges you will face.

EXPERIENTIAL ACTIVITY 12.1
Concluding Services

As you reflect on a client for who you believe concluding services will be especially difficult, how might you plan for termination with this client a month prior to your practicum end date? In might help to roleplay the session with a peer.

Follow-Up

An important part of ending work with clients is attention to the **follow-up** of services. This means that a professional or a member of the family has the responsibility to track the client progress. The purpose is to assure that the client's needs continue to be met and assessment and intervention are available if need be. Follow-up varies according to the needs of the client or the resources available. The type of follow-up with clients spans both time and intensity. If the client remains in the care of the site supervisor, then follow-up is not needed. If another staff member assumes the counseling responsibilities for your client, then the site supervisor might assume responsibility for follow-up. When the client is transferred to another agency or school or the services are concluded, then the site supervisor could provide follow-up.

What are the ways that follow-up can occur? It is helpful to think about a continuum of care model to envision follow-up. For instance, it can be as limited a one phone call or as elaborate as a monthly check-in with the client for six months to a year. Services can be as simple as conducting a survey about quality of services, gathering information about client well-being, or providing additional services.

In much of professional counseling, follow-up is minimal for a variety of reasons. Counselors and other staff are busy serving those on their current client case load, there are limited resources to allocate to past clients, and clients are often difficult to reach or reluctant to participate in post-counseling activities. Also, counselors may not view follow-up as part of the counseling responsibility, and the agency or school may not include follow-up as part of the job responsibility. In spite of the difficulties of follow-up, for CITs in practicum, it is particularly important. When you leave your practicum site, you will worry about the future of your clients. And, serving the clients or following up on their care will no longer be your responsibility. Developing a sound follow-up plan, even it is limited in scope, becomes an important piece of taking leave, and this helps you leave your practicum site with fewer concerns. Another benefit supports the assessment and evaluation of the delivery of services. Following up with clients may help counselors gain insight into their service delivery and client satisfaction. This information is important to document gains in evidence-based practice, program evaluation, and quality assessment.

The next section focuses on leave taking related to your practice site. This includes meeting your professional requirements, saying goodbye, and preparing for internship.

Taking leave from Your Practicum (Work) Site

You began your practicum with an interview, an orientation, and an introduction to an agency or school staff and facilities. In some ways, this initial activity resembles the beginning of a job. At the conclusion of practicum, taking leave also shares some commonalities with leaving a place of employment. Done well, others remaining at the work site can assume your responsibilities in a seamless way. And, your site supervisor and other staff will retain positive thoughts of your work and your contributions. Because of the importance of taking leave, you might begin the counting-down process about a month prior to your planned departure. A month out, you can remind your site supervisor and other staff of your last week and determine the date of your final day. Because of the crush of activities within any agency or school setting, you can remind individuals at your site of this date once a week. These reminders will help everyone be clear that practicum is time limited and that you are engaged in practicum in routine ways, as well as beginning transition activities.

Approaching leave taking in this manner creates an atmosphere of and impression of professionalism. Attending to the seven tasks described next will also help you perform and complete the assignments required in your practicum course work. In addition, the tasks related to taking leave will help you think critically about your practicum experience and professional growth.

RECORD PROJECTS. About a month before your practicum end date, record a list of your tasks and projects; you don't need to record client work, here. Once you construct the list, you will want to describe each effort and project and detail what has been achieved and what is yet to be completed. You will work with others (site supervisor and other staff) to decide whether the project might be continued. If the project is to be continued, you can help determine next steps and pass on any material or notes you might have to the appropriate staff members (Mosier, 2017). You can create this record of projects on a spreadsheet or document file. Don't include any client information on this list. It is best recorded in another data set, since client data is confidential.

REVIEW PROJECTS. A month out, you will want to follow a **record-and-review activity** by scheduling time with your site supervisor to discuss your efforts and projects. Talk about the viability of sustaining each after you leave. Be sure to discuss any new efforts you undertake and consider if each is realistic to begin or complete.

SUMMARIZE CLIENT WORK. This task is critical to ensure the welfare of your client, a responsibility you and your site supervisor share. Table 12.1 might be a useful tool to perform this task. Information you want to include relates to the name of the client or client group, goals, description of the counseling work, and suggested plan for transition. This document is a working document and will change with supervisor input and client progress during the final month of your internship. Remember, it is important to treat this as confidential information. You will share this **summary of work with individual clients and client groups** with your site supervisor and, if necessary, with your faculty supervisor.

TABLE 12.1. Summary of Work with Individual Clients and Client Groups

Client or client group	Goals	Description of counseling	Plan for transition

REVIEW CLIENT WORK. About a month prior to the end of practicum, begin reviewing your work with clients and client groups with your site supervisor. Although time remains for counseling, this discussion will help you and your supervisor prepare for a positive transition for clients. You and your site supervisor can also discuss what you and your client can reasonably expect to achieve during the remainder of the practicum experience.

It is important to note that during the last month of practicum, practicum students may experience an increased demand for their counseling services. As their visibility expands at the site and there develops a confirmation of and reliance on their skills and abilities, more staff and clients want them involved. There is always a balance between wanting to help clients and assuming more work with clients than can be accomplished.

OFFER FEEDBACK. Because you have spent an academic term at your agency or school as a practicum student, you have valuable insights about the agency and the ways it serves as a practicum site. You will want to **offer feedback**. Feedback might include the ways a practicum student is oriented to the agency, receives supervision, finds clients, has access to records, and is assigned physical space. Sharing both information about what you found particularly helpful and what you wish you had received provides your supervisor and other members of the site a more comprehensive view of your experience. This information helps them prepare for the next student. For instance, during your practicum, you may have developed some new materials or forms that helped work within the agency or school structure.

This might include an orientation check list, a map of the physical space, new formats for documentation or record keeping of client counseling sessions, time charts that facilitate client interaction, and material created for using counseling techniques and approaches. Sharing these materials makes them tangible resources you can leave for other staff members and practicum students.

One specific way to support your site supervisor's work and prepare the way for the next practicum student is to candidly complete your program's **evaluation of site and site supervisor form**; you may also choose to write a letter of greeting for the next practicum student (see Experiential Activity 12.2).

EXPERIENTIAL ACTIVITY 12.2
"Best Advice You Never Got"

What is the best advice you NEVER got regarding practicum that you would want to share with an upcoming practicum student?

EXPRESS APPRECIATION. The conclusion of practicum represents a perfect time to reflect on the growth you have experienced and identify the individuals who have contributed to your professional and personal development, in other words, to **express appreciation**. During this time of reflection, you might prepare a list of individuals at your practicum site who you wish to thank for their mentoring and support. To prepare for giving thanks, you will want to share good wishes, appreciation, and specific actions these individuals took and supportive gestures they made that contributed to your growth. Appreciation coupled with specific feedback increases the power of your taking leave message. Appreciation may be expressed in multiple ways: private conversations, public acknowledgement, written informal notes and formal letters, and e-mail or chat communication. Sharing snacks or cookies, accompanied by a note of thanks, in an office or work room might also be a way to express gratitude.

EXPRESS GOOD CHEER. Although taking leave is often associated with sadness or loss, you can approach taking leave with a positive and hopeful attitude. For many practicum students, taking leave is difficult. At their practicum site, after anxious moments as they began, they discovered or confirmed skills and abilities and found a professional home. Practicum students may have established good relationships with their site supervisors, colleagues, and clients. And they felt they had become important members of a team, going beyond the feeling of being just a practicum student.

Sadness at leaving is normal. The desire to stay where one is successful and appreciated is understandable. Expressing gratitude and making plans to remain connected will help soothe and smooth the transition. Even if the practicum experience was less than you had hoped for, a positive, upbeat attitude during taking leave is important. Unfortunately, for some practicum students, there are practicum sites, site supervisors, or experiences associated with negative feelings. Students may leave the site unsatisfied or feel less than successful. Perhaps the site was not able to provide a team atmosphere or an adequate number of clients. Possibly the site supervisor did not make time for supervision, was unable to provide concrete feedback, or did not offer you the support needed.

In these circumstances, ask your faculty supervisor to help you articulate what you gained from your practicum experience and how, during your practicum, you sought support from others.

Taking leave from Your Site Supervisor

As has been your experience, your site supervisor is a critical part of your practicum, including concluding your work with clients and other projects. There are also other aspects of taking leave you will want to address with your site supervisor. As with taking leave from your work site, beginning your leave taking with your site supervisor a month before your final day at your practicum site will help prepare them.

REVIEW PROJECTS. You will want to describe these projects to your site supervisor and provide a description in writing. Together, you will create a transition plan. You might review the project list weekly for a month prior to you last day of internship.

REVIEW CLIENT WORK. A month before you leave your practicum, you will create a client summary review sheet (see Table 12.1) and review it with your site supervisor. In this document, you record a transition of service plan for each client.

PREPARE COURSE CHECKLIST. A month prior to the end of the term, review your practicum course syllabus and create a calendar of assignments and due dates. These may include written papers, oral and written reports, evaluation forms, logs forms, journals, case studies, and other practicum-related assignments. Note the assignments that will involve your site supervisor and discuss those. Review this checklist weekly, involving your site supervisor as necessary.

SAY "MAYBE." As the last month approaches, you will be inclined or invited to assume more responsibility at your site. Be mindful of the time remaining and choose any new projects or clients with that time and effort in mind. Ask you site supervisor for help as you respond to requests (or your own wishes) in a realistic manner.

PLAN EVALUATIONS. Your course syllabus, faculty handbook, and faculty supervisor will help you understand the practicum evaluation process. While each academic program develops its own evaluation process for practicum, that process reflects CACREP standards of professional practice. Prior to your taking leave activities, in all likelihood, you will have participated in a midterm evaluation. Final evaluations are a part of taking leave.

It is important that your site supervisor has time to complete the final evaluation form and meet with you to discuss it. Early in the last month of your practicum, discuss the final evaluation process with your site supervisor, share a copy of the form, provide the due date, and schedule an evaluation meeting. If there are other evaluation forms (e.g., practicum student evaluation of site supervisor and practicum site) or forms to be signed (e.g., direct and indirect hour logs and summary sheet), alert your site supervisor.

PROVIDE FEEDBACK. Providing concrete feedback to those at your practicum site is important. Your site supervisor has invested much time and effort in making your practicum experience a positive one and supported your professional growth and development. You will want to plan to meet with your site supervisor to share your impressions about the supervision you received and the benefits you gained working at your site. Your program may require that you assess the supervision you received and the site in which you received it. Or, you may provide feedback in an informal manner. Whether the meeting relates to providing informal feedback or formal feedback, you will want to set aside a specific time, develop a written agenda and plan, and meet with your site supervisor in private.

The more concrete this feedback is, the better. Make a note of your site supervisor's observable behaviors and when you experience them and indicate what you learned from them. Equally important is sharing with your site supervisor the additional aspects of the site that supported your learning. Again, the more concrete and specific, the better.

What do concrete examples of feedback look like? For it to be meaningful, you will want to describe the context, be specific about the behavior you target, and explain how the behavior altered the way you thought, behaved, or felt. Noting two or three concrete examples that illustrate the feedback you provide will increase positive communication.

JOSE: I really learned so much for helping so many different clients and I appreciated all of the different cultures my clients represented. I learned that I had to use different cultural "languages." Working with the different cultures gave me an opportunity to be sure I asked the client to continually provide feedback about what help looks like in their cultural setting.

Even though this may seem to be a lot of information to share, this type of feedback is invaluable as the supervisor prepares to work with other interns. It may be more valuable for supervisors to hear a more in-depth account of one aspect of a positive internship experience, rather than learning about six aspects with little depth in any of them. Reflection Question 12.2 will help you prepare for sharing feedback.

REFLECTION QUESTION 12.2

FEEDBACK TO SUPERVISOR: PRACTICUM SITE AND SITE SUPERVISION

What feedback would you like to provide about the practicum site and site supervision relative to your growth?

PLAN YOUR FAREWELL. Each agency has a culture related to saying goodbye to practicum students. It is appropriate to ask your site supervisor if there is a traditional way for you to say goodbye to the agency or school staff as a group. If there is not a tradition of taking leave, you could bring in cookies or a small cake, accompanied by a card that expresses your thanks to everyone in the agency for helping you during your time with them.

Practicum Course: Guidelines for Taking leave

Your practicum course represents a second component of your practicum experience. There are three aspects of taking leave from the practicum course: your faculty supervisor, your practicum peers, and the subsequent internship. Figure 12.4 presents an overarching illustration of taking leave from the practicum course.

FIGURE 12.4. Overarching illustration of taking leave from the practicum course

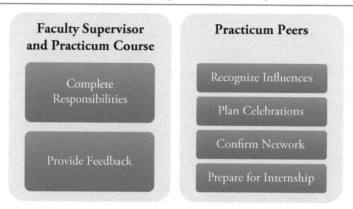

Taking leave From Your Faculty Supervisor and the Practicum Course

As the term comes to an end, it is important that you fulfill the requirements of your practicum course. This is a time you engage in reflection about your practicum experiences, note your knowledge and skill development, and describe your professional identity development. These reflections are critical to your professional preparation and help you assess your readiness for internship and establish your goals for that experience. Professional leave taking from your practicum course and your faculty supervisor helps you conclude the course in a positive way. Here are several guidelines that help you successfully complete the course. Because of your previous academic achievements, many aspects of the guidelines you may already practice.

COMPLETE RESPONSIBILITIES. A month prior to the end of the term, it is important for you to review your practicum syllabus. Note the specific requirements and the due dates. Make a chart of these assignments and note any questions you may have (see Table 12.2).

TABLE 12.2. Practicum Requirements

Requirements	Date due	Notes	Additional material needed
Liability insurance			
Professional disclosure statement			
Practicum contract			
Informed consent			
Midterm evaluation			
Notes from supervision			

Continued

TABLE 12.2. Practicum Requirements *Continued*

Requirements	Date due	Notes	Additional material needed
Client case notes			
Transcription of tapes/notes from one-on-one or triadic supervision			
Weekly journal			
Weekly taping			
Written case study			
Summary for case study presentation			
Final evaluation			
Weekly log (with signatures)			
Summary of hours (with signatures)			
Evaluation of site			
Evaluation of site supervision			
Practicum notebook			

PROVIDE FEEDBACK. It is important that you meet with your faculty supervisor to provide feedback about your professional growth and development. It is also a time to convey to your faculty supervisor the ways he or she supported your work and development. Similar to the suggested meeting with your site supervisor, the more concrete this feedback is, the better. Make note of your faculty supervisor's observable behaviors and when you experienced them and indicate what you learned from them.

Taking leave From Your Practicum Peers

By now you have formed strong relationships with your peers in your counseling program. Practicum has been a special time to learn from your peers, share a supervision experience, and seek help and receive support. You have seen how common values and education translate into counseling practice and have experienced critical reflection and disclosure. For the most part, you will not have to say goodbye to the peers with whom you shared practicum. But, you will want to mark the conclusion of practicum and thank them for the support they have provided.

RECOGNIZE INFLUENCES. As you reflect on the ways that your peers have influenced and supported your work in practicum, you might develop a plan to recognize these. Ask your faculty supervisor if there is time in class to express the contributions others have made in your practicum experience. You could also prepare thank-you notes or written messages of appreciation for peers that have been especially key in your development. Remember, the more specific you are about helpful behaviors, the more meaningful the feedback.

PLAN CELEBRATIONS. Practicum does represent the ending of one field experience and is often marked by a celebration dinner or small party, as a part of class or extracurricular activities.

Faculty supervisors may have a special way they help students mark the end of the class, and this is a good time to contribute to the ending. This might mean planning an informal event or taking some time in the final class to celebrate its conclusion. Built in to this could be a look to internship and beginning hopes and goals.

CONFIRM NETWORKS. The end of practicum provides a good opportunity to establish means of future communication. Many of our students form special Facebook pages, continue discussion board communication, or follow each other through other social media channels. In preparation for internship, often our students plan ways to meet and talk with members of their new internship class prior to the first day of class as a way to create a welcoming atmosphere.

PREPARE FOR INTERNSHIP. In some ways, your practicum experience is a pre-internship experience. The conclusion of practicum represents a time to assess your professional growth and counselor identity, learn about the upcoming internship, and assess your readiness for internship.

Summary

This chapter focused on the ways in which you conclude your practicum, highlighting the way that you will leave both your practicum site and your practicum course. Both are important. A thoughtful and well-ordered transition enhances your professional developmental. More important, you protect the clients your served, support the work of your practicum site, and honor those with whom you worked. Three aspects of taking leave facilitate a positive ending of practicum: concluding counseling, creating transitions, and planning follow-up. Concluding the additional projects and tasks you assumed during your practicum focuses on working with your site supervisor to review projects and client work and planning transitions. In addition, you will want to plan ways to express appreciate and say goodbye. Although you will miss your practicum site and the relationships you have developed, remember you will want to leave in a positive way.

Finally, it is important that you plan a positive and professional way to leave your site supervisor. You will want to summarize your work, confirm transitions, prepare and review the tasks and paperwork due related to your academic work, and plan your evaluation. You will also want to provide feedback to your site supervisor about the site and the supervision you received. Preparing and sharing this feedback is an important part of professional development. It also provides your site supervisor with concrete critical feedback about how to continue to work with practicum students and ways to improve.

It is also important to plan taking leave of your practicum class. This leave taking includes completing your responsibilities for your practicum class and giving and receiving feedback from your faculty supervisor. You will also want to conclude your practicum class by recognizing and acknowledging the ways others influenced your work. An end-of-the-term class celebration is one way to mark the conclusion of practicum and provides a time to confirm the network of peers you have established. Finally, taking leave in practicum is also a beginning as you start to prepare for your internship experience.

Key Terms

Beginning with the end in mind

Concluding counseling

Conducting follow-up

Counting down

Creating transitions

Evaluation of site and site supervisor form

Expression of appreciation

Follow-up

Offer feedback

Record-and-review activity

Summary of work with individual clients and client groups

Taking leave

Termination

Transition plan

Well-ordered transition

References

American Counseling Association (ACA). (2014). *2014 ACA Code of Ethics*. Alexandria, VA: Author.

Council for Accreditation of Counseling and Related Programs. (2016). *2016 CACREP Standards. (2018). Section 3: Professional Practice*. Retrieved from https://www.cacrep.org/section-3-professional-practice/

Howes, R. (September 30, 2008). Terminating therapy: Part I: What, why, how. *Psychology Today*. Retrieved from https://www.psychologytoday.com/blog/in-therapy/200809/terminating-therapy-part-i-what-why-how

Mosier, L. (2017). 6 things to do before leaving your job. *The Daily Muse*. Retrieved from https://www.themuse.com/advice/6-things-to-do-before-leaving-your-job.

Transition
TO INTERNSHIP

INTRODUCTION

You may be thinking as you read the title of this chapter, "What are they thinking? I am just finishing practicum and now I already have to think about internship?" The answer is yes, and you have likely been thinking about internship for some time. Now, it is time to transition from one developmental leap to the next. One aspect of the professional growth is leaving relationships, roles, and responsibilities with integrity. The second aspect of growth is to consolidate those prior lessons into wise, effective next steps. To make that transition, you need to know what that transition entails. Knowing what comes next can help you take advantage of your current experiences fully. At present, you are completing an experience that will mean something to you as you move forward. It is a cause for celebration. But, in that celebration, you will want to use that experience as a building block for the next step in the journey.

This time marks your movement from an earlier stage of development as a practicum student to a later, more advanced one as an internship student. Your feelings about beginning internship may be reminiscent of your feelings prior to practicum. You are both excited and anxious about working in a new setting! Thoughts such as, "I am nowhere ready to assume all of the responsibilities expected of me during internship" and, "I know that in internship, there will be more

CHAPTER 13 ▪ Transition to Internship **229**

client work and more difficult clients to counsel. I am not sure I am ready for these challenges" represent the uncertainty you feel about your skills and your abilities. At the same time, you reflect your excitement in thoughts such as these: "I can't wait to really be part of a team, working 20 hours a week at an agency" and, "Even though internship will be intense, it will be more like a real job. And I will learn so much more about the work place and a fuller range of responsibilities." These suggest your readiness for the next step in your preparation as a counselor. You will engage in a process referred to as **reflecting backward** and **reflecting forward**. This may seem a little unconventional at first, but as you look back on practicum with intention, you will be able to use those reflections to look forward into thinking critically about internship—before this practicum semester is even over. The goals of the chapter follow.

GOALS OF THE CHAPTER

- **Assess your professional growth and development**
- **Learn about your program's internship experience**
- **Prepare an assessment of your readiness for internship.**

RELATED CACREP GOALS

SECTION 3: PROFESSIONAL PRACTICE – Section 5.C.1-3 (CACREP, 2016)

Preparing for Internship

As you are aware, internship is the final field experience in your education and training as a professional counselor in your graduate academic program. During internship, you will be preparing for the world of work of the professional counselor as you assume various roles and responsibilities at your internship site. The internship is intended to be a meaningful and powerful experience in your identity development as a counselor and your professional skills development. You can follow a three step-process as you ready yourself for internship: (a) assess your current professional growth and development; (b) learn about internship responsibility; and (c) use the information from the first two steps to evaluate your readiness for internship.

Assessing Your Professional Growth and Development

Professional development is a lifelong journey. As such, there are several events or happenings that promote or encourage an assessment or evaluation of that development. These include taking leave from a field experience such as practicum, transitioning from one course of study to another, handling a work-related crisis, ending a job responsibility or experience, and assuming a new job responsibility or experience, to name a few. One way to reflect on each of these experiences is by using **reflection as action**.

REFLECTION AS ACTION. As you conclude your practicum experience, you will develop a comprehensive review of your professional growth as a counselor. To do so requires you gather materials that illustrate your work. These may include your experiences in practicum, the feedback you receive from your supervisors and peers, your written work related to practicum, and your self-reflections. As you begin to assess your practicum experience, you will use two types of reflection defined by Schön (1983) as reflection on action and reflection in action. **Reflection on action** requires you analyze an event after it has already occurred with the intent of describing the situation, your intervention, and the outcomes. For example, reflection on action outcomes include (a) an analysis of strengths and limits of your professional actions and (b) suggestions about what actions you might have taken in the past or what you might take in the future. Related to practicum, you will find the outcomes of reflection-on-action thinking in your midterm evaluation, final evaluation, case study, and summary of or material for special projects. There may also be a section of post-event reflection required in your written case notes and written faculty and site supervision notes. Let's look at Kaisha's reflection on action as her supervisor and peers review her case notes during group supervision (see Transcription 13.1)

TRANSCRIPTION 13.1. REFLECTION ON ACTION

Case notes as reflection on action, Kaisha, Session #3 Excerpt

Kaisha: "Client described feeling stressed about upcoming work project. He stated that he was 'overwhelmed' by the tasks, and has had trouble sleeping at night because of it. Counselor explored sleeping strategies to assist client in sleeping better."

Dr. Kim: Thank you for reading this excerpt from your case note (also called progress note). What, if anything, stands out to you?

Kaisha: In reviewing the note, it is obvious to me that I jumped from understanding the client's concern to problem-solving his ability to sleep.

Dr. Kim: At the very least, that is what your note communicated, right?

Kaisha: Yeah, I suppose that is true.

Dr. Kim: What would you like to do next time in this situation?

Kaisha: There's two things, I think. The first thing I would like to do is ensure that I'm hearing and understanding my client's concerns, rather than jumping to seek solutions. The second thing is that I'd like to be a little clearer in my written records.

Dr. Kim: These sound like fine goals. I would like to add that it is possible to be clearer in your written records without necessarily adding content or client details. How might you do that?

Kaisha: With this client, it turns out that the reason he is overwhelmed at work is that he hates his job and feels like it is not a good fit for him—that's the truer source of lost sleep. I might write next time something like, "Client identified work dissatisfaction as source of stress and stated that he would like to explore vocational options for himself. He expressed interest in exploring sleep strategies as well."

Dr. Kim: That is a different kind of note.

Kaisha: Well, it is clear to me now that pausing to listen a little longer to my client and to understand the fuller extent of his or her issue will also help me write a better progress note.

As you can see in the transcription with Kaisha, reflection on action can take both clinical skills and documentation to new levels. The transcription demonstrates how Dr. Kim guided Kaisha to reflect backward by thinking about her past behavior, and then helping her reflect forward by imagining what she would like to do differently next time. This way of thinking builds hope that mistakes or missteps can be changed going forward.

Another way engage in reflection is through **reflection in action**, which occurs in real time; this reflection can improve the incident or situation and, in fact, does so. Simply stated, this reflection and action occurs in the moment. During reflection in action, each situation is viewed as unique, requires something beyond your current knowledge or practiced skills, and occurs as you adapt or create a new response or approach. You will discover your reflections in action in your daily logs and notes, transcripts of counseling sessions, case notes, faculty and site supervision notes, and journaling entries. Here you will look for adjustments you made in the moment to improve your professional practice (Giaimo-Ballard & Hyatt, 2012). Read through Transcription 13.2 for a demonstration of reflection in action as Jose participates in a video-review session during group supervision.

TRANSCRIPTION 13.2. REFLECTION IN ACTION

This is a transcription of Jose's reflection in action during video review in group supervision.

Dr. Kim: I am going to stop the video right here. Jose, you appear as if you are going to say something, but stop yourself. You did this: (creates a mouth gesture that implies wanting to speak). Can you tell me about that?

Jose: I remember this moment clearly. Adele is my 15-year-old female client who has been engaging in non-suicidal self-injury. This is my first case of self-harm, so I had a lot of questions. I was about to ask her how it felt, but at that exact moment, I was aware that the question was more about my curiosity than it was about Adele's success. I caught myself and instead inserted a reflection of feeling, which comes next in the video.

Dr. Kim: That is quite a clear example of reflection in action, leading to being in the moment. You were able to quiet yourself and listen to your client while asking why you were about to engage in a behavior. In determining the self-focus rather than a client focus, you were able to shift course and listen to the client. Now, your facial expression makes more sense to me. As you view this now, how did it work?

Jose: That's the funny thing. You told us earlier in the semester that if we are patient and provide space for clients, they will tell us what is most important to them when they are ready. So, about 10 minutes later, Adele said that in a previous counseling relationship, the counselor seemed too interested in her cutting, asking lots of questions that frustrated her, so she clammed up. She told me she appreciated that I had just listened and did not try to figure out why she cuts. Ironically, that comment led to her describing the relationship she sees between her current self-harm and earlier sexual trauma she experienced.

Jose's experience of reflection in action shows how powerful this type of thinking can be with clients during a session. Identifying this process in supervision increases the likelihood that he will be able to continue using this in session. Did you catch the reflection forward in this transcription? Dr. Kim recognizes a course correction in Jose's video and provides an opportunity for him to tune into it and cement the experience. He was able to recognize how to take prior learning and use it in the moment and in the future.

REFLECTING ON REFLECTION. You have been engaged in critical reflection and making assessments of your personal growth and **professional counselor identity development** throughout practicum. Specifically, you have read, written, and learned about the various aspects of professional identity. These aspects reflected both personal and professional contexts and included values/beliefs, wellness and self-care, competencies, knowledge, professional organizations, ethical/multicultural considerations, and social justice. In Reflection Question 13.1, recall and revisit how practicum has influenced your professional identity development.

REFLECTION QUESTION 13.1

MY INTERACTIONS WITH THE ASPECTS OF PROFESSIONAL IDENTITY

What stands out to you about one of these times you (a) explored your own personal values and beliefs; (b) discussed and/or engaged in wellness and/or self-care activities; (c) participated in building counseling competencies and skills; (d) learned about or participated in professional organizations; (e) learned about or engaged in ethical decision making and ethical practice; (f) learned about or engaged in multicultural-related thoughts, feelings, and behaviors; or (g) learned about or engaged in advocacy and social justice?

Reviewing Your Professional Identity Development

Gibson and colleagues (2010) described the tasks required of students engaged in what the authors called identity transformation. Gibson and colleagues (2010) labeled these three tasks transformational tasks. These tasks include definition of counseling, responsibility for professional growth, and transformation to system identity. Each of these tasks is influenced by the amount of time CITs perform the work of a counselor and the experiences in which they engage. To assess your professional identity development at the end of practicum and to launch your internship process, you can engage in Reflection Question 13.2.

REFLECTION QUESTION 13.2

APPLYING THE PROCESS VIEW OF PROFESSIONAL COUNSELOR IDENTITY DEVELOPMENT TO YOUR OWN DEVELOPMENT

How would you

a. define the term and activity of counseling?

b. describe your professional growth as a counselor?

c. describe your identity as a counselor?

Determining Level of Success

Exploring the question, "How do I know if I am successful in my counseling work and professional development?" will help you begin to assess the specific practicum-related knowledge, skills, and professional behaviors you gained in your practicum experience (Carson & Bill, 2003; Sweitzer & King, 2013). As suggested earlier, the record of your work in practicum is critical to understanding your level of professional development and your counselor identity development. Discussions **Together** 13.1 and 13.2 can support this evaluation of your practicum work. In Discussion **Together** 13.1, you will compare your **definition of a professional counselor** with the work you completed during practicum.

DISCUSSION TOGETHER 13.1

Defining the Work of a Professional Counselor

How do the materials you've generated/accumulated during practicum—daily log, summary of indirect and direct hours, case notes, faculty and site supervision notes, journaling entries, transcripts of counseling sessions, midterm evaluation, final evaluation, case study, and summary of or material for special projects—assist you in defining what it means to be a counselor?

Using the IDM to Assess Your Levels of Competence

What do you think about your experience of these three areas at the three intervals that follow?

Areas of competence	Beginning of counseling program	Beginning of practicum	Project: End of practicum
Self- and other awareness			
Motivation			
Autonomy			

Now, let's determine your current professional knowledge, skills, and behavior that you will take into the beginning of internship.

Determining Professional Knowledge, Skills, and Behavior

Understanding your current professional knowledge, skills, and behaviors is important as you begin your internship. This assessment will help you prepare for internship, build on your strengths, and target your limitations for improvement. You can make an assessment of your current professional knowledge, skills, and behaviors in two ways. First, you can find information about your own assessment of your professional knowledge, skills, and behavior by reviewing your midterm and final evaluation that were completed by you and your site supervisor. The practicum evaluations specifically address the goals of practicum. As you review your own midterm and final evaluation documents related to practicum, you can make notes of the knowledge, skills, and behaviors that you and your supervisors conclude you have mastered (see Reflection Question 13.3.)

In addition, you will want to review the formal evaluation you received in practicum: the evaluation form used for a counseling internship course to measure your professional growth and development to date with expectations at the conclusion of internship. Components of this specific evaluation may include work place behaviors, personal-professional dispositions, counseling skills, and counseling specialty-specific outcomes (e.g., clinical mental health, school counseling). Reflection Question 13.3 guides you through this process of assessment.

REFLECTION QUESTION 13.3

REVIEWING YOUR FORMAL EVALUATIONS IN PRACTICUM

How might you use your evaluations from practicum to inform your plans for being successful in internship? How does your reflection on the IDM domains add to this process for you?

After you have completed Reflection Question 13.3, discuss your exploration with your future internship faculty and site supervisor. In these conversations, you will begin to establish your goals for an internship experience that will facilitate your professional development. In Discussion Together 13.3, you will engage in an exercise that facilitates communication among you, your future internship faculty, and your internship site supervisor about your professional development. During these conversations, you will begin to develop your goals for your upcoming internship.

DISCUSSION TOGETHER 13.3
Preparing for Conversations with Internship Faculty and Site Supervisor

As you reflect on your accomplishments during practicum, what professional knowledge, skills, and behaviors do you think these demonstrate?

With a clearer idea about your own professional growth and development, it is time for you to turn your sights to internship and its purposes and responsibilities. Guidelines for learning about internship reflect a similar approach you used when learning about practicum earlier in the text.

ETHICAL CONSIDERATION 13.1

Self-growth is an expectation of ethical counselors and counselor educators (ACA Code.F.8.c). As a matter of ethical practice and due process, you have the right to expect to be challenged to grow during practicum. To the extent that this has happened for you, identify how you might carry that forward into internship. If it has happened to a lesser degree for you during practicum, identify self-advocacy strategies to increase the likelihood that you will experience growth during internship.

Learning About Internship

Remember the thoughts and feelings you had prior to beginning your practicum experience. What do you know now that you wish you had known at the beginning of practicum? What steps could you have taken to obtain that knowledge? What could you have done to make yourself open to that knowledge in the event that it was available? Keep these questions in mind as you read through this section. You may be facing similar fears and anxieties as you approach internship. Information about the experience will help you prepare for internship—reflecting backward in order to reflect forward. Even though practicum is a building block for internship, expectations for internship are vastly different.

Focus of Internship

The counseling **internship** allows the counselor in training a more comprehensive experience as a counselor at a work site. The CIT is able to more fully develop assessment, client conceptualization, and individual and group counseling skills using ethically and multiculturally sensitive approaches. Faculty and students often determine internship sites based on the CIT's desired specialty, career interests, related setting, and population served. While a primary goal focuses on developing clinical counseling skills, the internship provides an opportunity for involvement in other professional roles such as client advocacy, professional advocacy, team participation, program planning, and program development, to name a few. CITs are encouraged to work more autonomously, make meaningful use of supervision, and develop a clearer professional identity. Specific professional goals for internship are required by CACREP and/or the academic program. Therefore, many professional counseling programs emphasize similar areas of focus for internship students such as opportunities for direct individual and group clinical contact, client assessment, taping or roleplaying, multicultural counseling, maintaining a client case load, report writing and documentation, case conceptualization, using theoretical approaches and intervention, goal setting, demonstrating oral and written communication, participating in teams, presenting cases, participating in continuing education, engaging in wellness activities, and participating in research activities. Many of these are reflected in the IDM specific domains, discussion in Chapter 9.

> **MULTICULTURAL CONSIDERATION 13.1**
>
> Consider the ways you can select an internship site that will expose you to diverse populations. Many times, students prefer to choose a site that has their target population (e.g., adolescents, substance use, adults, etc.); yet these target populations may not support your growth in the ways challenging populations might. Reflect on the population you feel most/least comfortable with and explore how you might challenge yourself in selecting a site.

CACREP REQUIREMENTS. As with practicum requirements, all CACREP accredited or CACREP compliant programs must meet the **CACREP standards** established for the counseling internship experience under the section "Professional Practice." These 2016 CACREP (2016) standards are as follows:

J. After successful completion of the practicum, students complete 600 clock hours of supervised counseling internship in roles and settings with clients relevant to their specialty area.

K. Internship students complete at least 240 clock hours of direct service.

L. Internship students have weekly interaction with supervisors that averages one hour per week of individual and/or triadic supervision throughout the internship, provided by (1) the site supervisor, (2) counselor education program faculty, or (3) a student supervisor who is under the supervision of a counselor education program faculty member.

M. Internship students participate in an average of 1½ hours per week of group supervision on a regular schedule throughout the internship. Group supervision must be provided by a counselor education program faculty member or a student supervisor who is under the supervision of a counselor education program faculty member.

Another way to prepare for internship is to review the internship syllabus. This syllabus will establish the guidelines for your work in this field-based experience. Describe what you consider the most important elements to understand now (at the beginning of your internship), based on what you wish you had known when entering practicum.

Assessing Readiness for Internship: Beginning with the End in Mind

As with any new endeavor, there exists anxiety over a sense of **readiness** for the activity or responsibility. This anxiety, as it relates to your development as a professional counselor, is no exception. Only a year ago, you were nervous about preparation and performance in counseling classes, especially roleplays and skill-building exercises. Earlier this term, you felt stress as you began your practicum experience. Internship expectations move you from the boundary of the profession into the context of broader professional activity and clinical work with clients (Woodside, Paulus, & Ziegler, 2009). Assessing your readiness for this work provides a way to channel your anxiety in a positive way. This activity and forward-thinking preparation, introduced earlier, is called "**beginning with the end in mind.**"

What does the term "beginning with the end in mind" mean in relationship to preparing for the internship experience? Before you begin your counseling internship, it is important to think about your academic program expectations and your own professional and personal goals for the conclusion of the internship experience by (a) reviewing the goals the counseling program and faculty supervisors have in mind, (b) reflecting on your knowledge, skills, and behaviors related to those goals, and (c) summarizing your strengths and identifying areas where need to begin to learn or need to improve.

In Experiential Activity 13.2, you can begin your assessment of your readiness for internship. In doing so, you will also discover some of your own personal and professional goals for the field experience.

EXPERIENTIAL ACTIVITY 13.2
Assessing Your Readiness for Internship

Review the goals the counseling program and faculty supervisors have in mind; reflect on your knowledge, skills, and behaviors related to those goals; summarize your strengths; and identify areas where you need to begin to learn or need to improve.

Summary

In this chapter, you begin to prepare for you next field-based experience, that of internship. Several guidelines described may help you engage in a positive experience.

Learn What Is Required of the Job and Go Beyond

As with any task, you want to work hard and go beyond the minimum expectations. For example, even though you know you can meet your required internship hours, offer to help when a need arises. For example, the agency just heard a major document due date has been moved up. Find out if there is a way you can help prepare the document under the new time constraints. You also want to observe and learn what the culture of the internship site requires. This means paying attention to a dress code, the meaning of punctuality, how talk in meetings, and the nature of a request or order from the director or principal. In addition, learn what knowledge, skills, and behaviors you need to assume certain responsibilities or perform a task. Be sure to ask for help if you need it.

Plan Your Goals

There will be many demands on your time during the internship term. You will have responsibilities with your academic course work, internship, and other work and social commitments and perhaps family responsibilities. It is important that your work in internship is intentional. This can mean choosing your responsibilities wisely. It can also mean asking for supervision to enhance your professional growth. Internships vary from those that demand all your time and to those where interns struggle to find enough work to engage in at the site. Whatever the situation, monitoring the work with which you are involved and the work that supports your professional goals requires continual awareness. For instance, if you would like to participate in a team staffing and present your work with clients, be specific with your site supervisor that that is a priority for you. If you work with children and you would like to work with parents, find ways to engage with them. Determine what opportunities are available, the skills you need to participate, and what level of participation is reasonable given your knowledge and skills level.

Seek Supervision

Seeking and engaging in supervision is important for your professional growth and development. The availability of a site supervisor is one of the many aspects of internship that distinguishes this work from a volunteer or a paid position. Having an experienced professional willing to spend time with you on a daily and weekly basis is valuable to help you develop as a professional. Even if, during internship, you become more autonomous, there is security in having another professional to seek out if you anticipate or encounter challenging situations or issues. If you actively seek supervision, you place yourself in a learning stance and challenge yourself to improve your work as a counselor. Another positive result of seeking supervision occurs as others see you as a responsible professional, willing to seek critical feedback and being open to multiple perspectives.

Seek Situations That Challenge You

Although you will naturally gravitate to tasks and responsibilities that use the skills and the strengths you have, working as an intern provides an excellent opportunity for you to assume new responsibilities that help you grow and develop. Once you become familiar with the work at the internship site and you know the culture of the site, you can volunteer for tasks that address your goals and objectives for internship. Another strategy for identifying responsibilities you would like to assume is to review the requirements and standards or competencies outlined in the final evaluation form. You can tell your site supervisor you would like an experience or responsibility that helps you address that requirement (e.g., work related to multicultural aspects of counseling; advocacy). And, remember, challenging work may require asking for help and supervision. So, when you need help with your work, be sure to ask for it.

Participate Openly in Reflection Activities

This chapter may seem like one big mirror, or a series of many smaller mirrors. That is because this chapter is the culmination of a theme that has run throughout this text: reflecting to grow. Growth is challenging because reflection is too. Yet, using these approaches to reflection, reflection in action, reflection on action, reflecting forward, reflecting backward, reflection on reflections, and reflections as action, you can continue your growth.

Practice Self-Care

Engaging in internship is a critical time for you to recognize the need for and practice for self-care. Many times in your academic program, you have discussed with faculty and peers the challenges professional counselors encounter related to burnout, vicarious trauma, and compassion fatigue. Integrated with a discussion of self-care has been a counselor's professional commitment. In the ACA Code of Ethics, Section C: Professional Responsibility: Introduction, "In addition, counselors engage in self-care activities to maintain and promote their own emotional, physical, mental, and spiritual well-being to best meet their professional responsibilities" (ACA, 2014, p. 8, col. 3, para 1). As mentioned earlier, self-care can include various aspects of wellness and a variety of activities including exercise, nutrition, mindfulness activities, social interaction, and spiritual engagement.

Discover a Work Setting That Is Right for You

One of the most important things that you have begun to discover in practicum and you can continue to explore during internship is the type of work setting in which you can thrive as a professional counselor. There are two aspects of work of particular importance; you might explore both of these aspects in light of previous work experiences, your practicum experience, and your future internship experience. First, ask yourself this question: "What is the type of work I like to do?" You can consider some elements of work, and if it requires or fosters "creativity, initiative, variety, orientation to detail, independence, structure, collaboration, competition, and/or hierarchy" (Ruttencutter, 2016, p. 351). Another question you might ask is, "What work environment provides benefits that are important to me?" Elements to consider include "professional growth, advancement, leadership, career ladder, stability, time flexibility, 24/7, or stable working hours" (Ruttencutter, 2016, p. 351).

Key Terms

Beginning with the end in mind

Cacrep standards

Definition of a professional counselor

Formal evaluation

Professional counselor identity development

Readiness

Refection in action

Reflecting backward

Reflecting forward

Reflection as action

Reflection on action

References

American Counseling Association (ACA). (2014). *2014 ACA Code of Ethics.* Alexandria, VA: Author.

Carson, L., & Bill, D. (2003). Utilizing the stages of internship to help students transition from interns to health education professionals. *The Health Educator, 35*(2), 9–15.

Council for Accreditation of Counseling and Related Program (2016). *2016 CACREP Standards: Section 3 Professional Practice.* Retrieved from http://www.cacrep.org/section-3-professional-practice/.

Giaimo-Ballard, C., & Hyatt, L. (2102). Reflection-in-action teaching strategies used by faculty to enhance teaching and learning. *Networks: An Online Journal for Teacher Research, 13*(2), 1–11. Retrieved from http://journals.library.wisc.edu/index.php/networks/article/viewFile/400/590

Gibson, D. M., Dollarhide, C. T., & Moss, J. M. (2010). Professional identity development: A grounded theory of transformational tasks of new counselors. *Counselor Education and Supervision, 50*(1), 21-38.

Ruttencutter, G. (2016). The professional voice and tips for practice. In M. Woodside (Ed.), *The human service internship experience: Helping students find their way* (p. 351). Thousand Oakes, CA: SAGE.

Schön, D. (1983). The reflective practitioner: How professionals think in action. London, UK: Temple Smith.

Sweitzer, F., & King, M. A. (2013). *The successful internship: Personal, professional, and civic development in experiential learning* (4th ed.). Pacific Grove, CA: Cengage.

Woodside, M., Paulus, T., & Ziegler, M. (2009). The experience of school counseling internship through the lens of communities of practice. *Counselor Education and Supervision, 49*(1), 20–38.

INDEX

CPSIA information can be obtained
at www.ICGtesting.com
Printed in the USA
LVHW060424060522
718043LV00001B/8

9 781516 531783